65.00   4

Decisions of the United States Supreme Court

1997-98 TERM

The Editorial Staff
United States Supreme Court Reports,
Lawyers' Edition

LEXIS®
LAW PUBLISHING

701 East Water Street
Charlottesville, VA 22902

ISBN 0-327-06328-9

7683510

CONTENTS

PREFACE

This volume is designed to serve as a quick-reference guide to the work of the United States Supreme Court during its 1997–1998 Term. Its important features are described below.

The Court's Personnel. A list of the Justices of the Supreme Court is accompanied by photographs and biographical sketches of each Justice serving during the Term.

Survey of the Term. A succinct narrative statement outlines the high spots of the Term.

Summaries of Decisions. Every important decision of the Supreme Court is individually summarized. These summaries (reprinted from Vols. 139–141 L Ed 2d) describe the manner in which the case came before the Court, the facts involved and issues presented, the holding of the Court and the reasons supporting that holding, the name of the Justice who wrote the opinion of the majority, and the names and views of those of the Justices who concurred or dissented.

The Summaries are printed in the order in which the cases were decided by the Court. Notations to Summaries indicate the volume and page at which the full opinion of the Court may be found in the official reports (US) published by the Federal Government, and the privately published United States Supreme Court Reports, Lawyers' Edition (L Ed 2d), and Supreme Court Reporter (S Ct).

Following each Summary is a listing of the attorneys who argued in behalf of the litigants.

Glossary. A glossary of common legal terms defines, in simple, nontechnical language, various legal words and phrases frequently used in the Supreme Court's decisions.

Table of Cases. A complete Table of Cases makes possible the location of the Summary of any case through the name of a party litigant.

Index. A detailed, alphabetical word index makes possible the location of the Summary of any case by consulting the index entries for appropriate factual and conceptual terms.

THE COURT'S PERSONNEL

JUSTICES

OF THE

SUPREME COURT OF THE UNITED STATES

_____

1997–98 Term

_____

Chief Justice
HON. WILLIAM H. REHNQUIST

Associate Justices
HON. JOHN P. STEVENS

HON. SANDRA DAY O'CONNOR

HON. ANTONIN SCALIA

HON. ANTHONY M. KENNEDY

HON. DAVID H. SOUTER

HON. CLARENCE THOMAS

HON. RUTH BADER GINSBURG

HON. STEPHEN BREYER

BIOGRAPHIES OF THE
JUSTICES

Chief Justice Rehnquist was born in Milwaukee, Wisconsin, on October 1, 1924, the son of William

B. and Margery P. Rehnquist. He married Natalie Cornell in 1953. They have three children, James, Janet, and Nancy.

Chief Justice Rehnquist attended public schools in Shorewood, Wisconsin, and received his B.A. degree, with great distinction, and an M.A. degree from Stanford University in 1948. He also earned an M.A. degree from Harvard University in 1950, and then returned to Stanford University, where he received his LL.B. degree in 1952.

From 1952 to 1953, he served as law clerk for Justice Robert H. Jackson, Supreme Court of the United States. From 1953 to 1969, Chief Justice Rehnquist engaged in private practice in Phoenix, Arizona, and in 1969, he was appointed Assistant Attorney General, Office of Legal Counsel, by President Nixon.

Chief Justice Rehnquist served in the United States Army Air Corps in this country and overseas from 1943 to 1946, and was discharged with the rank of sergeant.

Chief Justice Rehnquist was nominated to the position of Associate Justice of the United States Supreme Court by President Nixon on October 21, 1971, and took office on January 7, 1972. On June 17, 1986, he was nominated Chief Justice by President Reagan, and on September 26, 1986, he was sworn in as Chief Justice.

Chief Justice Rehnquist's professional activities have included membership in the American Bar Association, the Arizona Bar Association, the Maricopa County (Arizona) Bar Association (President, 1963), the National Conference of Lawyers and Realtors, the National Conference of Commissioners of Uniform State Laws, and the Council of the Administrative Conference of the United States.

Justice Stevens was born in Chicago, Illinois, on April 20, 1920. He is married to Maryan Mulholland Stevens

and has four children, John Joseph, Kathryn Stevens Tedlicka, Elizabeth Jane, and Susan Roberta.

Justice Stevens received an A.B. degree from the University of Chicago in 1941 and a J.D. degree, magna cum laude, from Northwestern University School of Law in 1947.

During the 1947–1948 Term of the United States Supreme Court, he was a law clerk to Justice Wiley Rutledge, and in 1949, he was admitted to practice law in Illinois. In 1951 and 1952, Justice Stevens was Associate Counsel to the Subcommittee on the Study of Monopoly Power of the Judiciary Committee of the United States House of Representatives, and from 1953 to 1955 he was a member of the Attorney General's National Committee to Study Anti-trust Law. From 1970 to 1975 he served as a Judge of the United States Court of Appeals for the Seventh Circuit.

Justice Stevens served in the United States Navy from 1942 to 1945.

Justice Stevens was appointed to the position of Associate Justice of the United States Supreme Court by President Ford on December 1, 1975, and took his seat on December 19, 1975.

Justice Stevens is a member of the Illinois Bar Association, Chicago Bar Association, Federal Bar Association, American Law Institute, and American Judicature Society.

Justice O'Connor was born in El Paso, Texas, on March 26, 1930, the daughter of Harold A. Day and Ada Mae Wilkey Day. She married John Jay O'Connor III in 1952. They have three children, Scott, Brian, and Jay.

Justice O'Connor graduated from Stanford University in 1950 with a B.A. degree, magna cum laude. She earned her LL.B. degree at Stanford in 1952.

Justice O'Connor served as a deputy county attorney in San Mateo County, California, from 1952 to 1953, and as a civilian attorney for the Quartermaster Market Center in Frankfurt, Germany, from 1954 to 1957. She was in the private practice of law in Maryvale, Arizona, from 1958 to 1960, and served as an Assistant Attorney General in Arizona from 1965 to 1969.

Justice O'Connor was a member of the Arizona State Senate from 1969 to 1975. She was a judge of the Maricopa County Superior Court in Phoenix, Arizona, from 1975 to 1979, and served on the Arizona Court of Appeals from 1979 to 1981.

Justice O'Connor was appointed to the position of Associate Justice of the United States Supreme Court by President Reagan on July 7, 1981, and took office on September 25, 1981.

Justice Scalia was born on March 11, 1936 in Trenton, New Jersey. He married Maureen McCarthy, September 10, 1960. They have  nine children: Ann Forrest, Eugene, John Francis, Catherine Elisabeth, Mary Clare, Paul David, Matthew, Christopher James, and Margaret Jane.

Justice Scalia attended Georgetown University and University of Fribourg (Switzerland), receiving his A.B. degree in 1957. He earned his LL.B. degree in 1960 from Harvard University.

Justice Scalia was admitted to the Ohio Bar, 1962, and the Virginia Bar, 1970. He was in private practice with Jones, Day, Cockley and Reavis, Cleveland, Ohio, from 1961 to 1967.

He served as general counsel, Office of Telecommunications Policy, Executive Office of the President, 1971 to 1972; chairman, Administrative Conference of the United States, 1972 to 1974; Assistant Attorney General, Office of Legal Counsel, U. S. Department of Justice, 1974 to 1977.

Justice Scalia was a professor of law at the University of Virginia from 1967 to 1974, a scholar in residence at the American Enterprise Institute in 1977, visiting professor of law at Georgetown University in 1977, professor of law at the University of Chicago from 1977 to 1982, and visiting professor of law at Stanford University from 1980 to 1981.

From 1982 to 1986, Justice Scalia served as a Judge of the United States Court of Appeals for the District of Columbia Circuit. He was nominated by President

Reagan as Associate Justice of the United States Supreme Court, and he took the oath of office on September 26, 1986.

Justice Kennedy was born in Sacramento, California, on July 23, 1936. He married Mary Davis on June 29,

1963, and they have three children, Justin Anthony, Gregory Davis, and Kristin Marie.

Justice Kennedy attended Stanford University and the London School of Economics, receiving a B.A. from Stanford in 1958. He then earned an LL.B. from Harvard Law School in 1961. From 1960 to 1961, he was on the board of student advisors, Harvard Law School.

Justice Kennedy was admitted to the California bar in 1962 and the United States Tax Court bar in 1971. From 1961 to 1963, he was an associate at Thelen, Marrin, Johnson & Bridges, San Francisco, then practiced as a sole practitioner in Sacramento from 1963 to 1967, and was a partner in Evans, Jackson & Kennedy, Sacramento, from 1967 to 1975. He was nominated to be a judge of the United States Court of Appeals for the Ninth Circuit by President Ford, and took the oath of office on May 30, 1975. In addition, Justice Kennedy has been a professor of constitutional law at McGeorge School of Law, University of the Pacific, from 1965 to 1988.

He has served in the California Army National Guard, 1961; the Judicial Conference of the United States Advisory Panel on Financial Disclosure Reports and Judicial Activities (subsequently renamed the Advisory Committee on Codes of Conduct), 1979 to 1987; and the board of the Federal Judicial Center, 1987 to 1988. He has been on the Committee on Pacific Territories, 1979 to 1988, and was named chairman 1982. He is a member of the American Bar Association,

Sacramento County Bar Association, State Bar of California, and Phi Beta Kappa.

Justice Kennedy was nominated by President Reagan as an Associate Justice of the Supreme Court, and took the oath of office on February 18, 1988.

Justice Souter was born in Melrose, Massachusetts on September 17, 1939, the son of Joseph Alexander and

Helen Adams Hackett Souter.

He graduated from Harvard College in 1961 with an A.B. degree. After two years as a Rhodes Scholar, Justice Souter received an A.B. in Jurisprudence from Oxford University in 1963. He earned an LL.B. degree from Harvard Law School in 1966 and an M.A. degree from Oxford University in 1989.

Justice Souter was an associate at the law firm of Orr and Reno in Concord, New Hampshire from 1966 to 1968. He then became an Assistant Attorney General of New Hampshire. In 1971, he became Deputy Attorney General, and in 1976, Attorney General of New Hampshire. Justice Souter was named Associate Justice of the Superior Court of New Hampshire in 1978. In 1983, he was appointed as an Associate Justice of the Supreme Court of New Hampshire.

On May 25, 1990, Justice Souter became a Judge of the United States Court of Appeals for the First Circuit. He was nominated by President Bush as an Associate Justice of the United States Supreme Court, and he took his seat on October 9, 1990.

Justice Souter is a member of the National Association of Attorneys General, the New Hampshire Bar Association, and the American Bar Association.

Justice Thomas was born in Pinpoint, Georgia on June 23, 1948. He married Virginia Lamp on May 30, 1987, and has one child, Jamal Adeen.

Justice Thomas attended Conception Seminary and Holy Cross College, receiving an A.B. degree, cum laude, from Holy Cross in 1971. He earned a J.D. degree from Yale Law School in 1974.

He was admitted to the Missouri Bar in 1974, and after serving as Assistant Attorney General of Missouri from 1974 to 1977, he was an attorney for the Monsanto Company from 1977 to 1979.

Justice Thomas served as a legislative assistant to Senator John C. Danforth of Missouri from 1979 to 1981, before serving as Assistant Secretary for Civil Rights for the United States Department of Education from 1981 to 1982 and Chairman of the United States Equal Employment Opportunity Commission from 1982 to 1990.

On March 12, 1990, Justice Thomas became a Judge of the United States Court of Appeals for the District of Columbia Circuit. He was nominated by President Bush as Associate Justice of the United States Supreme Court, and he took the oath of office on October 23, 1991.

Justice Ginsburg was born in Brooklyn, New York, on March 15, 1933, the daughter of Nathan Bader and  Celia Amster Bader. She married Martin D. Ginsburg in 1954, and they have two children, Jane and James.

She received a B.A. degree, with high honors in Government and distinction in all subjects, from Cornell University in 1954. She attended Harvard Law School and Columbia Law School, receiving her L.L.B. degree from Columbia in 1959.

Justice Ginsburg was admitted to the New York Bar in 1959 and the District of Columbia Bar in 1975. She served as a law clerk for Judge Edmund L. Palmieri of the United States District Court for the Southern District of New York from 1959 to 1961.

Justice Ginsburg was a professor at the Rutgers University School of Law from 1963 to 1972 and at Columbia Law School from 1972 to 1980. In addition, she served the American Civil Liberties Union as general counsel from 1973 to 1980 and as a member of the national board of directors from 1974 to 1980.

On June 30, 1980, Justice Ginsburg became a Judge of the United States Court of Appeals for the District of Columbia Circuit. She was nominated by President Clinton as an Associate Justice of the United States Supreme Court, and she took the oath of office on August 10, 1993.

Justice Breyer was born in San Francisco, California, on August 15, 1938. He married Joanna Hare on  September 4, 1967, and they have three children, Chloe, Nell, and Michael.

Justice Breyer received an A.B. degree, with Great Distinction, from Stanford University in 1959. He attended Oxford University as a Marshall Scholar and received a B.A. degree, with 1st Class Honors, in 1961. He earned his LL.B. degree from Harvard Law School, magna cum laude, in 1964.

During the 1964-1965 Term of the United States Supreme Court, he served as clerk to Justice Arthur Goldberg. He served as Special Assistant to the Assistant Attorney General (Antitrust), Department of Justice, 1965 to 1967; Assistant Special Prosecutor, Watergate Special Prosecution Force, 1973; Special Counsel to the U.S. Senate Judiciary Committee, 1974 to 1975; and Chief Counsel to the U.S. Senate Judiciary Committee, 1979 to 1980.

At Harvard University, Justice Breyer was an assistant professor from 1967 to 1970, a professor of law from 1970 to 1980, a professor at the Kennedy School of Government from 1977 to 1980, and a lecturer since 1980. He was a visiting professor at the College of Law, Sydney, Australia, in 1975, and the University of Rome in 1993.

He was appointed to the United States Court of Appeals for the First Circuit in 1980, and served as Chief Judge of that Court from 1990 to 1994. He was nominated by President Clinton as Associate Justice of the United States Supreme Court and took office on August 4, 1994.

SURVEY OF THE 1997-98 TERM

by

Gary Knapp, M.B.A., J.D.

§ 1. Generally; statistics

The Supreme Court's 1997-98 Term began on October 6, 1997. The court took a recess from June 26 until October 5, 1998, at which time the 1997-98 Term adjourned.

Statistics released by the Office of the Clerk of the Supreme Court reveal that (1) 7,692 cases appeared on the Supreme Court's docket for the 1997-98 Term, and (2) of these, 911 were carried over from the prior term, and 6,781 were docketed during the 1997-98 Term.

Of the 7,692 cases on the docket during the 1997-98 Term, 6,571 nonoriginal cases were disposed of by (1) the court's denial of review, (2) the court's dismissal, or (3) withdrawal. Another 50 nonoriginal cases were summarily decided. A total of 933 cases, including 6 original cases, were not acted upon, or remained undisposed of.

There were 138 cases available for argument during the 1997-98 Term, of which 96 cases were argued and 1 was dismissed or remanded without argument, leaving 41 cases still available for argument. Of the 96 cases which were argued, 93 were disposed of by signed opinion, 1 was disposed of by per curiam opinion, and 2 were dismissed under Supreme Court Rule 46.1.

Besides disposing of the 96 cases which were argued, the Supreme Court issued 8 per curiam opinions disposing of 11 unargued cases

§ 2. Landmark decisions

During the 1997-98 Term, the United States Supreme Court handed down a number of well-publicized landmark decisions. With respect to the free speech clause of the Federal Constitution's First Amendment, the Supreme Court held in one case that a state-owned public television broadcaster's decision to exclude from a televised congressional candidates' debate a third-party candidate who had little popular support was a reasonable viewpoint-neutral exercise of journalistic discretion that was consistent with the First Amendment's free speech protections (Arkansas Ed. Television Comm'n v Forbes (1998, US) 140 L Ed 2d 875, 118 S Ct 1633, infra § 44), and the court held in another case that a statutory provision, 20 USCS § 954(d)(1), that required the National Endowment for the Arts to consider "general standards of decency and respect for . . . diverse beliefs and values" in judging art grant applications was not facially invalid, as the provision neither inherently interfered with First Amendment rights nor violated constitutional vagueness principles (National Endowment for the Arts v Finley (1998, US) 141 L Ed 2d 500, 118 S Ct 2168, infra § 37).

Law enforcement officers' alleged violations of individuals' federal constitutional rights during the officers' performance of their duties were considered by the court during the Term. The court held that a police officer did not violate the substantive due process guarantee of the Constitution's Fourteenth Amendment by causing death through deliberate or reckless indifference to life in a high-speed automobile chase aimed at apprehending a suspected offender (County of Sacramento v Lewis (1998, US) 140 L Ed 2d 1043, 118 S Ct 1708, infra § 40). In addition, the court held that the federal exclusionary rule, which generally prohibits the introduction at a criminal trial of evidence obtained in violation of a defendant's right under the Constitution's Fourth Amendment to be free from unreasonable searches and seizures, does not apply in parole revocation hearings (Pennsylvania Bd. of Probation & Parole v Scott (1998, US) 141 L Ed 2d 344, 118 S Ct 2014, infra § 38).

The court also decided other significant cases involving individuals' federal constitutional rights. It was held, with respect to an accused's conviction under 31 USCS § 5316(a)(1)(A) for willfully failing to report that the accused was transporting more than $10,000 out of the United States, that forfeiture, pursuant to 18 USCS § 982(a)(1), of the full $357,144 in currency involved in the case would (1) constitute punishment and thus would be a "fine" within the meaning of the excessive fines clause of the Constitution's Eighth Amendment, and (2) violate the excessive fines clause, because such full forfeiture would be grossly disproportional to the gravity of the accused's reporting offense (United States v Bajakajian (1998, US) 141 L Ed 2d 314, 118 S Ct

2028, infra § 23). In another case, the Supreme Court held, with respect to a resident alien's refusal to answer questions stemming from the alien's possible participation in Nazi persecution during World War II, that the alien's asserted fear of foreign criminal prosecution was beyond the scope of the privilege against self-incrimination under the Constitution's Fifth Amendment (United States v Balsys (1998, US) 141 L Ed 2d 575, 118 S Ct 2218, infra § 51).

In cases concerning the President of the United States or other White House officials, the Supreme Court held that (1) certain parties had standing to challenge the validity, under the Federal Constitution, of the Line Item Veto Act, 2 USCS §§ 691 et seq., which allowed the President to cancel individual funding provisions contained in legislation enacted by Congress, and (2) the procedures set forth in the Act violated the Constitution's presentment clause, Art I, § 7, cl 2, which describes the procedures for enacting federal legislation (Clinton v City of New York (1998, US) 141 L Ed 2d 393, 118 S Ct 2091, infra § 32), and the court held that the notes written by a White House official's private attorney during an interview with the official shortly before the official's death were protected by the attorney-client privilege from subpoena by the Independent Counsel, who, after the official's death, sought to use the notes in a criminal investigation (Swidler & Berlin v United States (1998, US) 141 L Ed 2d 379, 118 S Ct 2081, infra § 6).

Three cases decided by the Supreme Court during the Term involved the issue of sex discrimination in employment, in violation of Title VII of Civil Rights Act of 1964 (42 USCS §§ 2000e et seq.). The court held that workplace sexual harassment is actionable as sex discrimination under a particular Title VII provision (42 USCS § 2000e-2(a)(1)), where the harasser and the harassed employee are of the same sex (Oncale v Sundowner Offshore Servs. (1998, US) 140 L Ed 2d 201, 118 S Ct 998, infra § 53). With respect to actions against an employer under Title VII by an employee who allegedly has been sexually harassed by a supervisor, the court held in one case that under Title VII, an employer may (1) without a showing of negligence or other fault on the part of the employer for a supervisor's actions, be subject to vicarious liability, for the supervisor's creation of a hostile workplace environment, to a sexually harassed employee who refuses the unwelcome and threatening sexual advances of the supervisor, yet suffers no adverse, tangible job consequences, but (2) raise an affirmative defense to liability or damages, subject to proof by a preponderance of the evidence (Burlington Indus. v Ellerth (1998, US) 141 L Ed 2d 633, 118 S Ct 2257, infra § 53); and the court made this same holding in a second case that was decided on the same day (Faragher v City of Boca Raton (1998, US) 141 L Ed 2d 662, 118 S Ct 2275, infra § 53).

As to sex discrimination against a party other than an employee, it was held that under Title IX of the Education Amendments of 1972, 20 USCS §§ 1681 et seq., monetary damages in an implied cause of action may not be recovered for a teacher's sexual harassment of a student, unless a school district official with authority to institute corrective measures on the district's behalf has actual notice of, and is deliberately indifferent to, the teacher's misconduct (Gebser v Lago Vista Indep. Sch. Dist. (1998, US) 141 L Ed 2d 277, 118 S Ct 1989, infra § 53). Moreover, as to yet another type of allegedly illegal discrimination, the Supreme Court held that the United States Court of Appeals for the First Circuit (1) was correct in determining that the asymptomatic HIV infection of a patient whom a dentist refused to treat was a "disability" under the Americans with Disabilities Act of 1990, 42 USCS §§ 12101 et seq., but (2) did not cite sufficient material to determine, as a matter of law, that the infection posed no direct threat to others' health and safety (Bragdon v Abbott (1998, US) 141 L Ed 2d 540, 118 S Ct 2196, infra § 24).

The court—overruling its prior antitrust decision in Albrecht v Herald Co. (1968) 390 US 145, 19 L Ed 2d 998, 88 S Ct 869—held that vertical maximum price fixing (1) is not a per se violation of the prohibition, in § 1 of the Sherman Act (15 USCS § 1), against contracts, combinations, or conspiracies in restraint of trade, and (2) instead, is subject to evaluation under the rule of reason (State Oil Co. v Khan (1997, US) 139 L Ed 2d 199, 118 S Ct 275, infra § 5).

It was held that that (1) abuse of discretion is the proper standard for an appellate court to apply in reviewing a Federal District Court's decision to admit or exclude expert scientific testimony at trial, and (2) because it was within the discretion of the District Court in the instant case, in which an electrician alleged that his on-the-job exposure to polychlorinated biphenyls (PCBs) had promoted his cancer, to conclude that the scientific studies upon which the electrician's experts relied were not sufficient to support the experts' conclusions that the electrician's exposure to PCBs contributed to his cancer, the District Court did not abuse its discretion in excluding the experts' testimony (GE v Joiner (1997, US) 139 L Ed 2d 508, 118 S Ct 512, infra § 16).

Finally, in a case that concerned an interpretation of § 109 of the Federal Credit Union Act (12 USCS § 1759) by the National Credit Union Administration (NCUA), which interpretation permitted credit unions to be composed of multiple unrelated employer groups, the Supreme Court held that (1) some banks and the American Bankers Association had standing under § 10(a) of the Administrative Procedure Act (5 USCS § 702) to seek federal court review of the NCUA's interpretation, and (2) the interpretation was impermissible (NCUA v First Nat'l Bank & Trust Co. (1998, US) 140 L Ed 2d 1, 118 S Ct 927, infra § 19).

§ 3. Admiralty and maritime law

The Supreme Court held that the Federal Constitution's Eleventh Amendment immunity of a state from suit in a federal court did not bar a Federal District Court's adjudication, in an in rem admiralty action filed by a company, of competing claims by the company and California to the historic wreck of a sunken vessel located several miles off the California coast. [California v Deep Sea Research (1998, US) 140 L Ed 2d 626, 118 S Ct 1464.]

It was held that because Congress has chosen not to authorize a survival action for a decedent's predeath pain and suffering in the Death on the High Seas Act (46 USCS §§ 761 et seq.), there can be no general maritime survival action for such damages. [Dooley v Korean Air Lines Co. (1998, US) 141 L Ed 2d 102, 118 S Ct 1890.]

§ 4. Age discrimination

An employee's release of claims against an employer under the Age Discrimination in Employment Act (29 USCS §§ 621 et seq.) was held to be unenforceable, where the release did not comply with the requirements of the Older Workers Benefit Protection Act (29 USCS § 626(f)). [Oubre v Entergy Operations (1998, US) 139 L Ed 2d 849, 118 S Ct 838.]

§ 5. Antitrust law

The court—overruling its prior antitrust decision in Albrecht v Herald Co. (1968) 390 US 145, 19 L Ed 2d 998, 88 S Ct 869—held that vertical maximum price fixing (1) is not a per se violation of the prohibition, in § 1 of the Sherman Act (15 USCS § 1), against contracts, combinations, or conspiracies in restraint of trade, and (2) instead, is subject to evaluation under the rule of reason. [State Oil Co. v Khan (1997, US) 139 L Ed 2d 199, 118 S Ct 275.]

§ 6. Attorneys

The Supreme Court held that interest earned on client funds deposited by an attorney in an Interest on Lawyers Trust Account (IOLTA) is the private property of the client for purposes of the requirement, under the Federal Constitution's Fifth Amendment, of just compensation for private property that is taken for public use. [Phillips v Washington Legal Found. (1998, US) 141 L Ed 2d 174, 118 S Ct 1925.]

It was held that the notes written by a White House official's private attorney during an interview with the official shortly before the official's death were protected by the attorney-client privilege from subpoena by the Independent Counsel, who, after the official's death, sought to use the notes in a criminal investigation. [Swidler & Berlin v United States (1998, US) 141 L Ed 2d 379, 118 S Ct 2081.]

§ 7. Bankruptcy

The court held that a creditor may not invoke the 11 USCS § 547(c)(3)(B) "enabling loan" exception—which prohibits a trustee in bankruptcy from avoiding, under 11 USCS § 547(b), a loan used to acquire property, if the creditor's security interest is perfected within 20 days after the debtor receives possession of the property—where the creditor performs the acts necessary to perfect its security interest more than 20 days after the debtor receives the property, but within a relation-back or grace period provided by the otherwise applicable state law. [Fidelity Fin. Servs. v Fink (1998, US) 139 L Ed 2d 571, 118 S Ct 651.]

A debt arising from a medical malpractice judgment attributable to negligent or reckless conduct was held not to be a debt for willful and malicious injury that was excepted from discharge in bankruptcy under 11 USCS § 523(a)(6). [Kawaauhau v Geiger (1998, US) 140 L Ed 2d 90, 118 S Ct 974.]

The Supreme Court held that 11 USCS § 523(a)(2)(A) excepted from discharge in bankruptcy all liability arising from specified fraud, including an award of treble damages (plus attorneys' fees and costs). [Cohen v de la Cruz (1998, US) 140 L Ed 2d 341, 118 S Ct 1212.]

§ 8. Bribery

The court held that for conviction of bribery in violation of 18 USCS § 666(a)(1)(B), the government is not required to prove that the bribe in question had any particular influence on federal funds. [Salinas v United States (1997, US) 139 L Ed 2d 352, 118 S Ct 469.]

§ 9. Confessions

It was held that the use of a nontestifying codefendant's redacted confession at a joint criminal trial, with the defendant's name replaced with obvious indications of alteration, fell within the protection of the rule of Bruton v United States (1968) 391 US 123, 20 L Ed 2d 476, 88 S Ct 1620, forbidding such use. [Gray v Maryland (1998, US) 140 L Ed 2d 294, 118 S Ct 1151.]

§ 10. Copyright

The Supreme Court held that a domestic distributor's importation and resale of a hair care manufacturer's products, with copyrighted labels attached, that the manufacturer had sold to a foreign distributor did not infringe, under 17 USCS § 602(a), the manufacturer's exclusive right to distribute the copyrighted labels in the United States, because § 602(a) was subject to 17 USCS § 109(a)'s limitation, on a copyright owner's exclusive right to vend, to first sales of works. [Quality King Distribs. v L'anza Research Int'l (1998, US) 140 L Ed 2d 254, 118 S Ct 1125.]

It was held that the Federal Constitution's Seventh Amendment provided a right to a jury trial on issues pertinent to an award when a copyright owner elected to recover statutory damages under 17 USCS § 504(c). [Feltner v Columbia Pictures TV (1998, US) 140 L Ed 2d 438, 118 S Ct 1279.]

§ 11. Death penalty

The court held that a Virginia trial court's failure to instruct the jury, in the selection phase of a defendant's capital sentencing process, on the concept of mitigation generally and on particular statutorily defined mitigating factors did not violate the defendant's right, under the Federal Constitution's Eighth and Fourteenth Amendments, to be free from arbitrary and capricious imposition of the death penalty. [Buchanan v Angelone (1998, US) 139 L Ed 2d 702, 118 S Ct 757.]

It was held that an Assimilative Crimes Act provision (18 USCS § 13(a))—which made state criminal statutes applicable to a wrongful act or omission of a person within a federal enclave in the state, where such an act or omission was not made punishable by any enactment of Congress—did not make Louisiana's first-degree murder statute, which concerned capital offenses, applicable in a federal prosecution involving the killing of a child on a federal army base in Louisiana, as Congress had made the charged acts in question punishable as federal second-degree murder under 18 USCS § 1111. [Lewis v United States (1998, US) 140 L Ed 2d 271, 118 S Ct 1135.]

Ohio's clemency procedures for state prison inmates under death sentences were held not to violate (1) due process under the Federal Constitution's Fourteenth Amendment, or (2) the right to remain silent under the Constitution's Fifth Amendment. [Ohio Adult Parole Auth. v Woodard (1998, US) 140 L Ed 2d 387, 118 S Ct 1244.]

The Supreme Court, in a per curiam decision, (1) held that a Virginia state prisoner who was a citizen of Paraguay and who had been sentenced to death by a Virginia state court was not entitled to federal habeas corpus review, where the prisoner (a) alleged that his rights under the Vienna Convention on Consular Relations (21 UST 77, TIAS No. 6820) had been violated at the time of his arrest, as the arresting authorities had failed to inform him that he had the right to contact his nation's consulate, but (b) had not asserted this claim in state court; and (2) denied (a) the prisoner's petition for an original writ of habeas corpus, (b) stay applications filed by the prisoner and Paraguay, and (c) other requested relief. [Breard v Greene (1998, US) 140 L Ed 2d 529, 118 S Ct 1352.]

It was held that the recall, by the United States Court of Appeals for the Ninth Circuit, of the court's mandate—which had denied all habeas corpus relief to an accused who had received a death sentence—2 days before the accused's scheduled execution, to revisit an earlier decision denying federal habeas corpus relief, was (1) consistent with the letter of the Antiterrorism and Effective Death Penalty Act of 1996, 110 Stat 1217, which set limits on successive federal habeas corpus applications, but (2) an abuse of discretion. [Calderon v Thompson (1998, US) 140 L Ed 2d 728, 118 S Ct 1489.]

The Supreme Court held that a federal habeas corpus claim by a prisoner who had received a death sentence from an Arizona state court, which claim—that the prisoner was incompetent to be executed—had been made in an earlier federal habeas corpus petition and had been dismissed as unripe, was not subject to 28 USCS § 2244(b)'s restriction on second or successive federal habeas corpus applications. [Stewart v Martinez-Villareal (1998, US) 140 L Ed 2d 849, 118 S Ct 1618.]

The court held that a declaratory judgment and injunctive relief action to determine what procedural rules would apply in federal habeas corpus cases filed by California state death-row prisoners with respect to the applicability of expedited habeas corpus review under 28 USCS §§ 2261-2266 was not a justiciable case under the Federal Constitution's Article III, as the action would not have completely resolved the underlying habeas corpus claims. [Calderon v Ashmus (1998, US) 140 L Ed 2d 970, 118 S Ct 1694.]

In a capital felony murder case, a state trial court in Nebraska was held not to have erred in failing to give jury instructions as to second-degree murder and manslaughter, where such offenses were not lesser included offenses of felony murder under state law. [Hopkins v Reeves (1998, US) 141 L Ed 2d 76, 118 S Ct 1895.] enalty

§ 12. Double jeopardy

The double jeopardy clause of the Federal Constitution's Fifth Amendment was held not to bar a federal criminal prosecution of three bank officials for alleged

conspiracy, misapplication of bank funds, and making
false bank entries, where the officials, in administrative
proceedings before the Office of the Comptroller of
the Currency, had (1) stipulated to monetary assessments of between $12,500 and $16,500 each, and (2)
agreed not to participate in the affairs of any banking
institution without agency authorization. [Hudson v
United States (1997, US) 139 L Ed 2d 450, 118 S Ct
488.]

The court held that the double jeopardy clause of the
Federal Constitution's Fifth Amendment, which clause
is applicable in the capital sentencing scheme, did not
extend to a California court's noncapital sentencing
proceeding to determine the truth of allegations supporting an enhanced sentence. [Monge v California
(1998, US) 141 L Ed 2d 615, 118 S Ct 2246.]

§ 13. Elections and voting

The Supreme Court held that a Georgia city was
entitled to conduct elections under the auspices of a
controlling state-law default rule that required a majority vote in a municipal election if the municipal charter
did not provide for plurality voting—which rule had
been passed by the state legislature in 1968 as part of a
comprehensive municipal election code that was still in
force—because the United States Attorney General had
approved and precleared the default rule under § 5 of
the Voting Rights Act of 1965, as amended (42 USCS
§ 1973c), when the state had submitted the 1968 code
to the Attorney General for preclearance. [City of
Monroe v United States (1997, US) 139 L Ed 2d 339,
118 S Ct 400.]

It was held that to the extent that Louisiana's "open
primary" statute was applied to select a federal congressional candidate in October, the state statute was void as
a result of conflicting with 2 USCS §§ 1 and 7, which

established the first Tuesday after the first Monday in November in even numbered years as the date for federal congressional elections. [Foster v Love (1997, US) 139 L Ed 2d 369, 118 S Ct 464.]

Texas' claim, seeking a declaration that state sanctions which could be applied against school districts were not subject to the federal preclearance requirement of § 5 of Voting Rights Act (42 USCS § 1973c), was held not to be ripe for adjudication. [Texas v United States (1998, US) 140 L Ed 2d 406, 118 S Ct 1257.]

The court (1) held that a group of voters had standing to challenge in the federal courts a Federal Election Commission (FEC) decision that an organization (a) was not a "political committee" as defined by 2 USCS § 431(4), and (b) was therefore not subject to disclosure requirements under the Federal Election Campaign Act of 1971, 2 USCS §§ 431 et seq.; and (2) remanded the case to await an FEC decision on the political committee issue under new FEC regulations. [FEC v Akins (1998, US) 141 L Ed 2d 10, 118 S Ct 1777.]

§ 14. Ellis Island

The Supreme Court held that the state of New Jersey, not the state of New York, had sovereign authority over approximately 24.5 acres of filled land that the Federal Government had added to Ellis Island, the former immigrant station in New York Harbor. [New Jersey v New York (1998, US) 140 L Ed 2d 993, 118 S Ct 1726.]

§ 15. Environmental protection

The Supreme Court held that an environmental protection organization lacked standing to maintain a suit under an Emergency Planning and Community Right-To-Know Act of 1986 citizen-suit provision (42 USCS § 11046(a)(1)), where none of the relief sought was likely to remedy the organization's alleged injury in fact. [Steel Co. v Citizens for a Better Env't (1998, US) 140 L Ed 2d 210, 118 S Ct 1003.]

It was held that a dispute concerning environmental organizations' challenge to the lawfulness of the United States Forest Service's plan, pursuant to the National Forest Management Act of 1976, 16 USCS §§ 1600 et seq., for Ohio's Wayne National Forest was not justiciable, because the dispute was not ripe for court review, given the procedural requirements that the Service would have to observe before it could permit logging under the plan. [Ohio Forestry Assn. v Sierra Club (1998, US) 140 L Ed 2d 921, 118 S Ct 1665.]

The court held that under § 107(a)(2) of the Comprehensive Environmental Response, Compensation, and Liability Act of 1980 (CERCLA), 42 USCS § 9607(a)(2)—which authorizes the United States to bring suit to recover the costs of cleaning up hazardous waste at a facility against a party that at the time of disposal of the waste owned or operated the facility—a parent corporation that actively participated in, and exercised control over, the operations of a subsidiary may not, without more, be held derivatively liable for cleanup costs as an operator of a polluting facility owned or operated by the subsidiary, unless the corporate veil may be pierced, but the parent corporation may be held directly liable for cleanup costs in its own right as an operator of the facility. [United States v Bestfoods (1998, US) 141 L Ed 2d 43, 118 S Ct 1876.]

§ 16. Expert scientific testimony

It was held that that (1) abuse of discretion is the proper standard for an appellate court to apply in reviewing a Federal District Court's decision to admit or exclude expert scientific testimony at trial; and (2) because it was within the discretion of the District Court in the instant case, in which an electrician alleged that his on-the-job exposure to polychlorinated biphenyls (PCBs) had promoted his cancer, to conclude that the scientific studies upon which the electrician's experts relied were not sufficient to support the experts' conclusions that the electrician's exposure to PCBs contributed to his cancer, the District Court did not abuse its discretion in excluding the experts' testimony. [GE v Joiner (1997, US) 139 L Ed 2d 508, 118 S Ct 512.]

§ 17. Extradition

The Supreme Court held that under the Federal Constitution's extradition clause (Art IV, § 2, cl 2), which is implemented by the Extradition Act (18 USCS § 3182), the Supreme Court of New Mexico—in upholding a grant of state habeas corpus relief to a parolee after New Mexico's governor issued a warrant for the parolee's extradition to Ohio, which sought to extradite the parolee as an alleged fugitive from justice—went beyond the scope of permissible inquiry in an extradition case and allowed the litigation of issues not open in New Mexico. [New Mexico ex rel. Ortiz v Reed (1998, US) 141 L Ed 2d 131, 118 S Ct 1860.]

§ 18. False statements

The conduct of a county prosecuting attorney in making allegedly false statements of fact in a certification for determination of probable cause—a document that summarized the evidence supporting an application for an arrest warrant—was held not to be protected by the doctrine of absolute prosecutorial immunity from liability pursuant to 42 USCS § 1983 for the deprivation of rights under federal law. [Kalina v Fletcher (1997, US) 139 L Ed 2d 471, 118 S Ct 502.]

The court held that neither the Civil Service Reform Act (5 USCS §§ 1101 et seq.) nor the due process clause of the Federal Constitution's Fifth Amendment precludes a federal agency from taking adverse action against a federal employee for making false statements in response to an underlying charge of employment-related misconduct. [Lachance v Erickson (1998, US) 139 L Ed 2d 695, 118 S Ct 753.]

It was held that there was no "exculpatory no" exception, for a false statement that consisted of a mere denial of wrongdoing, to criminal liability under 18 USCS § 1001 for making a false statement. [Brogan v United States (1998, US) 139 L Ed 2d 830, 118 S Ct 805.]

§ 19. Federal credit unions

The Supreme Court held—with respect to an interpretation of § 109 of the Federal Credit Union Act (12 USCS § 1759) by the National Credit Union Administration (NCUA), which interpretation permitted credit unions to be composed of multiple unrelated employer groups—that (1) some banks and the American Bankers Association had standing under § 10(a) of the Administrative Procedure Act (5 USCS § 702) to seek federal court review of the NCUA's interpretation, and (2) the interpretation was impermissible. [NCUA v First Nat'l Bank & Trust Co. (1998, US) 140 L Ed 2d 1, 118 S Ct 927].

§ 20. Federal Sentencing Guidelines

It was held that because the Federal Sentencing Guidelines, 18 USCS Appx, instructed "the judge" in a drug conspiracy case to determine the amount and kind of controlled substances involved and to base the sentence on those determinations, the judge, not the jury, in the instant case had to determine whether the drugs at issue—and how much of them—consisted of cocaine, crack, or both. [Edwards v United States (1998, US) 140 L Ed 2d 703, 118 S Ct 1475.]

§ 21. Federal taxes

The Supreme Court held that because the Harbor Maintenance Tax (26 USCS § 4461(a)) did not qualify as a user fee, the tax, as applied to goods loaded at United States ports for export, violated the Federal Constitution's export clause (Art I, § 9, cl 5), which provided that no tax or duty was to be laid on articles exported from any state. [United States v United States Shoe Corp. (1998, US) 140 L Ed 2d 453, 118 S Ct 1290.]

It was held that a Treasury Regulation (26 CFR § 1.846-3(c)) reasonably interpreted the term "reserve strengthening" as the term was used in § 1023(e)(3)(B) of the Tax Reform Act of 1986 (note following 26 USCS § 846) with respect to the taxation of property and casualty insurance companies' accounting reserves for unpaid losses, where the term was interpreted as generally including any increase in such companies' loss reserves, for purpose of an exception from a one-time federal income tax exclusion. [Atlantic Mut. Ins. Co. v Commissioner (1998, US) 140 L Ed 2d 542, 118 S Ct 1413.]

The federal priority statute, 31 USCS § 3713(a), which required that a claim of the United States be paid first when a decedent's estate could not pay all of its debts, was held not to require that federal tax liens against the property of a decedent's insolvent estate that consisted entirely of real property be given preference over a judgment lien against the decedent's real property that was perfected under state law before the Internal Revenue Service filed notices of the tax liens, where the Tax Lien Act of 1966, 26 USCS §§ 6321 et seq., provided in 26 USCS § 6323(a) that a federal tax lien was not valid until a prescribed notice had been given. [United States v Estate of Romani (1998, US) 140 L Ed 2d 710, 118 S Ct 1478.]

§ 22. Firearms

The court held that an accused was entitled to a hearing on the merits of his federal claim challenging, on collateral review, the validity of his prior guilty plea to a charge of using a firearm during and in relation to a drug trafficking crime, in violation of 18 USCS § 924(c)(1), if, on remand, the accused made the showing of actual innocence that was necessary to excuse his procedural default in raising the claim. [Bousley v United States (1998, US) 140 L Ed 2d 828, 118 S Ct 1604.]

In another case involving 18 USCS § 924(c)(1), it was held that the phrase "carries a firearm" in § 924(c)(1)—which, in addition to any punishment for the predicate offense, imposes a mandatory 5-year prison term upon a person who uses or carries a firearm during and in relation to a violent or drug trafficking crime—applies to a person who knowingly possesses and conveys a firearm in a vehicle, including in the locked glove compartment or trunk of a car, which the person accompanies. [Muscarello v United States (1998, US) 141 L Ed 2d 111, 118 S Ct 1911.]

The Supreme Court held that the term "willfully" in 18 USCS § 924(a)(1)(D)—which imposes a penalty for violation of 18 USCS § 922(a)(1)(A), which forbids firearms dealing without a federal license—requires proof only that an accused knew that the accused's conduct was unlawful, not that the accused also knew of the licensing requirement. [Bryan v United States (1998, US) 141 L Ed 2d 197, 118 S Ct 1939.]

The court held that a felon's prior conviction remained a predicate conviction for purposes of a federal conviction and enhanced sentence under 18 USCS

§§ 922(g) and 924(e) concerning possession of rifles and shotguns, where the state of conviction had restored the felon's civil rights but had restricted the felon's right to possess handguns. [Caron v United States (1998, US) 141 L Ed 2d 303, 118 S Ct 2007.]

§ 23. Forfeiture of currency

It was held, with respect to an accused's conviction under 31 USCS § 5316(a)(1)(A) for willfully failing to report that the accused was transporting more than $10,000 out of the United States, that forfeiture, pursuant to 18 USCS § 982(a)(1), of the full $357,144 in currency involved in the case would (1) constitute punishment and thus would be a "fine" within the meaning of the excessive fines clause of the Federal Constitution's Eighth Amendment, and (2) violate the excessive fines clause, because such full forfeiture would be grossly disproportional to the gravity of the accused's reporting offense. [United States v Bajakajian (1998, US) 141 L Ed 2d 314, 118 S Ct 2028.]

§ 24. HIV

The Supreme Court held that the United States Court of Appeals for the First Circuit (1) was correct in determining that the asymptomatic HIV infection of a patient whom a dentist refused to treat was a "disability" under the Americans with Disabilities Act of 1990, 42 USCS §§ 12101 et seq., but (2) did not cite sufficient material to determine, as a matter of law, that the infection posed no direct threat to others' health and safety. [Bragdon v Abbott (1998, US) 141 L Ed 2d 540, 118 S Ct 2196.]

§ 25. Home loans

It was held that (1) a Truth in Lending Act provision (15 USCS § 1635(f)) completely extinguished a borrower's right to rescind a home loan agreement after 3 years, and (2) thus, a borrower could not assert that right as an affirmative defense in a lender's collection action brought more than 3 years after the transaction's consummation. [Beach v Ocwen Fed. Bank (1998, US) 140 L Ed 2d 566, 118 S Ct 1408.]

§ 26. Immigration law

A provision of 8 USCS § 1326(b)(2) that authorized an increased sentence for a deported alien's illegal return if the deportation was subsequent to an aggravated felony conviction was held to be a penalty provision, so that the aggravated felony need not be charged in an indictment. [Almendarez-Torres v United States (1998, US) 140 L Ed 2d 350, 118 S Ct 1219.]

The Supreme Court affirmed, by a majority result without a majority opinion, a United States Court of Appeals for the District of Columbia Circuit decision which upheld the dismissal of a suit by an out-of-wedlock daughter of a Filipino national mother and a United States citizen father, in which suit the daughter had (1) sought a declaratory judgment that the daughter was a United States citizen, (2) sought an order requiring the United States State Department to grant her application for citizenship, and (3) argued that the naturalization requirement of 8 USCS § 1409(a)(4) that children born abroad and out of wedlock to citizen fathers and alien mothers obtain formal proof of paternity by age 18—which requirement did not apply to those born to citizen mothers and alien fathers—violated the equal protection component of the Federal Constitution's Fifth Amendment. [Miller v Albright (1998, US) 140 L Ed 2d 575, 118 S Ct 1428.]

§ 27. Immunity from suit

It was held that (1) local legislators are absolutely immune, with respect to their legislative activities, from suit under 42 USCS § 1983 for deprivation of federal rights; and (2) with respect to a city ordinance eliminating a city official's position pursuant to a proposed city budget, the actions of the city council's vice president in voting for the ordinance and the actions of the city's mayor in introducing the budget and signing the ordinance into law—in alleged violation of the official's civil rights—were protected by such absolute immunity, regardless of the subjective intent motivating such actions. [Bogan v Scott-Harris (1998, US) 140 L Ed 2d 79, 118 S Ct 966.]

As to the applicability in an admiralty action of the Federal Constitution's Eleventh Amendment immunity of a state from suit in a federal court, see California v Deep Sea Research (1998, US) 140 L Ed 2d 626, 118 S Ct 1464, supra § 3; and as to the effect of the Eleventh Amendment on removal of a state case to a federal court, see Wisconsin Dep't of Corrections v Schacht (1998, US) 141 L Ed 2d 364, 118 S Ct 2047, infra § 47.

As to a prosecuting attorney's immunity from liability for making false statements, see Kalina v Fletcher (1997, US) 139 L Ed 2d 471, 118 S Ct 502, supra § 18

§ 28. Indian tribes

The court held that the congressional intent of an 1894 surplus land act (28 Stat 286) was to diminish the Yankton Sioux Reservation so that unallotted lands, including a waste site, (1) were not Indian country as defined by 18 USCS § 1151(a), and (2) were thus under the primary jurisdiction of South Dakota. [South Dakota v Yankton Sioux Tribe (1998, US) 139 L Ed 2d 773, 118 S Ct 789.]

The Supreme Court held—in a case arising from an attempt by an Indian tribe in Alaska to impose a tax on nonmembers of the tribe who conducted business on land owned by the tribe's governing authority—that the land in question, which had constituted the tribe's reservation prior to the enactment of the Alaska Native Claims Settlement Act (43 USCS §§ 1601 et seq.) in 1971, was not "Indian country" within the meaning of 18 USCS § 1151, as the land did not fall within the category of "dependent Indian communities" for purposes of 18 USCS § 1151(b). [Alaska v Native Village of Venetie Tribal Gov't (1998, US) 140 L Ed 2d 30, 118 S Ct 948.]

Indian tribes were held to possess sovereign immunity from state court suits on the tribes' contracts, regardless of whether the contracts (1) involved governmental or commercial activities, and (2) were made on or off a reservation. [Kiowa Tribe v Manufacturing Techs. (1998, US) 140 L Ed 2d 981, 118 S Ct 1700.]

As to cases involving Indian tribes and state or local taxes, see Montana v Crow Tribe of Indians (1998, US) 140 L Ed 2d 898, 118 S Ct 1650, infra § 55, in which the Supreme Court held, with respect to severance taxes and gross proceeds taxes that had been paid by a non-Indian company to Montana and certain Montana counties concerning coal mined by the company on former reservation land to which the United States held mineral rights in trust for the Crow Tribe of Indians, that the restitution, sought by the tribe, of the full amount of such taxes paid for periods before the tribe had in place a valid severance tax of its own was not warranted; and see Cass County v Leech Lake Band of Chippewa Indians (1998, US) 141 L Ed 2d 90, 118 S Ct 1904, infra § 55, in which it was held that (1) an Indian tribe's repurchase of its former reservation land that had been made alienable by Congress and sold to non-Indians by the Federal Government did not cause the land to reassume the status of exemption from state taxation, and (2) therefore, the land was subject to a county's ad valorem property taxes.

§ 29. In forma pauperis proceedings

The Supreme Court, holding that an individual's filings were frivolous, denied the individual leave to proceed in forma pauperis in the Supreme Court on (1) a petition for certiorari to review a Federal Court of Appeals' dismissal of the individual's appeal after the individual's failure to pay a filing fee, and (2) future petitions for certiorari in noncriminal matters. [Brown v Williams (1997, US) 139 L Ed 2d 1, 118 S Ct 1.]

It was held that an individual would be denied leave to proceed in forma pauperis in the Supreme Court on (1) a petition for certiorari to review a Federal Court of Appeals' decision that affirmed a Federal District Court's dismissal of the individual's complaint for failure to amend his complaints, and (2) future petitions for certiorari in noncriminal matters [Arteaga v United States Court of Appeals for the Ninth Circuit (1998, US) 139 L Ed 2d 892, 118 S Ct 903.]

An individual was denied leave to proceed in forma pauperis in the Supreme Court on (1) a petition for certiorari to review a Federal Court of Appeals' decision that dismissed as frivolous claims by the individual concerning the individual's dispute with her landlord, and (2) future petitions for certiorari in noncriminal matters. [Glendora v Porzio (1998, US) 140 L Ed 2d 310, 118 S Ct 1124.]

§ 30. Jury trial

It was held that a Federal Court of Appeals' writ of mandamus, which required a Federal District Court to enter judgment for a lesser amount than that determined by the jury without allowing the option of new trial, was a violation of the Federal Constitution's Seventh Amendment right to a jury trial. [Hetzel v Prince William County (1998, US) 140 L Ed 2d 336, 118 S Ct 1210.]

As to the right to a jury trial in a copyright case, see § 10, supra.

§ 31. Labor unions

The court held that (1) the standard of the National Labor Relations Board (NLRB) for an employer's conduct of an internal poll of employee support for an incumbent union—under which standard such polling was an unfair labor practice unless the employer could show that the employer had a good-faith reasonable doubt about the union's majority support—was facially rational and consistent with the National Labor Relations Act (29 USCS §§ 151 et seq.); but (2) in the case at hand, the NLRB's factual finding that a particular employer lacked such a doubt was not supported by substantial evidence on the record as a whole. [Allentown Mack Sales & Serv. v NLRB (1998, US) 139 L Ed 2d 797, 118 S Ct 818.]

The Supreme Court held that because a labor union's complaint—which alleged that an employer had fraudulently induced the union to sign a collective bargaining agreement—alleged no violation of the agreement by either the union or the employer, the federal courts lacked subject matter jurisdiction over the case under § 301(a) of the Labor-Management Relations Act, 29 USCS § 185(a), which confers jurisdiction over only "suits for violation of contracts." [Textron Lycoming v Auto. Workers (1998, US) 140 L Ed 2d 863, 118 S Ct 1626.]

It was held that nonunion employees subject to an agency shop agreement—under which the employees had to pay an agency fee, that is, a monthly service charge to a union for representing the employees—who challenged a union's calculation of agency fees and who never agreed to submit fee disputes to arbitration could not be required by the union to exhaust an arbitration remedy before bringing the agency fee claims in federal court. [Air Line Pilots Ass'n v Miller (1998, US) 140 L Ed 2d 1070, 118 S Ct 1761.]

§ 32. Line item veto

The Supreme Court held that (1) certain parties had standing to challenge the validity, under the Federal Constitution, of the Line Item Veto Act, 2 USCS §§ 691 et seq., which allowed the President of the United States to cancel individual funding provisions contained in legislation enacted by Congress, and (2) the procedures set forth in the Act violated the Constitution's presentment clause, Art I, § 7, cl 2, which describes the procedures for enacting federal legislation. [Clinton v City of New York (1998, US) 141 L Ed 2d 393, 118 S Ct 2091.]

§ 33. Long distance telephone service

The court held that a long distance telephone services reseller's state-law claims against a federally regulated long distance carrier for breach of contract and tortious interference with contractual relations were pre-empted by the filed-tariff doctrine of § 203 of the Communications Act of 1934, 47 USCS § 203, under which doctrine a carrier's filed tariff rate is the only lawful charge. [AT&T v Central Office Tel. (1998, US) 141 L Ed 2d 222, 118 S Ct 1956.]

§ 34. Medicare

It was held that the "reaudit" rule, which permits a second audit of a hospital's base-year graduate medical education (GME) costs in order to insure accurate future provider reimbursements (1) is not impermissibly retroactive, and (2) is a reasonable interpretation of Medicare's GME Amendment, 42 USCS § 1395ww(h). [Regions Hosp. v Shalala (1998, US) 139 L Ed 2d 895, 118 S Ct 909.]

§ 35. Money laundering

The Supreme Court held that Missouri was not a proper venue for an accused's trial on counts of an indictment which charged the accused with money laundering—specifically, with conducting a financial transaction to avoid the transaction-reporting requirement of 18 USCS § 1956(a)(1)(B)(ii) and with engaging in monetary transactions in criminally derived property in violation of 18 USCS § 1957—where although the allegedly laundered money allegedly derived from illegal cocaine sales by others in Missouri, the counts at issue alleged acts occurring entirely in Florida. [United States v Cabrales (1998, US) 141 L Ed 2d 1, 118 S Ct 1772.]

§ 36. Multidistrict litigation

It was held that where several civil actions with common issues of fact are transferred to one Federal District Court pursuant to 28 USCS § 1407(a) for coordinated or consolidated pretrial proceedings, the District Court may not invoke 28 USCS § 1404(a) to assign a transferred case to itself for trial. [Lexecon Inc. v Milberg Weiss Bershad Hynes & Lerach (1998, US) 140 L Ed 2d 62, 118 S Ct 956.]

§ 37. National Endowment for the Arts

A statutory provision, 20 USCS § 954(d)(1), that required the National Endowment for the Arts to consider "general standards of decency and respect for . . . diverse beliefs and values" in judging art grant applications was held not to be facially invalid, as the provision neither inherently interfered with rights under the Federal Constitution's First Amendment nor violated constitutional vagueness principles. [National Endowment for the Arts v Finley (1998, US) 141 L Ed 2d 500, 118 S Ct 2168.]

§ 38. Parole revocation

The court held that the end of a federal habeas corpus petitioner's state prison term caused the petition—which challenged the validity of the petitioner's parole revocation—to be moot, as the petition no longer presented a case or controversy for purposes of the Federal Constitution's Article III. [Spencer v Kemna (1998, US) 140 L Ed 2d 43, 118 S Ct 978.]

The Supreme Court held that the federal exclusionary rule, which generally prohibits the introduction at criminal trial of evidence obtained in violation of a defendant's right under the Federal Constitution's Fourth Amendment to be free from unreasonable searches and seizures, does not apply in parole revocation hearings. [Pennsylvania Bd. of Probation & Parole v Scott (1998, US) 141 L Ed 2d 344, 118 S Ct 2014.]

§ 39. Pensions and retirement funds

It was held that (1) the 6-year limitations period set forth by 29 USCS § 1451(f)(1) concerning civil actions under the Multiemployer Pension Plan Amendments Act of 1980 (MPPAA) did not begin to run until an employer missed a payment according to the schedule for withdrawal liability payments set by the plan trustees pursuant to 29 USCS § 1399(b)(1); and (2) the fund's action to collect unpaid withdrawal liability from the employer under the MPPAA was timely, for purposes of § 1451(f)(1), as to any payments that came due during the 6 years preceding the suit, but the fund could not recover the employer's first installment payment, which came due prior to such time. [Bay Area Laundry & Dry Cleaning Pension Trust Fund v Ferbar Corp. (1997, US) 139 L Ed 2d 553, 118 S Ct 542.]

The Supreme Court held that for purposes of some provisions (29 USCS §§ 1161 et seq.) of the Employee Retirement Income Security Act of 1974 (ERISA), as amended by the Consolidated Omnibus Budget Reconciliation Act of 1985 (COBRA)—which provisions authorize a qualified beneficiary of an employer's group health plan to obtain continued coverage under the plan when the beneficiary might otherwise lose that benefit for certain reasons, such as the termination of employment—29 USCS § 1162(2)(D)(i) (later amended) does not allow an employer to deny COBRA continuation coverage to a qualified beneficiary who is covered under another group health plan at the time that the beneficiary makes a COBRA election. [Geissal v Moore Med. Corp. (1998, US) 141 L Ed 2d 64, 118 S Ct 1869.]

The court held, in a challenge under the due process and takings clauses of the Federal Constitution's Fifth Amendment, that a Coal Industry Retiree Health Benefit Act of 1992 provision, 26 USCS § 9706(a)(3), that allocated liability for funding health care benefits for coal industry retirees and their dependents was unconstitutional as applied to a former coal mine operator that left the coal industry in 1965. [Eastern Enters. v Apfel (1998, US) 141 L Ed 2d 451, 118 S Ct 2131.]

§ 40. Police chases

The Supreme Court held that a police officer did not violate the substantive due process guarantee of the Federal Constitution's Fourteenth Amendment by causing death through deliberate or reckless indifference to life in a high-speed automobile chase aimed at apprehending a suspected offender. [County of Sacramento v Lewis (1998, US) 140 L Ed 2d 1043, 118 S Ct 1708.]

§ 41. Polygraph tests

Military Rule of Evidence 707, which made polygraph evidence inadmissible in court-martial proceed-

1

ings, was held not to abridge an accused's right, under the Federal Constitution, to present a defense. [United States v Scheffer (1998, US) 140 L Ed 2d 413, 118 S Ct 1261.]

§ 42. Prisoners' rights

The court held that a prison inmate who, in a civil rights action under 42 USCS § 1983, alleged that a corrections officer had retaliated against the inmate for the inmate's exercise of his free speech rights under the Federal Constitution's First Amendment was not required, in order to defeat the officer's motion for summary judgment, to adduce clear and convincing of improper motive with respect to the allegedly retaliatory act. [Crawford-El v Britton (1998, US) 140 L Ed 2d 759, 118 S Ct 1584.]

It was held that Title II of the Americans with Disabilities Act of 1990, 42 USCS §§ 12131 et seq., which prohibits a "public entity" from discriminating against a "qualified individual with a disability" on account of that individual's disability, applies to inmates in state prisons. [Pennsylvania Dep't of Corrections v Yeskey (1998, US) 141 L Ed 2d 215, 118 S Ct 1952.]

§ 43. Products liability

The Supreme Court held that the Federal Constitution's full faith and credit clause, Art IV, § 1, did not bar an automobile manufacturer's former employee from testifying in a Missouri state court products liability action in which the employee had been subpoenaed to testify against the manufacturer, where previously, in settlement of claims and counterclaims precipitated by the manufacturer's discharge of the employee, the employee and the manufacturer had stipulated to a Michigan state court permanent injunction prohibiting the employee from testifying in any litigation involving the manufacturer as an owner, seller, manufacturer, or designer. [Baker by Thomas v GMC (1998, US) 139 L Ed 2d 580, 118 S Ct 657.]

§ 44. Public television

A state-owned public television broadcaster's decision to exclude from a televised congressional candidates' debate a third-party candidate who had little popular support was held to be a reasonable viewpoint-neutral exercise of journalistic discretion that was consistent with the free speech protections of the Federal Constitution's First Amendment. [Arkansas Ed. Television Comm'n v Forbes (1998, US) 140 L Ed 2d 875, 118 S Ct 1633.]

§ 45. Race discrimination

The court held that a white criminal defendant had the requisite standing to raise objections, under the equal protection and due process clauses of the Federal Constitution's Fourteenth Amendment, to alleged discrimination against black persons in the selection of Louisiana grand jurors. [Campbell v Louisiana (1998, US) 140 L Ed 2d 551, 118 S Ct 1419.]

§ 46. Racketeer Influenced and Corrupt Organizations Act (RICO)

The Supreme Court held that to be convicted, under 18 USCS § 1962(d), of conspiracy to violate the Racketeer Influenced and Corrupt Organizations Act (RICO), a party need not have committed or agreed to commit the two or more predicate acts requisite to an underlying substantive RICO offense under 18 USCS § 1962(c). [Salinas v United States (1997, US) 139 L Ed 2d 352, 118 S Ct 469.]

§ 47. Removal of state case

The court held that (1) landowners' state law administrative claims against a city's landmarks commission fell within a Federal District Court's original jurisdiction over federal questions under 28 USCS § 1331; (2) the claims had thus been properly removed from a state court to the District Court under 28 USCS § 1441(a); and (3) the District Court could exercise supplemental jurisdiction over the state claims, which constituted "other claims" that formed "part of the same case or controversy" for purposes of 28 USCS § 1367(a); but (4) a remand to the Federal Court of Appeals that earlier had addressed the jurisdiction issue was necessary in order to allow the Court of Appeals to address, in the first instance, the questions whether (a) abstention principles required the District Court to decline to exercise supplemental jurisdiction, or (b) the District Court should have refused to exercise supplemental jurisdiction under 28 USCS § 1367(c). [City of Chicago v International College of Surgeons (1997, US) 139 L Ed 2d 525, 118 S Ct 523.]

Claim preclusion by reason of prior orders of a federal court was held to be a defensive plea that provided no basis for removal of a case from a Louisiana state court to a Federal District Court, where (1) such a defense was properly made in state proceedings, and (2) the state courts' disposition was subject to the Supreme Court's ultimate review. [Rivet v Regions Bank (1998, US) 139 L Ed 2d 912, 118 S Ct 921.]

It was held that (1) the presence, in a case that was otherwise removable to a Federal District Court under 28 USCS § 1441(a), of claims that were barred from assertion in the District Court by the Federal Constitution's Eleventh Amendment did not destroy the District Court's removal jurisdiction, and (2) the District Court therefore could decide the claims in the case that were not barred by the Eleventh Amendment. [Wisconsin Dep't of Corrections v Schacht (1998, US) 141 L Ed 2d 364, 118 S Ct 2047.]

§ 48. Review by Supreme Court—generally

The Supreme Court was held to have jurisdiction under 28 USCS § 1254(1) to review a denial by a judge or panel of a Federal Court of Appeals of an application under 28 USCS § 2253(c)(1) for a certificate of appealability concerning a Federal District Court's denial of an accused's motion under 28 USCS § 2255 to vacate a federal conviction. [Hohn v United States (1998, US) 141 L Ed 2d 242, 118 S Ct 1969.]

See Rivet v Regions Bank (1998, US) 139 L Ed 2d 912, 118 S Ct 921, supra § 47, in which it was held that claim preclusion by reason of prior orders of a federal court was a defensive plea that provided no basis for removal of a case from a Louisiana state court to a Federal District Court, where (1) such a defense was properly made in state proceedings, and (2) the state courts' disposition was subject to the Supreme Court's ultimate review.

As to in forma pauperis proceedings in the Supreme Court, see § 29, supra.

§ 49. —Dismissal of writ of certiorari

A writ of certiorari to the Supreme Court of Alabama concerning the Alabama court's decision, on interlocutory appeal in a 42 USCS § 1983 action, that had ordered a remand for further proceedings was dismissed, because the decision was not a final judgment within the meaning of 28 USCS § 1257(a). [Jefferson v City of Tarrant (1997, US) 139 L Ed 2d 433, 118 S Ct 481.]

The Supreme Court dismissed, as improvidently granted, a writ of certiorari to review a Federal Court of Appeals decision, where (1) certiorari had been granted as to a question whether the failure to instruct the jury on an element of an offense constituted harmless error, and (2) six members of the Supreme Court, although unable to agree on an opinion, agreed that the question on which the Supreme Court had granted certiorari was not fairly presented by the lower court record. [Rogers v United States (1998, US) 139 L Ed 2d 686, 118 S Ct 673.]

The Supreme Court also dismissed as improvidently granted a writ of certiorari to review a decision by the United States Court of Appeals for the Seventh Circuit involving the question whether it was reasonable, under the Federal Constitution's Fourth Amendment guarantee against unreasonable searches and seizures, for police officers of an Illinois village to make a full custodial arrest of an individual for allegedly operating a business without a license, in violation of a village ordinance, where such a violation assertedly was punishable by only a fine and did not involve a breach of the peace. [Ricci v Village of Arlington Heights (1998, US) 140 L Ed 2d 789, 118 S Ct 1693.]

§ 50. Search and seizure

It was held that (1) the Federal Constitution's Fourth Amendment does not hold police officers to a higher standard than the test articulated in Richards v Wisconsin (1997) 520 US 385, 137 L Ed 2d 615, 117 S Ct 1416—that a no-knock entry is justified if police have a reasonable suspicion that knocking and announcing will be dangerous or futile, or will inhibit the effective investigation of the crime—when a no-knock entry results in the destruction of property; (2) this same standard is the measure to determine the applicability of the knock-and-announce requirement's exigent circumstances exception codified in 18 USCS § 3109; and (3) in the instant case, police officers, who broke a garage window while executing a no-knock warrant at a home, did not violate the Fourth Amendment or § 3109. [United States v Ramirez (1998, US) 140 L Ed 2d 191, 118 S Ct 992.]

See Pennsylvania Bd. of Probation & Parole v Scott (1998, US) 141 L Ed 2d 344, 118 S Ct 2014, supra § 38, in which the court held that the federal exclusionary rule, which generally prohibits the introduction at criminal trial of evidence obtained in violation of a defendant's right under the Federal Constitution's Fourth Amendment to be free from unreasonable searches and seizures, does not apply in parole revocation hearings.

Also, see Ricci v Village of Arlington Heights (1998, US) 140 L Ed 2d 789, 118 S Ct 1693, supra § 49, in which the Supreme Court dismissed as improvidently granted a writ of certiorari to review a decision by the United States Court of Appeals for the Seventh Circuit involving the question whether it was reasonable, under the Federal Constitution's Fourth Amendment guarantee against unreasonable searches and seizures, for police officers of an Illinois village to make a full custodial arrest of an individual for allegedly operating a business without a license, in violation of a village ordinance, where such a violation assertedly was punishable by only a fine and did not involve a breach of the peace.

§ 51. Self-incrimination

The Supreme Court held, with respect to a resident alien's refusal to answer questions stemming from the alien's possible participation in Nazi persecution during World War II, that the alien's asserted fear of foreign criminal prosecution was beyond the scope of the privilege against self-incrimination under the Federal Constitution's Fifth Amendment. [United States v Balsys (1998, US) 141 L Ed 2d 575, 118 S Ct 2218.]

§ 52. Settlement agreements

It was held that neither Rule 60(b) of the Federal Rules of Civil Procedure, concerning relief from a judgment, nor the Quiet Title Act, 28 USCS § 2409a, gave a federal court jurisdiction to reopen a settlement agreement in which title to disputed land had been quieted in the United States in return for a payment to the land's former owners, who were seeking to reopen the agreement. [United States v Beggerly (1998, US) 141 L Ed 2d 32, 118 S Ct 1862.]

§ 53. Sex discrimination

The court held that workplace sexual harassment is actionable as sex discrimination under a provision of Title VII of Civil Rights Act of 1964 (42 USCS § 2000e-2(a)(1)), where the harasser and the harassed employee are of the same sex. [Oncale v Sundowner Offshore Servs. (1998, US) 140 L Ed 2d 201, 118 S Ct 998.]

The Supreme Court held that under Title IX of the Education Amendments of 1972, 20 USCS §§ 1681 et seq., monetary damages in an implied cause of action may not be recovered for a teacher's sexual harassment of a student, unless a school district official with authority to institute corrective measures on the district's behalf has actual notice of, and is deliberately indifferent to, the teacher's misconduct. [Gebser v Lago Vista Indep. Sch. Dist. (1998, US) 141 L Ed 2d 277, 118 S Ct 1989.]

With respect to actions against an employer under Title VII of the Civil Rights Act of 1964, 42 USCS §§ 2000e et seq., by an employee who allegedly has been sexually harassed by a supervisor, the court held in one case that under Title VII, an employer may (1) without a showing of negligence or other fault on the part of the employer for a supervisor's actions, be subject to vicarious liability, for the supervisor's creation of a hostile workplace environment, to a sexually harassed employee who refuses the unwelcome and threatening sexual advances of the supervisor, yet suffers no adverse, tangible job consequences, but (2) raise an affirmative defense to liability or damages, subject to proof by a preponderance of the evidence [Burlington Indus. v Ellerth (1998, US) 141 L Ed 2d 633, 118 S Ct 2257]; and the court made this same holding in a second case that was decided on the same day [Faragher v City of Boca Raton (1998, US) 141 L Ed 2d 662, 118 S Ct 2275].

§ 54. Social Security disability benefits

The Supreme Court held that a Federal District Court's order, remanding a case in which the Social Security Administration had denied an individual's application for disability benefits under § 223 of the Social Security Act, 42 USCS § 423, was appealable under 28 USCS § 1291 and 42 USCS § 405(g). [Forney v Apfel (1998, US) 141 L Ed 2d 269, 118 S Ct 1984.]

§ 55. State and local taxes

It was held that a New York state statutory provision, which effectively denied only nonresidents a state income tax deduction for alimony paid, violated the privileges and immunities clause in Art IV, § 2 of the Federal Constitution. [Lunding v New York Tax Appeals Tribunal (1998, US) 139 L Ed 2d 717, 118 S Ct 766.]

A Florida state court was held to have erred, under Reich v Collins (1994) 513 US 106, 130 L Ed 2d 454, 115 S Ct 547, in denying a magazine access to an adequate postpayment remedy for a refund of the state sales tax that the magazine had paid under a scheme that unconstitutionally exempted newspapers but not magazines from state sales tax. [Newsweek, Inc. v Florida Dep't of Revenue (1998, US) 139 L Ed 2d 888, 118 S Ct 904.]

The Supreme Court held, with respect to severance taxes and gross proceeds taxes that had been paid by a non-Indian company to Montana and certain Montana counties concerning coal mined by the company on former reservation land to which the United States held mineral rights in trust for the Crow Tribe of Indians, that the restitution, sought by the tribe, of the full amount of such taxes paid for periods before the tribe had in place a valid severance tax of its own was not warranted. [Montana v Crow Tribe of Indians (1998, US) 140 L Ed 2d 898, 118 S Ct 1650.]

The court held that (1) an Indian tribe's repurchase of its former reservation land that had been made alienable by Congress and sold to non-Indians by the Federal Government did not cause the land to reassume the status of exemption from state taxation, and (2) therefore, the land was subject to a county's ad valorem property taxes. [Cass County v Leech Lake Band of Chippewa Indians (1998, US) 141 L Ed 2d 90, 118 S Ct 1904.]

§ 56. State procedural default

It was held that a Federal Court of Appeals, in reviewing a Federal District Court's habeas corpus decision with respect to a state prisoner's conviction, was not required to raise—on the Court of Appeals' own motion—the issue of the prisoner's state procedural default, that is, a critical failure to comply with state procedural law. [Trest v Cain (1997, US) 139 L Ed 2d 444, 118 S Ct 478.]

§ 57. Student loans

The Supreme Court held that specific intent to injure or defraud someone, whether the United States or another, was not an element of the misapplication of funds proscribed, prior to 1992, by 20 USCS § 2097(a) (later amended), which then made it a felony "knowingly and willfully" to misapply student loan funds insured under the federal Guaranteed Student Loan program (later renamed) of Title IV of the Higher Education Act of 1965 (20 USCS §§ 1070 et seq.). [Bates v United States (1997, US) 139 L Ed 2d 215, 118 S Ct 285.]

SUMMARIES OF DECISIONS

CARSON LYNN BROWN, Petitioner
v
R. WILLIAMS et al.

522 US —, 139 L Ed 2d 1, 118 S Ct 1

[No. 97-5370]

Decided October 20, 1997.

Decision: Person denied leave to proceed in forma pauperis on (1) petition for certiorari to review Federal Court of Appeals' dismissal of appeal after person's failure to pay filing fee, and (2) future petitions for certiorari in noncriminal matters.

SUMMARY

An individual sought leave to proceed in forma pauperis in the United States Supreme Court with respect to a petition for certiorari to review a decision of the United States Court of Appeals for the Sixth Circuit dismissing the individual's appeal after he had failed to pay the required filing fee. During an 8-year period, the Supreme Court had denied, without recorded dissent, each of the eight petitions filed by the individual in the Supreme Court and had, in one instance, denied the individual leave to proceed in forma pauperis by invoking Supreme Court Rule 39.8—which authorizes the Supreme Court to deny such leave with respect to frivolous petitions—after which, according to the Supreme Court, the individual

1

had continued filing frivolous petitions in the Supreme Court. The instant petition alleged that certain prison officials had conspired to violate the individual's federal constitutional rights by such means as denying him access to the courts and sabotaging his laundry, and that the federal district judge below was biased against the individual as an "African Jew."

In a per curiam opinion expressing the view of REHNQUIST, Ch. J., and O'CONNOR, SCALIA, KENNEDY, SOUTER, THOMAS, GINSBURG, and BREYER, XC, JJ., the Supreme Court (1) commenting that the allegations in the instant petition were frivolous, (a) denied the individual leave to proceed in forma pauperis, and (b) allowed the individual a specified period within which to pay the docketing fee required by Supreme Court Rule 38(a) and to submit his petition in compliance with Supreme Court Rule 33.1; and (2) commenting that the individual had a history of abusing the Supreme Court's certiorari process, directed the Clerk of the Supreme Court not to accept any further petitions for certiorari in noncriminal matters from the individual unless he first complied with Rules 33.1 and 38(a).

STEVENS, J., dissented for the reasons expressed in a previous Supreme Court case involving some similar issues.

STATE OIL COMPANY, Petitioner

v

BARKAT U. KHAN and KHAN & ASSOCIATES, INC.

522 US —, 139 L Ed 2d 199, 118 S Ct 275

[No. 96-871]

Argued October 7, 1997.
Decided November 4, 1997.

Decision: Vertical maximum price fixing held (1) not to be per se antitrust violation of § 1 of Sherman Act (15 USCS § 1), and (2) instead, to be subject to evaluation under rule of reason.

SUMMARY

In Albrecht v Herald Co. (1968) 390 US 145, 19 L Ed 2d 998, 88 S Ct 869, which involved a newspaper publisher's alleged attempt to fix the maximum resale price of newspapers, the United States Supreme Court held that vertical maximum price fixing was a per se violation of § 1 of the Sherman Act (15 USCS § 1), which prohibits contracts, combinations, or conspiracies in restraint of trade. An individual and his corporation entered into an agreement with an oil company to lease and operate a gas station owned by the oil company. The agreement included a provision that if the retail price charged for gasoline sold was higher than a price suggested by the oil company, then the excess was to be rebated to the oil company. After a dispute arose, the individual and his corporation (1) sued the oil company in the United States District Court for the Northern District of Illinois, and (2) included a claim that the oil company had engaged in

3

price fixing in violation of § 1. However, the District Court found that the complaint's allegations did not state a per se violation of the Sherman Act. Subsequently, the District Court, on cross-motions, entered summary judgment for the oil company on the Sherman Act claim, as the court concluded that the individual and his corporation had failed to demonstrate antitrust injury or harm to competition (907 F Supp 1202, 1995 US Dist LEXIS 17068). The United States Court of Appeals for the Seventh Circuit, in reversing in pertinent part, expressed the view that (1) the agreement fixed maximum prices by making it worthless to exceed the suggested retail price, and (2) under Albrecht v Herald Co., the oil company's maximum pricing scheme was a per se antitrust violation (93 F3d 1358, 1996 US App LEXIS 22504).

On certiorari, the Supreme Court vacated and remanded. In an opinion by O'CONNOR, J., expressing the unanimous view of the court, it was held—expressly overruling Albrecht v Herald Co.—that (1) vertical maximum price fixing is not a per se violation of § 1; (2) instead, vertical maximum price fixing is to be evaluated under the rule of reason; and (3) under the circumstances in the case at hand, the Court of Appeals ought to review in the first instance the question whether the individual and his corporation were entitled to recover damages on the basis of the oil company's conduct.

COUNSEL

John Baumgartner argued the cause for petitioner.

Joel I. Klein argued the cause for the United States, as amicus curiae, by special leave of court.

Anthony S. Divincenzo argued the cause for respondents.

Pamela J. Harbour argued the cause for the state of New York, as amicus curiae, by special leave of court.

GARRIT BATES, Petitioner

v

UNITED STATES

522 US —, 139 L Ed 2d 215, 118 S Ct 285

[No. 96-7185]

Argued October 7, 1997.
Decided November 4, 1997.

Decision: Specific intent to injure or defraud someone, whether United States or another, held not to be element of misapplication of federal Guaranteed Student Loan funds proscribed by 20 USCS § 1097(a) (later amended) prior to 1992.

SUMMARY

A federal indictment charged an accused with pre-1992 violations of 20 USCS § 1097(a) (later amended), which, prior to 1992, made it a felony knowingly and willfully to misapply student loan funds insured under the federal Guaranteed Student Loan (GSL) program (later renamed) of Title IV of the Higher Education Act of 1965 (20 USCS §§ 1070 et seq.). Allegedly, the accused was the chief financial officer of a technical school which failed to make to lenders some required partial refunds of GSL proceeds for students who had withdrawn before the end of a term—thus allegedly leaving the students, and if the students defaulted, the Federal Government, liable for the full amount of those loans. However, a Federal District Court, in dismissing the indictment in response to a pretrial motion by the accused, expressed the view that (1) a conviction under § 1097(a) required an allegation of the accused's intent

6

to injure or defraud the United States, and (2) the indictment lacked such an allegation. On appeal, the United States Court of Appeals for the Seventh Circuit, in vacating the District Court's judgment and in reinstating the prosecution, expressed the view at the time of the accused's alleged wrongdoing, § 1097(a) required the government to prove only that the accused had misapplied Title IV funds and that the accused had done so knowingly and willfully (96 F3d 964, 1996 US App LEXIS 24828).

On certiorari, the United States Supreme Court affirmed. In an opinion by GINSBURG, J., expressing the unanimous view of the court, it was held that with respect to the § 1097(a) charges, the Federal Government was not required to allege and prove, in addition to a knowledge requirement, that the accused had an intent to injure or defraud anyone, because specific intent to injure or defraud someone, whether the United States or another, was not an element of the misapplication of funds proscribed by § 1097(a) prior to 1992.

COUNSEL

C. Richard Oren argued the cause for petitioner.
Lisa S. Blatt argued the cause for respondent.

CITY OF MONROE et al., Petitioners

v

UNITED STATES

522 US —, 139 L Ed 2d 339, 118 S Ct 400

[No. 97-122]

Decided November 17, 1997.

Decision: State-law rule requiring majority vote to win election held to have been precleared for purposes of § 5 of Voting Rights Act of 1965, as amended (42 USCS § 1973c), and Georgia city held entitled to conduct elections under such rule.

SUMMARY

A Georgia city was covered by § 5 of the Voting Rights Act of 1965, as amended (42 USCS § 1973c), which required the preclearance of certain voting changes. Prior to 1966, the city's charter did not specify whether a majority vote or a plurality vote was needed to win a mayoral election. In practice, the city changed in 1966 from using a plurality-voting requirement to using a majority-voting requirement. The United States (1) brought suit against the city and some of its officials in the United States District Court for the Middle District of Georgia; (2) included a claim that the city had not sought preclearance of the change to majority voting, as required by § 5; and (3) sought, among other matters, to enjoin such majority voting and to require the city to return to plurality voting. The District Court, in granting summary judgment and injunctive relief in favor of the United States, expressed the view that the change to majority voting had not been precleared in

8

accordance with § 5 (962 F Supp 1501, 1997 US Dist
LEXIS 5449). On a motion by the city, the United States
Supreme Court granted a stay pending appeal (521 US
——, 138 L Ed 2d 1046, 118 S Ct 14).

On appeal, the Supreme Court reversed. In a per
curiam opinion expressing the view of REHNQUIST,
Ch. J., and STEVENS, O'CONNOR, KENNEDY, THOMAS,
and GINSBURG, JJ., it was held that the city was entitled
to conduct elections under the auspices of a controlling
state-law default rule that required a majority vote in a
municipal election if the municipal charter did not
provide for plurality voting—which rule had been
passed by the state's legislature in 1968 as part of a
comprehensive municipal election code—because the
United States Attorney General had approved and
precleared the default rule when the state had submitted the 1968 code to the Attorney General for preclearance, for among other matters, the submission had
given the Attorney General an adequate opportunity to
determine the purpose of the default-rule electoral
changes and whether they would adversely affect mi-
nority voting.

SCALIA, J., concurring in the judgment, expressed
the view that (1) with respect to the submission of the
1968 code, the Attorney General ought to have known
that a switch to majority voting in some municipalities
was being approved; and (2) if that had seemed possi-
bly troublesome, then the burden was upon the Attorney General to inquire further.

SOUTER, J., joined by BREYER, J., dissenting, expressed
the view that (1) neither the city nor the state had
disclosed the pre-1966 city charter silence on which the
1968 code's default rule might operate to provide a
new majority-voting requirement, and (2) it was unrea-

9

sonable to suppose that the Attorney General's approval of the 1968 code had been meant to preclear its undisclosed applications.

BREYER, J., joined by SOUTER, J., dissenting, expressed the view that Supreme Court ought to reject the city's preclearance argument on the basis of a 1980 Supreme Court precedent which—in rejecting a similar preclearance argument by another Georgia city—had turned upon the practical fact that the Attorney General, in preclearing the 1968 code, would not have intended to preclear earlier and potentially unlawful local changes of which the Attorney General had not been specifically told.

MARIO SALINAS, Petitioner

v

UNITED STATES

522 US —, 139 L Ed 2d 352, 118 S Ct 469

[No. 96-738]

Argued October 8, 1997.
Decided December 2, 1997.

Decision: Bribery conviction under 18 USCS
§ 666(a)(1)(B) held not to require proof that
bribe had any particular influence on federal
funds; RICO conspiracy conviction under 18 USCS
§ 1962(d) held not to require proof that defendant
committed or agreed to commit predicate acts.

SUMMARY

Under 18 USCS § 666(a)(1)(B) together with other
provisions of 18 USCS § 666, an agent of an organization, a state, local, or Indian tribal government, or any
agency thereof is prohibited from accepting or agreeing to accept anything of value from any person,
intending to be influenced or rewarded in connection
with any business, transaction, or series of transactions
of such organization, government, or agency that involves anything of value of $5,000 or more, when the
organization, government, or agency receives, in any
1-year period, benefits in excess of $10,000 under a
federal program. The United States Marshals Service
and a Texas county entered into some agreements
under which the county would take custody of federal
prisoners, in exchange for payments from the Federal
Government. One of the federal prisoners who was

11

housed in the county jail pursuant to these agreements allegedly paid monetary bribes to the county sheriff to allow the prisoner contact visits with the prisoner's wife or girlfriend, while a deputy allegedly (1) arranged for the contact visits when the sheriff was not available; (2) on occasion, stood watch outside the room where the visits took place; and (3) received from the prisoner, in return for assisting with the scheme, a pair of designer watches and a pickup truck. In a subsequent federal prosecution of the sheriff and the deputy on the basis of this alleged scheme, the deputy was charged with (1) two counts of bribery in violation of § 666(a)(1)(B); (2) one substantive count, under 18 USCS § 1962(c), of violating the Racketeer Influenced and Corrupt Organizations Act (RICO); and (3) one RICO count, under 18 USCS § 1962(d), of conspiracy to violate § 1962(c). The jury acquitted the deputy on the substantive RICO count, but convicted him on the bribery counts and the RICO conspiracy count. On appeal, the United States Court of Appeals for the Fifth Circuit, in affirming the deputy's convictions, expressed the view that (1) the case at hand was within the scope of conduct which Congress intended to encompass within § 666, (2) a RICO conspirator did not need to agree to perform personally the two predicate acts of racketeering activity that comprised the substantive violation of RICO, and (3) there was sufficient evidence to convict the deputy of RICO conspiracy (89 F3d 1185, 1996 US App LEXIS 21873).

On certiorari, the United States Supreme Court affirmed. In an opinion by KENNEDY, J., expressing the unanimous view of the court, it was held that (1) as a matter of statutory construction, for purposes of charging bribery, § 666(a)(1)(B) does not require the government to prove that the bribe in question had any particular influence on federal funds; (2) under this

12

construction, § 666(a)(1)(B) was constitutional as applied to the case at hand, in that such an application did not extend federal power beyond its proper bounds; (3) in order for a RICO defendant to be convicted under § 1962(d) for conspiring to violate § 1962(c), it is not required that the defendant commit or agree to commit two or more predicate acts that are needed for a substantive conviction under § 1962(c); and (4) there was ample evidence to support the deputy's RICO conspiracy conviction.

COUNSEL

Francisco J. Enriquez argued the cause for petitioner.
Paul R. Q. Wolfson argued the cause for respondent.

MURPHY J. FOSTER, JR., Governor of Louisiana, et
al., Petitioners

v

G. SCOTT LOVE, PAUL S. BERGERON, KATHLEEN
B. BALHOFF, and BENNIE BAKER-BOURGEOIS

522 US —, 139 L Ed 2d 369, 118 S Ct 464

[No. 96-670]

Argued October 6, 1997.
Decided December 2, 1997.

Decision: Louisiana's "open primary" statutory
scheme for electing United States senators and
representatives held violative of 2 USCS §§ 1 and 7.

SUMMARY

The date for the election of United States representatives is established for all states by 2 USCS § 7, which
sets such date as the Tuesday after the first Monday in
November of every even-numbered year. The same rule
is set for the election of United States senators by 2
USCS § 1, which provides that senators are to be
elected at the same election that representatives are
chosen—and hence on the same federal election day. A
separate federal statute, 2 USCS § 8, provides that the
states may prescribe the time for holding elections for
a United States representative to fill a vacancy where
such vacancy is caused by a failure to elect at the time
prescribed by law. Under a Louisiana statutory scheme
which took effect in 1978, (1) an election popularly
known as an "open primary" is to be held in October
of a federal election year; (2) in such open primary, (a)
all candidates for congressional offices appear on the
14

same ballot, regardless of party, and (b) all voters, with like disregard of party, are entitled to vote; (3) if no candidate for a given office receives a majority in the open primary, a runoff between the two top votegetters is held on the federal election day; and (4) if a candidate receives a majority in the open primary, such candidate "is elected," and no further action is taken on the federal election day to fill the office in question. Since 1978, more than 80 percent of the contested congressional elections in Louisiana ended with the open primary. In 1995, several individuals who were registered to vote in Louisiana filed an action in the United States District Court for the Middle District of Louisiana against Louisiana state officials. The voters alleged that the Louisiana open primary system violated §§ 1 and 7. The District Court granted the state officials' motion for summary judgment. On appeal, a panel of the United States Court of Appeals for the Fifth Circuit, in reversing and in ordering a remand, expressed the view that Louisiana's system conflicted with §§ 1 and 7 (90 F3d 1026, 1996 US App LEXIS 18733). The Court of Appeals then denied rehearing by the panel and en banc (100 F3d 413, 1996 US App LEXIS 29932).

On certiorari, the United States Supreme Court affirmed. In an opinion by SOUTER, J., expressing the unanimous view of the court in pertinent part, it was held that Louisiana's "open primary" statutory scheme for electing congressional officials violated §§ 1 and 7, and that such scheme was void to the extent that it conflicted with federal law, in part because (1) §§ 1 and 7 referred to the combined actions of voters and officials meant to make a final selection of an office-holder, subject only to the possibility of a later runoff election pursuant to § 8; (2) by establishing a particular day as "the day" on which such actions must take place,

§§ 1 and 7 regulated the time of the election, a matter on which the Federal Constitution's elections clause (Art I, § 4, cl 1) explicitly gave Congress the final say; and (3) a contested selection of candidates for a congressional office that was concluded as a matter of law before the federal election day, with no act in law or in fact to take place on the date chosen by Congress, violated § 7.

COUNSEL

Richard P. Ieyoub argued the cause for petitioners.
M. Miller Baker argued the cause for respondents.

———

MELVIN JEFFERSON, Individually and as Administrator of the Estate of Alberta K. Jefferson, Deceased, et al., Petitioners

v

CITY OF TARRANT, ALABAMA

522 US —, 139 L Ed 2d 433, 118 S Ct 481

[No. 96-957]

Argued November 4, 1997.
Decided December 9, 1997.

Decision: Writ of certiorari to Alabama Supreme Court concerning its decision, on interlocutory appeal in 42 USCS § 1983 action, dismissed, because decision was not final judgment within meaning of 28 USCS § 1257(a).

SUMMARY

Two survivors of a person who died in a fire brought in an Alabama state trial court against an Alabama city a suit asserting, with respect to the actions of city firefighters, state law claims for wrongful death and for the tort of outrage and claims under 42 USCS § 1983—under which, the United States Supreme Court has held, punitive damages may not be recovered against a municipality—for violation of the due process and equal protection clauses of the Federal Constitution's Fourteenth Amendment. The trial court denied in its entirety the city's motion for summary judgment on all claims and denied in part the city's motion for judgment on the pleadings on the § 1983 claims, where, with respect to the § 1983 claims, the trial court ruled that, notwithstanding the punitive-damages-only

17

limitation in the state's wrongful death act, the survivors could recover compensatory damages upon proof that the city had violated the decedent's federal constitutional rights. The trial court certified the damages question to the Supreme Court of Alabama for immediate review, and the Supreme Court of Alabama granted the city permission to appeal from the denial of its motion for judgment on the pleadings. On interlocutory appeal, the Supreme Court of Alabama reversed the trial court's judgment and remanded for further proceedings consistent with the opinion of the Supreme Court of Alabama (682 So 2d 29).

On certiorari to resolve the question whether, when a decedent's death is alleged to have resulted from a deprivation of federal rights occurring in the state, the state's wrongful death act governs the recovery by the representative of the decedent's estate under § 1983, the United States Supreme Court dismissed the writ of certiorari as improvidently granted for want of jurisdiction. In an opinion by GINSBURG, J., joined by REHNQUIST, Ch. J., and O'CONNOR, SCALIA, KENNEDY, SOUTER, THOMAS, and BREYER, JJ., it was held—where the city, in its brief on the merits, for the first time had asserted that the Supreme Court lacked jurisdiction to review the interlocutory order of the state's highest court—that the Supreme Court lacked jurisdiction under 28 USCS § 1257(a), because the state's highest court had not yet rendered a final judgment within the meaning of § 1257(a), since (1) the state's highest court had answered a single certified question that affected only two of the four counts in the survivors' complaint; (2) absent settlement or further dispositive motions, the proceedings on remand would include a trial on the merits of the state law claims; and (3) the instant case did not come within the limited set of situations in which the Supreme Court had found

18

finality as to the federal issue despite the ordering of further proceedings in the lower state courts.

STEVENS, J., dissenting, expressed the view that (1) as to jurisdiction, the instant case was governed by the United States Supreme Court's 1987 holding that a particular state court judgment resolving a federal question was final within the meaning of § 1257(a), even though the federal question could have been (a) relitigated in the state court if the appeals had been dismissed, and (b) raised in a second appeal to the Supreme Court after the conclusion of further proceedings in the state courts; and (2) on the merits, the judgment of the Supreme Court of Alabama ought to be reversed.

COUNSEL

Dennis G. Pantazis argued the cause for petitioners. John G. Roberts argued the cause for respondent.

———————

RICHARD F. TREST, Petitioner

v

BURL CAIN, Warden

522 US —, 139 L Ed 2d 444, 118 S Ct 478

[No. 96-7901]

Argued November 10, 1997.
Decided December 9, 1997.

Decision: Federal Court of Appeals held not required, in habeas corpus case, to raise—on court's own motion—issue of state prisoner's procedural default, that is, critical failure to comply with state procedural law.

SUMMARY

A prisoner, alleging that his conviction in a Louisiana state court for armed robbery had been defective under the Federal Constitution, petitioned for habeas corpus relief in a Federal District Court, which denied the petition. The United States Court of Appeals for the Fifth Circuit, in affirming the District Court's judgment, expressed the view that (1) because the prisoner had failed to raise his federal claims on time in state court, the state court would refuse to consider his claims; (2) such state procedural default amounted to an adequate and independent state ground for denying the prisoner relief; and (3) in the absence of special circumstances, a federal habeas corpus court could not reach the merits of the prisoner's federal claims (94 F3d 1005). The parties themselves had neither raised nor argued the procedural default issue in the Court of Appeals and were not given an opportunity for argument on that issue.

On certiorari, the United States Supreme Court vacated the Court of Appeals' judgment and remanded the case for further proceedings. In an opinion by BREYER, J., expressing the unanimous view of the court, it was held that (1) a Court of Appeals, in reviewing a District Court's habeas corpus decision with respect to a state prisoner's conviction, is not required to raise, on the Court of Appeals' own motion, the issue of the prisoner's state procedural default; and (2) under the circumstances presented, it was not appropriate for the Supreme Court to examine the question whether the Court of Appeals was permitted, although not required, to raise the procedural default issue.

COUNSEL

Rebecca L. Hudsmith argued the cause for petitioner.

Kathleen E. Petersen argued the cause for respondent.

JOHN HUDSON, LARRY BARESEL, and JACK BUT-
LER RACKLEY, Petitioners

v

UNITED STATES

522 US —, 139 L Ed 2d 450, 118 S Ct 488

[No. 96-976]

Argued October 8, 1997.
Decided December 10, 1997.

Decision: Double jeopardy clause held not to bar
prosecution for allegedly illegal lending transactions, where individuals had stipulated to sanctions
in prior administrative proceedings involving
transactions.

SUMMARY

In February 1989, the Office of the Comptroller of
the Currency (OCC) issued a notice which alleged that
three individuals who held positions as officers and/or
directors of two Oklahoma banks had violated 12 USCS
§§ 84 and 375b by using the individuals' banking
positions to arrange a series of loans to third parties.
Pursuant to such notice, the OCC assessed a monetary
penalty of $100,000 against one of the individuals and
penalties of $50,000 each against the other two indi-
viduals. In addition, the OCC issued a notice, pursuant
to the authority of 12 USCS § 1818(e), that the OCC
intended to bar the individuals from further participation in the conduct of any insured depository institution. In October 1989, the individuals resolved the
OCC proceedings against them by each entering into a
stipulation and consent order which provided that the

individuals agreed (1) to pay assessments of between
$12,500 and $16,500 each, and (2) not to participate in
the affairs of any banking institution without the written authorization of the OCC and all other relevant
regulatory agencies. In August 1992, the individuals
were indicted in the United States District Court for the
Western District of Oklahoma on charges of conspiracy,
misapplication of bank funds, and making false bank
entries. The violations charged in the indictment rested
on the same lending transactions that formed the basis
for the prior administrative actions brought by the
OCC. The individuals moved to dismiss the indictment
on grounds that the indictment violated the double
jeopardy clause of the Federal Constitution's Fifth
Amendment. The District Court ultimately granted the
individuals' motion to dismiss (879 F Supp 1113, 1994
US Dist LEXIS 20357). On appeal, the United States
Court of Appeals for the Tenth Circuit, reversing,
expressed the view that under United States v Halper
(1989) 490 US 435, 104 L Ed 2d 487, 109 S Ct 1892—in
which the United States Supreme Court had ruled that
a civil sanction that could not be said solely to serve a
remedial purpose, but rather could be explained only
as also serving either retributive or deterrent purposes,
was punishment for purposes of the double jeopardy
clause—the monetary sanctions imposed on the individuals were not so grossly disproportional to the
proven damages to the government as to render such
sanctions punishment for double jeopardy purposes
(92 F3d 1026, 1996 US App LEXIS 19982).

On certiorari, the Supreme Court affirmed. In an
opinion by REHNQUIST, Ch. J., joined by O'CONNOR,
SCALIA, KENNEDY, and THOMAS, JJ., it was
held—expressly disavowing in large part the method of
analysis that had been used in United States v
Halper—that the double jeopardy clause was not a bar

23

to the federal criminal prosecution of the three individuals, because (1) Congress had intended that the OCC money penalties and occupational debarment sanctions imposed for violations of §§ 84 and 375b be civil in nature, and (2) there was little evidence—much less the "clearest proof" required under the Supreme Court's decision in United States v Ward (1980) 448 US 242, 65 L Ed 2d 742, 100 S Ct 2636—to suggest that either the OCC money penalties or debarment sanctions were so punitive in form and effect as to render them criminal despite Congress' intent to the contrary.

SCALIA, J., joined by THOMAS, J., concurring, expressed the view that (1) the double jeopardy clause prohibited successive prosecution, not successive punishment, and (2) the Supreme Court's multiple punishments jurisprudence essentially duplicated the correct law under the double jeopardy clause so long as a requirement of successive criminal prosecutions was maintained.

STEVENS, J., concurring in the judgment, expressed the view that (1) the case at hand should have been decided by application of the "same-elements" test, under the Supreme Court's decision in Blockburger v United States (1932) 284 US 299, 76 L Ed 306, 52 S Ct 180, to identify the same offense for double jeopardy purposes; (2) accordingly, a re-examination of the Supreme Court's decision in United States v Halper was not required in the case at hand; and (3) the government could not use the "civil" label for a sanction to escape entirely the double jeopardy clause's command.

SOUTER, J., concurring in the judgment, expressed the view that (1) where a successive prosecution under the Supreme Court's decision in Blockburger v United States was permissible even on the assumption that each penalty was criminal, the double jeopardy issue

24

was necessarily settled; and (2) the requisite "clearest proof" under the Supreme Court's decision in United States v Ward that a penalty was criminal for double jeopardy purposes should be read to be a function of the strength of the countervailing indications of the penalty's civil nature.

BREYER, J., joined by GINSBURG, J., concurring in the judgment, expressed the view that (1) the proper approach for determining whether a penalty was criminal for double jeopardy purposes would have been under the nonexclusive list of factors set forth in the Supreme Court's decision in Kennedy v Mendoza-Martinez (1963) 372 US 144, 9 L Ed 2d 644, 83 S Ct 554; (2) it was possible that a statute that provided for a punishment that normally was civil in nature could nonetheless amount to a criminal punishment as applied in special circumstances; and (3) in the case at hand, (a) the statutory penalty was not on its face a criminal penalty, and (b) the application of the statute to the individuals did not amount to criminal punishment.

COUNSEL

Bernard J. Rothbaum argued the cause for petitioners.

Michael R. Dreeben argued the cause for respondent.

———————

LYNNE KALINA, Petitioner

v

RODNEY FLETCHER

522 US —, 139 L Ed 2d 471, 118 S Ct 502

[No. 96-792]

Argued October 7, 1997.

Decided December 10, 1997.

Decision: Conduct of prosecuting attorney in making allegedly false statements of fact in document supporting application for arrest warrant held not protected by absolute prosecutorial immunity from 42 USCS § 1983 liability.

SUMMARY

A deputy prosecuting attorney for King County, Washington, commenced a criminal proceeding against a suspect by filing in the King County Superior Court (1) an unsworn information charging the suspect with burglary, (2) an unsworn motion for an arrest warrant, and (3) a certification for determination of probable cause, in which document the prosecutor summarized the evidence supporting the charge and swore to the truth of the alleged facts under penalty of perjury. Although state law required an arrest warrant to be supported by either an affidavit or sworn testimony establishing the grounds for issuing the warrant, neither federal, state, nor county law made it necessary for the prosecutor herself to make the certification. On the basis of the certification, the Superior Court found probable cause, and the suspect was arrested and spent a day in jail, but the charges were ultimately dismissed.

26

The suspect, alleging that the certification had contained inaccurate factual statements, brought a damages action in the United States District Court for the Western District of Washington against the prosecutor under 42 USCS § 1983 on the basis of the alleged violation of the suspect's constitutional right to be free from unreasonable seizures. The prosecutor moved for summary judgment on the theory that the three documents that she had filed were protected by the doctrine of absolute prosecutorial immunity. The District Court denied the motion, and the United States Court of Appeals for the Ninth Circuit affirmed (93 F3d 653, 1996 US App LEXIS 21488).

On certiorari, the United States Supreme Court affirmed. In an opinion by STEVENS, J., expressing the unanimous view of the court, it was held that (1) a prosecutor's conduct in making allegedly false statements of fact in a certification for determination of probable cause is not protected by the doctrine of absolute prosecutorial immunity, as the prosecutor, in making such a certification, performs a function of a complaining witness rather than an advocate; and (2) thus, § 1983 may, under some circumstances, provide a damages remedy against such a prosecutor.

SCALIA, J., joined by THOMAS, J., concurring, (1) agreed that the prosecutor was not entitled to absolute immunity under the Supreme Court's precedents, and (2) expressed the view that for reasons of stare decisis, the Supreme Court's functional approach to immunity questions ought not to be abandoned, although that approach made adherence to the common law embodied in § 1983 difficult.

COUNSEL

Norman Maleng argued the cause for petitioner.

Patricia A. Millett argued the cause for the United States, as amicus curiae, by special leave of court.

Timothy K. Ford argued the cause for respondent.

GENERAL ELECTRIC COMPANY, et al., Petitioners

v

ROBERT K. JOINER et ux.

522 US —, 139 L Ed 2d 508, 118 S Ct 512

[No. 96-188]

Argued October 14, 1997.

Decided December 15, 1997.

Decision: Abuse of discretion held to be proper standard for review of Federal District Court's decision to admit or exclude expert scientific testimony, and court held not to have abused discretion in excluding such testimony.

SUMMARY

An electrician, who alleged that his small cell lung cancer was promoted by on-the-job exposure to polychlorinated biphenyls (PCBs) and to furans and dioxins (some PCB derivatives), sued in a Georgia state court the manufacturers of the products through which the exposure had occurred. After the manufacturers removed the case to the United States District Court for the Northern District of Georgia, the District Court—in excluding the proffered scientific testimony of the electrician's experts indicating a link between exposure to PCBs and small cell lung cancer, and in granting the manufacturers' summary judgment motion—expressed the view that (1) there was no genuine issue as to whether the electrician had been exposed to furans and dioxins, and (2) the expert testimony did not rise above subjective belief or unsupported speculation (864 F Supp 1310). The United States Court of Appeals

29

for the Eleventh Circuit, in reversing the District Court's judgment, expressed the view that (1) the Court of Appeals would apply a particularly stringent standard of review to a trial judge's exclusion of expert testimony, and (2) under that standard, the District Court had erred in excluding the testimony of the electrician's experts (78 F3d 524).

On certiorari, the United States Supreme Court reversed and remanded. In an opinion by REHNQUIST, Ch. J., expressing the unanimous view of the court as to holding 1 below, and joined by O'CONNOR, SCALIA, KENNEDY, SOUTER, THOMAS, GINSBURG, and BREYER, JJ., as to holding 2 below, it was held that (1) abuse of discretion is the proper standard for an appellate court to apply in reviewing a Federal District Court's decision to admit or exclude expert scientific testimony at trial; and (2) because it was within the discretion of the District Court in the instant case to conclude that the animal studies and the four epidemiological studies upon which the experts relied were not sufficient, whether individually or in combination, to support the experts' conclusions that the electrician's exposure to PCBs contributed to his cancer, the District Court did not abuse its discretion in excluding the experts' testimony.

BREYER, J., concurring, expressed the view that given the offer of cooperative effort from the scientific to the legal community, and given the various methods authorized under the Federal Rules of Evidence and the Federal Rules of Civil Procedure for facilitating the trial courts' task as the gatekeepers insuring that scientific testimony or evidence admitted at trial is relevant and reliable, the gatekeeping requirement would not prove inordinately difficult to implement.

STEVENS, J., concurring in part and dissenting in part, (1) agreed that abuse of discretion was the proper standard for an appellate court's review of a Federal District Court's admission or exclusion of expert scientific evidence at trial, but (2) as to the question whether the District Court in the instant case had properly held the expert testimony to be inadmissible, expressed the view that (a) it was not certain that the parties had adequately briefed the question or that the Supreme Court had adequately explained why the Court of Appeals' disposition was erroneous, and (b) the case ought to have been remanded to the Court of Appeals for application of the proper standard of review.

COUNSEL

Steven R. Kuney argued the cause for petitioners.

Lawrence G. Wallace argued the cause for the United States, as amicus curiae, by special leave of court.

Michael H. Gottesman argued the cause for respondents.

CITY OF CHICAGO, et al., Petitioners

v

INTERNATIONAL COLLEGE OF SURGEONS et al.

522 US —, 139 L Ed 2d 525, 118 S Ct 523

[No. 96-910]

Argued October 14, 1997.

Decided December 15, 1997.

Decision: Federal District Court held to have supplemental jurisdiction under 28 USCS § 1367(a) over landowners' state law administrative claims against city's landmarks commission, where complaints included federal constitutional claims.

SUMMARY

Some Chicago landowners planned to demolish all but the facades of two mansions in a designated landmark district and to construct a high-rise condominium tower. Chicago's landmarks commission twice denied a permit for the proposed demolition. Following each of the commission's decisions, the landowners filed actions in the Circuit Court of Cook County, Illinois, against the commission, the city of Chicago, and various city officials for on-the-record judicial review of the commission's decisions pursuant to Illinois' administrative review law. Both complaints raised a number of federal constitutional claims as well, including claims that the city's landmarks and designation ordinances, both on their face and as applied, violated the due process and equal protection clauses of—and effected a taking of property without just compensation under—the Constitution's Fifth and Fourteenth

32

Amendments. The defendants removed both lawsuits to the United States District Court for the Northern District of Illinois on the basis of federal question jurisdiction. The District Court, having exercised supplemental jurisdiction over the state law claims pursuant to 28 USCS § 1367(a), granted summary judgment in favor of the defendants. The United States Court of Appeals for the Seventh Circuit, in reversing the District Court's judgment and in ordering a remand to state court, concluded that the District Court was without jurisdiction, as (1) some of the claims involved deferential review of the commission's decisions, and (2) the case thus could not be termed a "civil action" of which the District Courts had original jurisdiction within the meaning of the federal removal statute (28 USCS § 1441(a)) (91 F3d 981, 1996 US App LEXIS 18988).

On certiorari, the United States Supreme Court reversed and remanded. In an opinion by O'CONNOR, J., joined by REHNQUIST, Ch. J., and SCALIA, KENNEDY, SOUTER, THOMAS, and BREYER, JJ., it was held that (1) the landowners' actions fell within the District Court's original jurisdiction over federal questions under 28 USCS § 1331; (2) the actions had thus been properly removed to the District Court under § 1441(a); and (3) the District Court could exercise supplemental jurisdiction over the state claims, which constituted "other claims" that formed "part of the same case or controversy" for purposes of § 1367(a); but (4) a remand was necessary in order to allow the Court of Appeals to address, in the first instance, the questions whether (a) abstention principles required the District Court to decline to exercise supplemental jurisdiction, or (b) the District Court should have refused to exercise supplemental jurisdiction under 28 USCS § 1367(c).

GINSBURG, J., joined by STEVENS, J., dissenting, expressed the view that allowing "cross-system" appeals—that is, the shifting of on-the-record review of a local agency's actions from the appropriate state tribunal to a federal court of first instance at the option of either party—in cases involving federal question or diversity jurisdiction enlarged the District Courts' authority in a way that was unauthorized by Congress.

COUNSEL

Benna Ruth Solomon argued the cause for petitioners.

Richard J. Brennan argued the cause for respondents.

_____

BAY AREA LAUNDRY AND DRY CLEANING PEN-
SION TRUST FUND, Petitioner

v

FERBAR CORPORATION OF CALIFORNIA, INC.,
and STEPHEN BARNES

522 US —, 139 L Ed 2d 553, 118 S Ct 542

[No. 96-370]

Argued November 10, 1997.
Decided December 15, 1997.

Decision: 6-year limitations period under 29 USCS
§ 1451(f)(1) held not to commence until employer misses installment payment of withdrawal
liability to multiemployer pension plan; action
held timely as to payments due within period.

SUMMARY

Under 29 USCS § 1381(a), a provision of the Multiemployer Pension Plan Amendments Act of 1980 (MP-
PAA), 29 USCS §§ 1381-1461, most employers who
withdraw from underfunded multiemployer pension
plans are required to pay "withdrawal liability"—that is,
the employer's proportionate share of the plan's un-
funded vested benefits, subject to certain
adjustments—upon complete withdrawal from a plan.
Under 29 USCS § 1399(b)(1), the trustees of a multiemployer pension plan must set an installment schedule and demand payment as soon as practicable after
an employer's withdrawal from the plan. After contrib-
uting for several years to a multiemployer pension fund
for laundry workers, an employer ceased making contributions in March 1985. In December 1986, the fund

trustees sent the employer a letter which (1) demanded payment of the employer's withdrawal liability, which the fund calculated to be $45,570.80; and (2) gave the employer the option of either (a) paying the entire liability as a lump sum within 60 days of receiving the letter, or (b) paying $345.50 per month for 240 months, beginning February 1, 1987. Thereafter, the employer asked the trustees to review their decision and filed a notice of initiation of arbitration. However, no payments were made by the employer. On February 9, 1993, the fund filed an action in the United States District Court for the Northern District of California against the employer. The fund sought to recover the employer's entire withdrawal liability. Pursuant to 29 USCS § 1451(f), civil actions under the MPPAA may not be brought after the later of (1) 6 years after the date on which the cause of action arose (29 USCS § 1451(f)(1)); or (2) 3 years after the earliest date on which the plaintiff acquired or should have acquired actual knowledge of the existence of such cause of action (29 USCS § 1451(f)(2)). The District Court, granting the employer's motion for summary judgment, ruled that (1) the fund's action was time barred under § 1451(f)(2), since the action was filed more than 3 years after the fund had become aware of the employer's delinquency in making payments on the employer's withdrawal liability under the MPPAA; and (2) alternatively, the fund's action was time barred under § 1451(f)(1), since the applicable 6-year period had begun to run on February 1, 1987. On appeal, the United States Court of Appeals for the Ninth Circuit, affirming, expressed the view that (1) the applicable limitations period in the case at hand was 6 years, which was "the later of" the two limitations periods in § 1451(f); and (2) the limitations period on the fund's action had begun to run from March 1985, the date of the employer's complete withdrawal from the fund (73 F3d 971, 1996 US App LEXIS 470).

On certiorari, the United States Supreme Court reversed and remanded. In an opinion by GINSBURG, J., expressing the unanimous view of the court, it was held that (1) the 6-year limitations period set forth by § 1451(f)(1) did not begin to run until the employer missed a payment according to the schedule for withdrawal liability payments set by the plan trustees pursuant to § 1399(b)(1); and (2) the fund's action to collect unpaid withdrawal liability from an employer under the MPPAA was timely, for purposes of § 1451(f)(1), as to any payments that came due during the 6 years preceding the suit, but the fund could not recover the employer's first installment payment of $345.50, which came due prior to such time.

COUNSEL

Marsha S. Berzon argued the cause for petitioner.

Edward C. Dumont argued the cause for the United States, as amicus curiae, by special leave of court.

William F. Terheyden argued the cause for respondents.

FIDELITY FINANCIAL SERVICES, INC., Petitioner

v

RICHARD V. FINK, Trustee

522 US —, 139 L Ed 2d 571, 118 S Ct 651

[No. 96-1370]

Argued November 3, 1997.

Decided January 13, 1998.

Decision: Security interest held to be "perfected" under 11 USCS § 547(c)(3)(B) on date that secured party has completed necessary steps to perfect its interest, for purposes of "enabling loan" exception to avoiding preferential transfers.

SUMMARY

An individual purchased an automobile in Missouri and gave a loan company a promissory note for the purchase price, secured by the new automobile. The loan company mailed the security interest perfection papers 21 days after the purchase. The purchaser later filed for bankruptcy and the trustee in bankruptcy moved to set aside the security interest on the ground that (1) the loan was a voidable preference under 11 USCS § 547(b); and (2) the "enabling loan" exception in 11 USCS § 547(c)(3)—which could prohibit the trustee from displacing a security interest for a loan used to acquire the encumbered property—was not appropriate, because the loan company had allegedly failed to perfect its security interest within 20 days after the purchase of the property as mandated by 11 USCS § 547(c)(3)(B). The loan company argued that under Missouri law, a lien on a motor vehicle was treated as

38

perfected on the date of its creation if the creditor filed the necessary documents within 30 days after the purchaser/debtor took possession. The Bankruptcy Court for the Western District of Missouri (1) set aside the lien as a voidable preference, and (2) expressed the view that Missouri's relation-back provision could not extend the 20-day perfection period imposed by § 547(c)(3)(B) (183 BR 857). The District Court for the Western District of Missouri affirmed on substantially the same grounds, as did the Court of Appeals for the Eighth Circuit (102 F3d 334).

On certiorari, the United States Supreme Court affirmed. In an opinion by SOUTER, J., expressing the unanimous view of the court, it was held that a transfer of a security interest is "perfected" under § 547(c)(3)(B) on the date that the secured party has completed the steps necessary to perfect its interest, so that a creditor may invoke the enabling loan exception only by satisfying state-law perfection requirements within the 20-day period provided by the federal statute.

COUNSEL

Michael P. Gaughan argued the cause for petitioner. Richard V. Fink argued the cause for respondent.

KENNETH LEE BAKER and STEVEN ROBERT
BAKER, by his Next Friend, MELISSA THOMAS, Petitioners

v

GENERAL MOTORS CORPORATION

522 US —, 139 L Ed 2d 580, 118 S Ct 657

[No. 96-653]

Argued October 15, 1997.
Decided January 13, 1998.

Decision: National full faith and credit command held
not to bar witness from testifying under subpoena
in Missouri product-liability suit, despite Michigan
court's injunction purportedly barring such testimony.

SUMMARY

An engineering analyst brought a wrongful-discharge
suit in a Michigan court against an automobile company. In a counterclaim, the company alleged that the
analyst had breached his fiduciary duty, when testifying
in product-liability litigation in a Georgia court, by
disclosing privileged and confidential information
about the company. In settlement of the suit, the
company and the analyst agreed to a permanent
injunction—entered by the Michigan court—generally
prohibiting the analyst from testifying, without the
prior written consent of the company, as a witness in
litigation involving the company as an owner, seller,
manufacturer, or designer. However, the injunction, by
its terms, did not operate to interfere with the jurisdiction of the Georgia court, where the case in which the

analyst had testified was still pending. Also, the company separately agreed not to institute contempt or breach-of-contract proceedings in the Michigan court against the analyst for giving subpoenaed testimony in another court or tribunal. Subsequently, plaintiffs who had not been parties to the Michigan litigation subpoenaed the analyst to testify in a product-liability action against the company—which action was commenced in a Missouri state court and removed by the company to the United States District Court for the Western District of Missouri—but the company, objecting to the analyst's appearance as a deponent or trial witness, asserted that the Michigan injunction barred the analyst's testimony. The District Court allowed the plaintiffs to depose the analyst and to call him as a witness at trial, on the grounds that (1) enforcement of the Michigan court's injunction would violate Missouri's public policy, which assertedly shielded from disclosure only privileged or otherwise confidential information; and (2) just as the injunction could be modified in Michigan, so a court elsewhere could modify the decree. After a jury trial, the District Court entered judgment in the plaintiffs' favor (159 FRD 519, 1994 US Dist LEXIS 19161). The United States Court of Appeals for the Eighth Circuit, in reversing, reasoned that (1) assuming the existence of a public policy exception to the full faith and credit command, the District Court erroneously relied on Missouri's policy favoring disclosure of relevant, nonprivileged information, for Missouri had an equally strong public policy in favor of full faith and credit; and (2) the evidence was insufficient to show that the Michigan court would have modified the injunction barring the analyst's testimony (86 F3d 811, 1996 US App LEXIS 14510).

On certiorari, the United States Supreme Court reversed and remanded. In an opinion by GINSBURG, J.,

41

joined by REHNQUIST, Ch. J., and STEVENS, SOUTER, and BREYER, JJ., it was held that notwithstanding the Michigan court's injunction, the national full faith and credit command did not bar the analyst from giving subpoenaed testimony in the Missouri product-liability action under the circumstances presented, for the Michigan court lacked authority to control courts elsewhere by precluding such courts—in actions brought by strangers to the wrongful-discharge suit—from determining for themselves what witnesses would be competent to testify and what evidence would be relevant and admissible.

SCALIA, J., concurring in the judgment, expressed the view that neither the Federal Constitution's full faith and credit clause (Art IV, § 1) nor the federal statute implementing the clause (28 USCS § 1738) required Missouri to execute the Michigan court's injunction, for enforcement measures did not travel with sister-state judgments as preclusive effects did.

KENNEDY, J., joined by O'CONNOR and THOMAS, JJ., concurring in the judgment, expressed the view that (1) Michigan law would not have sought to bind the Missouri plaintiffs to the Michigan court's injunction; and (2) determining as a threshold matter the extent to which Michigan law gave preclusive effect to the injunction would have eliminated the need to decide (a) whether full faith and credit applied to equitable decrees as a general matter, or (b) the extent to which the general rules of full faith and credit were subject to exceptions.

COUNSEL

Laurence H. Tribe argued the cause for petitioners.
Paul T. Cappuccio argued the cause for respondent.

GEORGE G. ROGERS, Petitioner

v

UNITED STATES

522 US —, 139 L Ed 2d 686, 118 S Ct 673

[No. 96-1279]

Argued November 5, 1997.

Decided January 14, 1998.

Decision: Writ of certiorari dismissed as improvidently granted where question to be addressed was not fairly presented by lower court record.

SUMMARY

The knowing possession of an unregistered and unserialized firearm is a violation of 26 USCS §§ 5861(d) and (i). Upon the arrest of an individual for driving while intoxicated, a silencer to a firearm was found in a canvas bag in his motor vehicle. Although he denied knowing that the item found was in his motor vehicle, the individual—during questioning to the police and in criminal trial testimony in the United States District Court for the Southern District of Florida—repeatedly acknowledged that the item found was a silencer. The acknowledgement was confirmed by the individual's lawyer during argument to the jury. During jury instructions, the trial judge denied the individual's request for an instruction that defined the government's burden of establishing "knowing possession" as proof that the individual's acknowledgment of the silencer was the knowing and willful possession of a firearm. The trial court convicted the individual on various firearm violations. A panel of the United States

44

Court of Appeals for the Eleventh Circuit, in affirming the individual's conviction for violating §§ 5861(d) and (i), expressed the view that it was harmless error for the District Court to fail to give a jury instruction relating to an element of the crime that the individual admitted (94 F3d 1519, 1996 US App LEXIS 24311).

The United States Supreme Court dismissed, as improvidently granted, a writ of certiorari to review the Court of Appeals decision. Although unable to agree on an opinion, six members of the court agreed that the issue which the court had granted certiorari to address was not fairly presented by the lower court record.

STEVENS, J., announced the judgment of the court and, in an opinion joined by THOMAS, GINSBURG, and BREYER, JJ., expressed the view that (1) the mens rea element of a violation of § 5861(d) requires the government to prove that a defendant had knowledge that he was in possession of an item that possessed firearm characteristics, not that the defendant knew that possession was unlawful; (2) in the case at hand, since the individual admitted that the item in his possession was a silencer and that it was a firearm, this knowledge was enough to satisfy the mens rea element; (3) the grant of certiorari involved whether it was harmless error for the trial judge to fail to give adequate jury instructions regarding the mens rea element of the offense; (4) the jury instructions had informed the jurors that they had to find that the individual knew that the item was a silencer; and (5) therefore, the lower court record did not adequately present the question on which certiorari had been granted.

O'CONNOR, J., joined by SCALIA, J., concurring in the result, expressed the view that (1) the question presented on certiorari was not squarely presented by the lower court record, and (2) trial courts should explain the mens rea requirement more carefully in jury instructions than was done in the case at hand.

KENNEDY, J., joined by REHNQUIST, Ch. J., and SOUTER, J., dissenting, expressed the view that (1) the trial court, defendant's counsel, and the Court of Appeals had interpreted the jury instructions as telling the jury that it had to find that the defendant knew that he possessed the device in question, but not that he knew that it was a silencer; (2) the interpretation by the opinion of STEVENS, J., of the jury instructions suggested that all convictions based on this form of instruction had to be affirmed; and (3) this was a substantive point that had been neither briefed nor argued and was not the subject of the grant of certiorari.

COUNSEL

Javier R. Rubenstein argued the cause for petitioner.

Jonathan E. Nuechterlein argued the cause for respondent.

———————

JANICE R. LaCHANCE, Acting Director, Office of
Personnel Management, Petitioner

v

LESTER E. ERICKSON, Jr., et al.

522 US —, 139 L Ed 2d 695, 118 S Ct 753

[No. 96-1395]

Argued December 2, 1997.
Decided January 21, 1998.

Decision: Neither Civil Service Reform Act nor due
process held to preclude federal agency from
taking adverse action against employee for making
false statements in response to underlying charge
of employment-related misconduct.

SUMMARY

Five employees worked for various federal agencies.
The employees allegedly made false statements to
agency investigators with respect to some misconduct
with which the employees had been charged. In each
case, the agency additionally charged the alleged false
statement as a ground for adverse action, and the
action eventually taken was based in part on the added
charge. The employees separately appealed to the
Merit Systems Protection Board (MSPB), which (1) in
each case, upheld the portion of the penalty based on
the underlying charge, but overturned the false statement charge; and (2) expressed the view that (a) an
employee's false statements cannot be used for the
purpose of impeaching the employee's credibility, (b)
an employee's false statements cannot be considered in
setting the appropriate punishment for underlying

47

misconduct, and (c) an agency may not charge an employee with failure to report an act of fraud when reporting such fraud would tend to implicate the employee in employment-related misconduct (62 MSPR 586; 63 MSPR 80; 64 MSPR 570; 65 MSPR 186; 66 MSPR 564). In a consolidated appeal, the United States Court of Appeals for the Federal Circuit (1) affirmed the MSPB's decisions with respect to four of the employees; and (2) expressed the view that (a) an agency may not charge an employee with falsification or a similar charge on the ground of the employee's denial of another charge or of underlying facts relating to that other charge, and (b) denials of charges and related facts may not be considered in determining a penalty (89 F3d 1575, 1996 US App LEXIS 17473). Then, in a separate decision, the Court of Appeals affirmed the MSPB's (1) reversal of the false-statement charge against the fifth employee, and (2) conclusion that an employee's false statements may not be considered even for purposes of impeachment (92 F3d 1208, reported in full 1996 US App LEXIS 18002).

On certiorari, the United States Supreme Court reversed the judgments of the Court of Appeals. In an opinion by REHNQUIST, Ch. J., expressing the unanimous view of the court, it was held that neither the Civil Service Reform Act (5 USCS §§ 1101 et seq.) nor the due process clause of the Federal Constitution's Fifth Amendment precludes a federal agency from taking adverse action against an employee for making false statements in response to an underlying charge of employment-related misconduct.

COUNSEL

Seth P. Waxman argued the cause for petitioner.
Paul E. Marth argued the cause for respondents.

DOUGLAS McARTHUR BUCHANAN, Jr., Petitioner

v

RONALD J. ANGELONE, Director, Virginia Department of Corrections, et al.

522 US —, 139 L Ed 2d 702, 118 S Ct 757

[No. 96-8400]

Argued November 3, 1997.
Decided January 21, 1998.

Decision: Virginia trial court's failure to instruct capital sentencing jury on concept of mitigation generally and on particular mitigating factors held not to violate defendant's rights under Federal Constitution's Eighth and Fourteenth Amendments.

SUMMARY

After a jury trial in the Circuit Court of Amherst County, Virginia, an accused was convicted of capital murder. In a separate sentencing hearing, the prosecution sought the death penalty on the basis of the crime's alleged "vileness," an aggravating factor under Virginia law. The accused's counsel, having told the jury that the accused should not be executed in light of mitigating evidence, discussed at length four statutorily defined mitigating factors, involving the accused's (1) lack of prior criminal activity, (2) extreme mental or emotional disturbance at the time of the offense, (3) significantly impaired capacity to appreciate the criminality of his conduct or to conform his conduct to the law's requirements, and (4) youth. The prosecution, while admitting the existence of mitigating evidence and agreeing that the jury had to weigh that evidence
50

against the accused's conduct, argued that the circumstances warranted the death penalty. The prosecution and the accused's counsel agreed that the court should instruct the jury with Virginia's pattern capital sentencing instruction, which stated, among other matters, that (1) before the death penalty could be fixed, the prosecution had to prove beyond a reasonable doubt that the conduct was vile; (2) if the jury found that this condition was met, then the jury could fix the punishment at death or—if the jury believed from all the evidence that the death penalty was not justified—life imprisonment; and (3) if the jury did not find the condition met, then the jury had to impose a life sentence. The accused's counsel requested additional instructions specifically directing the jury to consider each of the four mitigating factors that had been argued and also any other facts in mitigation of the offense, but the court refused to give these instructions. The jury returned with a verdict for the death penalty. The death penalty verdict form stated that the jury had unanimously found the accused's conduct to be vile and had considered the mitigating evidence. The court imposed the sentence fixed by the jury. On direct appeal, the Supreme Court of Virginia affirmed the conviction and death sentence (238 Va 389, 384 SE2d 757, cert den 493 US 1063, 107 L Ed 2d 963, 110 S Ct 880). The accused then petitioned the United States District Court for the Western District of Virginia for federal habeas corpus relief. The District Court denied the petition, and the Court of Appeals for the Fourth Circuit affirmed, on the ground that Virginia's sentencing procedure—by allowing the jury to consider all relevant mitigating evidence—satisfied the requirement, under the Federal Constitution's Eighth Amendment, of individualized sentencing in capital cases (103 F3d 344, 1996 US App LEXIS 33869).

On certiorari, the United States Supreme Court affirmed. In an opinion by REHNQUIST, Ch. J., joined by O'CONNOR, SCALIA, KENNEDY, SOUTER, and THOMAS, JJ., it was held that the trial court's failure to instruct the jury on the concept of mitigation generally and on the four mitigating factors did not violate the accused's rights under the Constitution's Eighth and Fourteenth Amendments, as (1) the court's instructions, by directing the jury to base the decision on "all the evidence," afforded the jurors an opportunity to consider mitigating evidence and did not constrain the manner in which the jury was able to give effect to mitigation; (2) the court's instructions did not mislead the jury to think that life imprisonment could be imposed only if the jury did not find the aggravating factor proved; and (3) in the context of the case, there was not a reasonable likelihood that the jurors understood the court's instructions to preclude consideration of relevant mitigating evidence offered by the accused.

SCALIA, J., concurring, (1) agreed that there was no reasonable likelihood that the jurors had understood the challenged instructions to preclude consideration of relevant mitigating evidence, and (2) expressed the view that the Eighth Amendment did not require that sentencing juries be given discretion to consider mitigating evidence.

BREYER, J., joined by STEVENS and GINSBURG, JJ., dissenting, expressed the view that in light of the instructions and the context taken together, the judge's instructions had created a reasonable likelihood that the jury had applied the challenged instruction in a way that prevented the consideration of constitutionally relevant evidence.

COUNSEL

Gerald T. Zerkin argued the cause for petitioner. Katherine P. Baldwin argued the cause for respondents.

CHRISTOPHER H. LUNDING, et ux., Petitioners

v

NEW YORK TAX APPEALS TRIBUNAL et al.

522 US —, 139 L Ed 2d 717, 118 S Ct 766

[No. 96-1462]

Argued November 5, 1997.
Decided January 21, 1998.

Decision: New York state statutory income tax provision effectively denying only nonresidents deduction for alimony paid held to violate privileges and immunities clause in Art IV, § 2 of Federal Constitution.

SUMMARY

A New York state statutory income tax provision, by disallowing any deduction for alimony paid at one of the several steps used to calculate nonresidents' tax on their income earned in the state, effectively denied only nonresident taxpayers a state income tax deduction for alimony paid, where in some circumstances, the provision would result in a nonresident's tax liability being greater than if the nonresident was a resident. A nonresident married couple (1) filed a New York nonresident income tax return on which the couple reported the husband's income earned in New York; and (2) rather than complying with the statutory provision, deducted the portion of the alimony paid by the husband that corresponded to the percentage of the couple's total income that was earned in New York. After the state's denial of the pro rata alimony deduction resulted in an increase in the couple's tax liability,

the couple was unsuccessful in seeking state administrative relief from the denial of the deduction on the
basis, among others, that the state tax provision violated
the privileges and immunities clause in Art IV, § 2 of
the Federal Constitution. The couple commenced an
action before the Third Department of the Appellate
Division of the New York Supreme Court, which expressed the view that the tax provision violated the
privileges and immunities clause (218 App Div 2d 268,
639 NYS2d 519). The New York Court of Appeals, in
reversing, expressed the view that the provision did not
violate the privileges and immunities clause, as substantial reasons for the disparity in tax treatment were
apparent on the face of the statutory scheme (89 NY 2d
283, 675 NE2d 816).

On certiorari, the United States Supreme Court
reversed and remanded. In an opinion by O'CONNOR,
J., joined by STEVENS, SCALIA, SOUTER, THOMAS, and
BREYER, JJ., it was held that the New York statutory
provision violated the privileges and immunities clause,
because the state had not presented a substantial
justification for the discriminatory treatment of nonresidents effected by the provision, where (1) there was
no reasonable explanation or substantial justification in
the rationale adopted by the New York Court of Appeals in upholding the provision, (2) the provision
violated the rule of substantial equality of treatment
described by the Supreme Court in an earlier case, and
(3) as a personal obligation that generally correlated
with a taxpayer's total income or wealth, alimony bore
some relationship to earnings regardless of their
source.

GINSBURG, J., joined by REHNQUIST, Ch. J., and
KENNEDY, J., dissenting, expressed the view that the
state statutory provision did not offend the nondiscrim-
ination principle embodied in the privileges and im-

55

munities clause, as (1) with respect to the treatment of
alimony, the state statutory provision was a fair adapta-
tion, at the state level, of the current federal system,
and (2) the privileges and immunities clause did not
require that all personal income tax deductions be
allowed in the proportion that in-state income bore to
total income.

COUNSEL

Christopher H. Lunding argued the cause for petitioners.

Andrew D. Bing argued the cause for respondents.

SOUTH DAKOTA, Petitioner

v

YANKTON SIOUX TRIBE et al.

522 US —, 139 L Ed 2d 773, 118 S Ct 789

[No. 96-1581]

Argued December 8, 1997.
Decided January 26, 1998.

Decision: Congress held to have diminished Yankton
Sioux Reservation in 1894 surplus land act, so that
unallotted lands, including waste site, were (1) not
Indian country, and (2) thus, under primary jurisdiction of South Dakota.

SUMMARY

An 1894 federal statute (28 Stat 286) incorporated
the Yankton Sioux Tribe's agreement to "cede, sell,
relinquish, and convey to the United States," in return
for a single payment of $600,000, all of the unallotted
lands on the tribe's reservation in South Dakota that
had been established pursuant to an 1858 treaty (11
Stat 743) between the United States and the tribe. The
statute contained a saving clause that purported to
preserve the provisions of the treaty. A waste management district that had been formed by several South
Dakota counties acquired from a non-Indian, for the
purpose of creating a waste disposal landfill, a site
located within the lands ceded under the 1894 statute.
After the state's Sixth Judicial Circuit affirmed a state
administrative decision that granted the waste district a
state permit for the landfill, the United States District
Court for the District of South Dakota—while declining

to grant the tribe's request that construction of the landfill be enjoined—granted the tribe a declaratory judgment that (1) the 1894 statute did not alter the 1858 reservation boundaries, and (2) consequently, the waste site was within an Indian reservation where federal environmental regulations applied (890 F Supp 878). On appeal concerning the declaratory judgment, the United States Court of Appeals for the Eighth Circuit, in affirming, expressed the view that Congress intended by the statute that the tribe sell its surplus lands but not the tribe's governmental authority over the lands (99 F3d 1439).

On certiorari, the United States Supreme Court reversed and remanded. In an opinion by O'CONNOR, J., expressing the unanimous view of the court, it was held that the 1894 statute diminished the reservation, so that the unallotted lands, including the waste site, ceded under the statute no longer constituted Indian country as defined by 18 USCS § 1151(a), and thus, South Dakota had primary jurisdiction over the waste site and other lands ceded under the 1894 statute, where (1) the statute, as a negotiated agreement providing for the total surrender of tribal claims in exchange for a fixed payment, bore the hallmarks of congressional intent to diminish a reservation, (2) a reasonable interpretation of the statute's saving clause did not conflict with a conclusion that precise cession and sum certain language indicated diminishment, and (3) the context of the statute did not rebut the almost insurmountable presumption of diminishment that arose from the statute's plain terms.

COUNSEL

Mark W. Barnett argued the cause for petitioner.

James G. Abourezk argued the cause for respondents.

Barbara B. McDowell argued the cause for the United States, as amicus curiae, by special leave of court.

ALLENTOWN MACK SALES AND SERVICE, INC.,
Petitioner

v

NATIONAL LABOR RELATIONS BOARD

522 US —, 139 L Ed 2d 797, 118 S Ct 818

[No. 96-795]

Argued October 15, 1997.
Decided January 26, 1998.

Decision: National Labor Relations Board's finding
that employer lacked objective reasonable doubt
about union's majority status—and thus should
not have conducted poll as to employees' support
of union—held not supported by evidence.

SUMMARY

A truck company's factory branch in Allentown,
Pennsylvania, was sold to a successor company, which
hired 32 of the predecessor's 45 employees. During the
period before and immediately after the sale, a number
of employees made statements to the prospective owners of the successor company to the effect that the
union which had represented the predecessor's employees had lost support among employees in the
bargaining unit. Specifically, (1) eight employees made
statements at least arguably indicating that they personally no longer supported the union; (2) an employee
who was a shop steward and a member of the union's
bargaining committee told management that it was his
feeling that the employees did not want a union, and
that with a new company, if a vote was taken, the union
would lose; and (3) an employee on the night shift told

a manager that the entire night shift, then five or six employees, did not want the union. The union asked to be recognized as the employees' collective bargaining representative and to begin negotiations for a contract. The successor company, in rejecting the request, (1) claimed to have a "good faith doubt" as to support of the union among the employees, and (2) announced that an independent poll would be conducted to determine employee support for the union. The union lost the poll 19 to 13. Shortly thereafter, the union filed an unfair-labor-practice charge with the National Labor Relations Board (NLRB). An administrative law judge (ALJ) of the NLRB concluded that (1) the successor company had inherited the predecessor's bargaining obligation and a presumption of continuing majority support for the union, and (2) the poll violated §§ 8(a)(1) and 8(a)(5) of the National Labor Relations Act (NLRA) (29 USCS §§ 158(a)(1), 158(a)(5)), because the successor company had not had an "objective reasonable doubt" about the majority status of the union. The NLRB adopted the ALJ's findings and ordered the successor company to recognize and bargain with the union (316 NLRB 1199, 1995 NLRB LEXIS 323). On review, the United States Court of Appeals for the District of Columbia Circuit enforced the NLRB's bargaining order (317 US App DC 435, 83 F3d 1483, 1996 US App LEXIS 11520).

On certiorari, the United States Supreme Court reversed the Court of Appeals' judgment and remanded the case with instructions to deny enforcement of the bargaining order. In an opinion by SCALIA, J., joined in pertinent part (as to holding 1 below) by STEVENS, SOUTER, GINSBURG, AND BREYER, JJ., and joined in pertinent part (as to holding 2 below) by REHNQUIST, Ch. J., and O'CONNOR, KENNEDY, and THOMAS, JJ., it was held that (1) the NLRB's standard for an employer's conduct of an internal poll of employee support for an incumbent union—under which standard such polling was an unfair labor practice unless the employer could show that the employer had a good-faith reasonable doubt about the union's majority support—was facially rational and consistent with the NLRA, but (2) in the case at hand, the NLRB's factual finding that the successor company lacked such a doubt was not supported by substantial evidence on the record as a whole.

REHNQUIST, Ch. J., joined by O'CONNOR, KENNEDY, and THOMAS, JJ., concurring in part and dissenting in part, (1) agreed that the NLRB's findings were not supported by substantial evidence, and (2) expressed the view that (a) the NLRB's standard for employee polling was not rational or consistent with the NLRA, and (b) such polling ought to be allowed where the polling did not tend to coerce or restrain employees.

BREYER, J., joined by STEVENS, SOUTER, and GINS-BURG, JJ., concurring in part and dissenting in part, (1) concurred in the Supreme Court's view that the NLRB's standard for employee polling was rational and consistent with the NLRA, and (2) expressed the view that the NLRB's conclusion in the case at hand was well within the NLRB's authority to make findings and to reach conclusions on the basis of record evidence.

COUNSEL

Stephen D. Shawe argued the cause for petitioner.

Jonathan E. Nuechterlein argued the cause for respondent.

JAMES BROGAN, Petitioner

v

UNITED STATES

522 US —, 139 L Ed 2d 830, 118 S Ct 805

[No. 96-1579]

Argued December 2, 1997.

Decided January 26, 1998.

Decision: "Exculpatory no" exception, for false statement that consisted of mere denial of wrongdoing, held not to exist with respect to criminal liability under 18 USCS § 1001 for making false statement.

SUMMARY

At the time pertinent to the case at hand, 18 USCS § 1001, a criminal statute, prohibited knowingly and willfully making "any" false statement in any matter within the jurisdiction of any department or agency of the United States. However, many—but not all—of the Federal Courts of Appeals had adopted an "exculpatory no" doctrine, which, with some variations, provided that simple denials of guilt did not come within § 1001. In the case at hand, an individual who was a labor union officer accepted cash payments from a company whose employees were represented by the union. When federal investigatory agents, who were visiting the individual at his home, asked whether he had received any cash or gifts from the company when he was a union officer, he replied "no." The individual was (1) indicted for (a) accepting unlawful cash payments from an employer, in violation of federal labor law, and (b) making a false statement within the jurisdiction of a federal agency, in violation of § 1001; (2) tried, along with several codefendants, before a jury in the United States District Court for the Southern District of New York; and (3) found guilty. On appeal, the United States Court of Appeals for the Second Circuit, in affirming in pertinent part, rejected the exculpatory no doctrine as a defense to a false-statement charge under § 1001 (96 F3d 35, 1996 US App LEXIS 24261).

On certiorari, the United States Supreme Court affirmed. In an opinion by SCALIA, J., joined by REHN-QUIST, Ch. J., and O'CONNOR, KENNEDY, and THOMAS, JJ., and joined in pertinent part by SOUTER, J., it was held that—under the plain language of § 1001 as it read at the time that the individual falsely replied "no" to the government investigators' question—there was no exculpatory no exception, for a false statement that consisted of the mere denial of wrongdoing, to criminal liability under § 1001 for making a false statement, where the individual did not contest that his utterance was false or that it was made knowingly and willfully.

Souter, J., concurring in part and concurring in the judgment, (1) joined the court's opinion except for its response to the individual's argument premised on the potential for prosecutorial abuse of § 1001 as written, and (2) on that point, joined the opinion of GINSBURG, J.

Ginsburg, J., joined by SOUTER, J., concurring in the judgment, expressed the view that (1) a false denial fit the unqualified language of § 1001; (2) Congress had, perhaps unwittingly, conferred extraordinary authority on prosecutors to manufacture crimes; and (3) after the Supreme Court's decision in the case at hand, given that an array of recommendations had been made to refine § 1001, Congress might advert to the exculpatory no doctrine and to the problem that had prompted the doctrine's formulation.

Stevens, J., joined by BREYER, J., dissenting, expressed the view that—while a false denial fit within the unqualified language of § 1001—(1) it seemed clear that Congress had not intended to make every exculpatory no a felony, and (2) even if that were not clear, the Supreme Court ought to show greater respect for the virtually uniform understanding of the bench and bar that had persisted for decades as to the existence of the exculpatory no doctrine.

COUNSEL

Stuart A. Holtzman argued the cause for petitioner. Seth P. Waxman argued the cause for respondent.

DOLORES M. OUBRE, Petitioner

v

ENTERGY OPERATIONS, INC.

522 US —, 139 L Ed 2d 849, 118 S Ct 838

[No. 96-1291]

Argued November 12, 1997.

Decided January 26, 1998.

Decision: Employee's release of claims under Age Discrimination in Employment Act (29 USCS §§ 621 et seq.) held unenforceable, where release did not comply with requirements of Older Workers Benefit Protection Act (29 USCS § 626(f)).

SUMMARY

Under the Older Workers Benefit Protection Act (OWBPA) (29 USCS § 626(f)), (1) an individual may not waive any right or claim under the Age Discrimination in Employment Act (ADEA) (29 USCS §§ 621 et seq.) unless the waiver is knowing and voluntary, and (2) a waiver may not be considered knowing and voluntary without satisfying various enumerated minimum requirements. A Louisiana power plant employee, pursuant to a termination agreement, signed a release of all claims against her employer. In consideration for the release, the employee received severance pay in installments. The release did not comply with the requirements for a release under the OWBPA in at least three respects, in that (1) the employer did not give the employee enough time to consider her options, (2) the employer did not give the employee 7 days after she signed the release to change her mind, and (3) the
66

release made no specific reference to claims under the ADEA. The employee filed an age discrimination charge with the Equal Employment Opportunity Commission, which dismissed the charge on the merits but issued a right-to-sue letter. The employee, alleging constructive discharge on the basis of her age in violation of the ADEA and state law, filed suit against the employer in the United States District Court for the Eastern District of Louisiana. The employer moved for summary judgment on the ground that the employee had ratified the defective release by failing to return or offer to return the monies that she had received. The District Court, agreeing, entered summary judgment for the employer (20 EBC 2772, 73 BNA FEP Cas 984). The United States Court of Appeals for the Fifth Circuit affirmed (112 F3d 787, 1996 US App LEXIS 41288, 1996 US App LEXIS 41679).

On certiorari, the United States Supreme Court reversed and remanded. In an opinion by KENNEDY, J., joined by STEVENS, O'CONNOR, SOUTER, GINSBURG, and BREYER, J., it was held that (1) the employee's release of claims was unenforceable against the employee, insofar as the release purported to waive or release ADEA claims, because the release did not comply with the requirements of the OWBPA; (2) the employee's retention of the severance pay monies did not amount to a ratification of the release as to the ADEA claims; and (3) tendering back the monies was not a precondition to filing suit as to the ADEA claims.

BREYER, J., joined by O'CONNOR, J., concurring, expressed the view that (1) the employee was free to bring the age discrimination suit without tendering back the employer's payment as a precondition, and (2) the OWBPA's provisions were consistent with viewing an invalid release of an ADEA claim as voidable, rather than void.

SCALIA, J., dissenting, expressed the view that (1) the OWBPA did not abrogate the common-law doctrines of "tender back" and ratification, (2) the Court of Appeals' judgment ought to have been affirmed because no tender back had been made by the employee, and (3) ratification was not a second basis for affirmance in the case at hand.

THOMAS, J., joined by REHNQUIST, Ch. J., dissenting, expressed the view that (1) the OWBPA, although abrogating the common-law definition of a "knowing and voluntary" waiver where ADEA claims were involved, did not abrogate the common-law doctrine of ratification and the doctrine that a party must tender back consideration received under a release of legal claims before bringing suit; and (2) there was no reason to think that the Court of Appeals had erred in determining that the employee had ratified her release.

COUNSEL

Barbara G. Haynie argued the cause for petitioner.

Beth S. Brinkmann argued the cause for the United States, as amicus curiae, by special leave of court.

Carter G. Phillips argued the cause for respondent.

NEWSWEEK, INC., Petitioner

v

FLORIDA DEPARTMENT OF REVENUE et al.

522 US —, 139 L Ed 2d 888, 118 S Ct 904

[No. 97-663]

Decided February 23, 1998.

Decision: Florida court held to have erred in denying taxpayer access to state postpayment remedy for refund of taxes paid under unconstitutional sales tax exemption scheme.

SUMMARY

Effective in 1988, a Florida statutory provision exempted newspapers from sales tax, but did not exempt magazines. In 1990, the Florida Supreme Court found this classification invalid under the First Amendment of the Constitution of the United States. Based on the 1990 ruling, a magazine filed a claim for a refund of the sales tax it had paid between 1988 and 1990. The department of revenue denied the refund and the magazine filed suit, alleging that the state's failure to accord the magazine retroactive relief was a violation of due process. A Florida trial court granted summary judgment against the magazine. The District Court of Appeal of Florida, First District, in affirming, expressed the view that the magazine was afforded due process, as the magazine could have pursued a prepayment remedy—filing an action and paying the contested amount into the court registry, posting a bond, or obtaining a court order approving an alternative arrangement—without suffering onerous penalties (689 So 2d 361).

The United States Supreme Court granted certiorari, vacated the judgment of the District Court of Appeal, and remanded the case for further proceedings. In a per curiam opinion expressing the unanimous view of the court, it was held that the District Court of Appeals' decision improperly (1) failed to consider the decision in Reich v Collins (1994) 513 US 106, 130 L Ed 2d 454, 115 S Ct 547, concerning the due process clause of the Constitution's Fourteenth Amendment; and (2) denied the magazine access to a Florida postpayment remedy for the refund of taxes paid under the sales tax exemption scheme, as due process prevented the state from applying a requirement to litigate first and pay later to taxpayers, like the magazine, who had reasonably relied on the availability of a postpayment refund when paying the tax.

LORENZO ARTEAGA, Petitioner

v

UNITED STATES COURT OF APPEALS FOR THE
NINTH CIRCUIT

LORENZO ARTEAGA, Petitioner

v

PETE WILSON, Governor of California, et al.

522 US —, 139 L Ed 2d 892, 118 S Ct 903

[No. 97-6749]

Decided February 23, 1998.

Decision: Person denied leave to proceed in forma
pauperis on (1) petition for certiorari to review
Federal Court of Appeals' affirmance of dismissal
of person's complaint, and (2) future petitions for
certiorari in noncriminal matters.

SUMMARY

An individual sought leave to proceed in forma
pauperis in the United States Supreme Court with
respect to a petition for certiorari to review a United
States Court of Appeals for the Ninth Circuit decision
that affirmed a Federal District Court's dismissal with
prejudice of the individual's complaint for failure to
amend his complaints pursuant to the District Court's
instructions. The individual had filed in the Supreme
Court 20 petitions, including 16 within two terms, and
the Supreme Court had (1) denied all the petitions
without recorded dissent, and (2) in one instance,
denied the individual leave to proceed in forma pauperis by invoking Supreme Court Rule 39.8, which

71

authorizes the Supreme Court to deny such leave with respect to frivolous petitions.

In a per curiam opinion expressing the view of REHNQUIST, Ch. J., and O'CONNOR, SCALIA, KENNEDY, SOUTER, THOMAS, GINSBURG, and BREYER, JJ., the Supreme Court (1) indicating that the instant petition was frivolous, (a) denied the individual leave to proceed in forma pauperis, and (b) allowed the individual a specified period within which to pay the docketing fee required by Supreme Court Rule 38 and to submit his petition in compliance with Supreme Court Rule 33.1; and (2) directed the Clerk of the Supreme Court not to accept any further petitions for certiorari in noncriminal matters from the individual unless he first complied with Rules 33.1 and 38.

STEVENS, J., dissented for the reasons expressed in a previous Supreme Court case involving some similar issues.

REGIONS HOSPITAL, Petitioner

v

DONNA E. SHALALA, Secretary of Health and Human Services

522 US —, 139 L Ed 2d 895, 118 S Ct 909

[No. 96-1375]

Argued December 1, 1997.
Decided February 24, 1998.

Decision: Reaudit rule permitting second audit of graduate medical education (GME) costs in order to insure accurate future provider reimbursements held not impermissibly retroactive and held reasonable interpretation of Medicare's "GME Amendment."

SUMMARY

Section 9202(a) of the Medicare and Medicaid Budget Reconciliation Amendments of 1985 (42 USCS § 1395ww(h)) (the "GME Amendment") (1) required the Secretary of Health and Human Services to reimburse teaching hospitals for the graduate medical education (GME) costs—allowable costs for which a hospital may receive reimbursement—attributable to Medicare services, 42 USCS §§ 1395 et seq.; and (2) directed the Secretary to use a hospital's fiscal year 1984 GME costs "recognized as reasonable," adjusted for inflation, to calculate a hospital's GME reimbursement for subsequent years. The Secretary issued a reaudit rule (42 CFR § 413.86(e)) which interpreted the GME Amendment to permit a second audit of the 1984 GME costs in order to insure accurate future reimbursements, even though the GME costs had been audited previously. By another regulation (42 CFR § 405.1885(a)), the Secretary could reopen, within 3 years, any determination of a hospital's GME costs in order to revise such costs. In 1986, a teaching hospital's 1984 GME costs were assessed at $9,892,644. Although this decision became final in 1989, in 1991, this determination was reopened and a reaudit commenced, where the hospital's 1984 GME costs were reduced to $5,916,868. The Secretary sought (1) to use this recomputed amount to determine reimbursements for future years and past years within the 3-year reopening window, and (2) not to recoup excessive reimbursement paid to the hospital for its 1984 GME costs, for the 3-year window had already closed on that year. The hospital, challenging the validity of the reaudit rule, appealed to the Provider Reimbursement Review Board, which responded that it lacked the authority to invalidate the Secretary's regulation. The hospital sought judicial review. On cross-motions for summary judgment, the United States District Court for the District of Minnesota ruled for the Secretary, as the court concluded that (1) the language of the GME Amendment was ambiguous, (2) the reaudit rule reasonably interpreted congressional intent, and (3) the reaudit rule did not impose an impermissible "retroactive rule." The United States Court of Appeals for the Eighth Circuit affirmed (91 F3d 57).

On certiorari, the United States Supreme Court affirmed the Court of Appeals' judgment. In an opinion by GINSBURG, J., joined by REHNQUIST, Ch. J., and STEVENS, KENNEDY, SOUTER, and BREYER, JJ., it was held that (1) the reaudit rule reflected not an impermissibly retroactive rule, and (2) although the congressional intent of the GME Amendment's phrase "recognized as reasonable" was ambiguous, the reaudit rule was a
74

reasonable interpretation of the GME Amendment that merited the Supreme Court's approbation.

SCALIA, J., joined by O'CONNOR and THOMAS, JJ., dissenting, expressed the view that (1) the 1984 GME costs "recognized as reasonable" in the GME Amendment had to be the "reasonable costs" for which the Secretary actually reimbursed the hospital in 1984, and (2) the words "recognized as reasonable," viewed in their entire context, could not reasonably be understood to authorize a new composite cost determination.

COUNSEL

Ronald N. Sutter argued the cause for petitioner.
Lisa S. Blatt argued the cause for respondent.

MARY ANNA RIVET, et al., Petitioners

v

REGIONS BANK OF LOUISIANA et al.

522 US —, 139 L Ed 2d 912, 118 S Ct 921

[No. 96-1971]

Argued January 21, 1998.

Decided February 24, 1998.

Decision: Case brought in Louisiana state court held improperly removed, under 28 USCS § 1441(b), to Federal District Court, where basis for removal was defendants' assertion that action was precluded by prior orders of federal court.

SUMMARY

Congress has provided, under 28 USCS § 1441(b), for the removal of a case from state court to federal court on the basis of the Federal District Courts' original jurisdiction over federal questions. Several individuals (1) brought suit in a Louisiana state court against defendants including a bank, (2) sought recognition and enforcement of a mortgage involving real property located in Louisiana, and (3) relied exclusively on Louisiana law. The dispute involved only Louisiana parties. However, the defendants, invoking § 1441(b), removed the case to the United States District Court for the Eastern District of Louisiana on the basis of the defendants' assertion that the individuals' action was precluded by some prior orders of a federal bankruptcy court. The District Court, in denying a motion by the individuals to remand the case to state court, expressed the view that (1) the prior bankruptcy orders completely precluded the individuals' cause of action, and (2) this complete preclusion made removal of the case proper (1995 US Dist LEXIS 5670). On appeal, a panel of the United States Court of Appeals for the Fifth Circuit, in affirming, expressed similar views concerning the removal of the case (108 F3d 576, 1995 US App LEXIS 4708, 1995 US App LEXIS 12775). The Court of Appeals then denied a panel rehearing and rehearing en banc (114 F3d 1185, 1997 US App LEXIS 11989).

On certiorari, the United States Supreme Court reversed and remanded. In an opinion by GINSBURG, J., expressing the unanimous view of the court, it was held that (1) even though § 1441(b) provides for removal of a case when a plaintiff's complaint alleges a claim arising under federal law, it was improper to remove, under § 1441(b), the case at hand from the Louisiana state court to the District Court on the basis of the defendants' assertion concerning the prior bankruptcy orders, because claim preclusion—also known as res judicata—by reason of a prior federal judgment is a defensive plea that provides no proper basis for removal under § 1441(b); and (2) instead, such a defense of claim preclusion is properly made in the state proceedings, and the state courts' disposition of the defense is subject to the Supreme Court's ultimate review.

COUNSEL

John G. Odom argued the cause for petitioners.

Charles L. Stern, Jr. argued the cause for respondents.

NATIONAL CREDIT UNION ADMINISTRATION,
Petitioner

v

FIRST NATIONAL BANK AND TRUST CO. et al.
(No. 96-843)

AT&T FAMILY FEDERAL CREDIT UNION, et al.,
Petitioners

v

FIRST NATIONAL BANK AND TRUST CO. et al.
(No. 96-847)

522 US —, 140 L Ed 2d 1, 118 S Ct 927

[Nos. 96-843 and 96-847]

Argued October 6, 1997.
Decided February 25, 1998.

Decision: Commercial banks held to have prudential standing to challenge administrative interpretation of 12 USCS § 1759 permitting federal credit unions to be composed of unrelated employer groups; interpretation held impermissible.

SUMMARY

In 1982, the National Credit Union Administration (NCUA) began to interpret a provision of § 109 of the Federal Credit Union Act (12 USCS § 1759)—that membership in occupationally defined federal credit unions be limited to groups having a common bond of occupation—as permitting federal credit unions to be composed of multiple unrelated employer groups, each having its own distinct common bond of occupation. After the NCUA approved a series of amendments to the charter of a federal credit union that added several unrelated employer groups, five commercial banks and a bankers association brought, under § 10(a) of the Administrative Procedure Act (5 USCS § 702) — providing that a person suffering legal wrong because of agency action, or adversely affected or aggrieved by agency action within the meaning of a relevant statute, was entitled to judicial review thereof—an action alleging that the new employer groups did not share with the federal credit union's existing members the common bond of occupation required under § 109. After the United States District Court for the District of Columbia dismissed the complaint on the basis that because the interests of the banks and the bankers association were not within the zone of interests to be protected by § 109, the parties lacked prudential standing to challenge the NCUA's action (772 F Supp 609), the United States Court of Appeals for the District of Columbia Circuit reversed (988 F2d 1272). On remand, the District Court, entering a summary judgment against the banks and the bankers association, expressed the view that the NCUA had permissibly interpreted § 109 (863 F Supp 9). The Court of Appeals, again reversing, expressed the view that the NCUA's interpretation of § 109 was impermissible (90 F3d 525).

On certiorari, the United States Supreme Court affirmed. In an opinion by THOMAS, J., joined by REHNQUIST, Ch. J., and KENNEDY and GINSBURG, JJ., and joined in pertinent part by SCALIA, J., it was held that (1) the banks and the bankers association had prudential standing, under § 10(a), to challenge the NCUA's interpretation of § 109, where the interest of the banks and the bankers association, as competitors of federal credit unions, in limiting the markets that federal credit unions could serve was arguably within the zone of interests to be protected by § 109; and (2) the NCUA's interpretation was impermissible, because such interpretation was contrary to the unambiguously expressed intent of Congress that the same common bond of occupation had to unite all members of an occupationally defined federal credit union.

O'CONNOR, J., joined by STEVENS, SOUTER, and BREYER, JJ., dissenting, expressed the view that (1) the pertinent question under the zone-of-interests test was whether Congress intended to protect certain interests through a particular provision, and (2) the competitive interest sought by the banks and the bankers association to be protected was not arguably within the zone of interests intended by Congress to be protected by § 109's common-bond-of-occupation provision.

COUNSEL

Seth P. Waxman argued the cause for petitioner in No. 96-843.

John G. Roberts, Jr. argued the cause for petitioners in No. 96-847.

Michael S. Helfer argued the cause for respondents in both cases.

ALASKA, Petitioner

v

NATIVE VILLAGE OF VENETIE TRIBAL GOVERN-
MENT et al.

522 US —, 140 L Ed 2d 30, 118 S Ct 948

[No. 96-1577]

Argued December 10, 1997.
Decided February 25, 1998.

Decision: Land owned by Alaska Native tribe's governing authority held not to be "Indian country"
within meaning of 18 USCS § 1151, where land did
not fall within category of "dependent Indian
communities" within meaning of 18 USCS
§ 1151(b).

SUMMARY

In 1971, Congress enacted the Alaska Native Claims
Settlement Act (ANCSA) (43 USCS §§ 1601 et seq.),
which, among other matters, (1) revoked all but one of
the reservations previously set aside for Alaska Native
use by legislative or executive action, (2) authorized the
transfer of federal funds and Alaska lands to state-
chartered private business corporations to be formed
by Alaska Natives, and (3) allowed such corporations to
opt out of ANCSA by receiving fee simple title to
former reservation lands in return for forgoing ANC-
SA's monetary payments and transfers of nonreserva-
tion lands. In 1973, the United States conveyed fee
simple title to the land constituting an Alaska Native
tribe's former reservation to two Native corporations,
which transferred title to the tribe's governing author-

ity. In 1986, the state of Alaska entered into a joint venture with a private contractor to construct a public school in one of the tribe's villages. After the contractor and the state refused the authority's demand for approximately $161,000 in taxes for conducting business on tribal land, the authority filed suit in the tribe's tax court to collect the taxes. The state brought suit in the United States District Court for the District of Alaska to enjoin collection of the tax. The District Court concluded that (1) the authority's ANCSA lands were not "Indian country" within the meaning of 18 USCS § 1151(b), and (2) the authority thus lacked the power to impose a tax upon nonmembers of the tribe. On appeal, the United States Court of Appeals for the Ninth Circuit (1) expressed the view that the tribe's land was Indian country, as the land qualified under § 1151(b)'s inclusion of "dependent Indian communities"; (2) reversed the District Court's judgment; and (3) remanded the case to the District Court to determine whether the authority had the power to impose the tax under the circumstances presented (101 F3d 1286, 1996 US App LEXIS 29991).

On certiorari, the United States Supreme Court reversed. In an opinion by Thomas, J., expressing the unanimous view of the court, it was held that the land in question was not Indian country within the meaning of 18 USCS § 1151, for (1) the land did not fall within the category of "dependent Indian communities" within the meaning of § 1151(b), as the land (a) had not been set aside by the Federal Government for the use of Indians as Indian land, and (b) was not under the superintendence of the Federal Government; and (2) no Indian allotments, within the meaning of 18 USCS § 1151(c), were at issue.

COUNSEL

John G. Roberts, Jr. argued the cause for petitioner. Heather R. Kendall argued the cause for respondents.

———————

RANDY G. SPENCER, Petitioner

v

MIKE KEMNA, Superintendent, Western Missouri
Correctional Center, et al.

523 US —, 140 L Ed 2d 43, 118 S Ct 978

[No. 96-7171]

Argued November 12, 1997.
Decided March 3, 1998.

Decision: End of term of imprisonment held to cause
federal habeas corpus petition, which challenged
validity of state's parole revocation, to be moot as
no longer presenting case or controversy.

SUMMARY

On October 17, 1990, an accused began serving
concurrent 3-year Missouri sentences on convictions
for felony stealing and burglary, which sentences were
due to expire on October 16, 1993. He was released on
parole on April 16, 1992, but that parole was later
revoked on September 24, 1992, for alleged drug use
and forcible rape. On being returned to prison, the
accused sought to invalidate the parole revocation by
filing state habeas corpus petitions which were rejected
by the Circuit Court of DeKalb County, the Missouri
Court of Appeals, and the Missouri Supreme Court.
The accused then filed a petition for a writ of habeas
corpus, under 28 USCS § 2254, in the United States
District Court for the Western District of Missouri, on
April 1, 1993, just over 6 months before the expiration
of his 3-year sentence. On August 7, 1993, petitioner
was rereleased on parole. On August 23, 1995, the

District Court dismissed the habeas corpus petition, as
the District Court expressed the view that the accused's
claim for relief was moot, since the accused was no
longer in custody within the meaning of § 2254. The
United States Court of Appeals for the Eighth Circuit
affirmed the District Court's judgment, as the Court of
Appeals concluded that the accused's claim had become moot since he suffered no collateral consequences to the parole revocation (91 F3d 1114).

On certiorari, the United States Supreme Court
affirmed the Court of Appeals' judgment. In an opinion by SCALIA, J., joined by REHNQUIST, Ch. J., and
O'CONNOR, KENNEDY, SOUTER, THOMAS, GINSBURG,
and BREYER, JJ., it was held that (1) although incarcera-
tion or parole always satisfies the federal judicial requirement under Article III, § 2 of the United States
Constitution for a case or controversy when challenging
the validity of a conviction, in the case of parole, a
continuing injury—other than a now-ended incarcera-
tion or parole—in the form of collateral consequences
must be proven if the suit is to be maintained; and (2)
in the case at hand, the accused's subsequent release as
having completed the entire term of imprisonment
underlying the parole revocation caused the accused's
petition to be moot, where the accused failed to
demonstrate adequate collateral consequences as a
result of the revocation.

SOUTER, J., joined by O'CONNOR, GINSBURG, and
BREYER JJ., concurring, expressed the view—as an
added reason not reached by the court—that a former
prisoner, no longer in custody, may bring a 42 USCS
§ 1983 action establishing the unconstitutionality of a
conviction or confinement without being bound to
satisfy a favorable-termination requirement that it
would be impossible as a matter of law to satisfy.

GINSBURG, J., concurring, expressed the view that although a state prisoner may not maintain an action under § 1983 if the direct or indirect effect of granting relief would be to invalidate the state sentence being served, nevertheless, individuals without recourse to the habeas corpus statute because they are not "in custody" fit within the broad reach of § 1983.

STEVENS, J., dissenting, expressed the view that since the Supreme Court in previous cases had held that an interest in vindicating one's reputation was sufficient to confer standing, then it necessarily followed that such an interest was also sufficient to defeat a claim of mootness.

COUNSEL

John W. Simon argued the cause for petitioner.

James R. Layton argued the cause for respondents.

_____

LEXECON INC. et al., Petitioners

v

MILBERG WEISS BERSHAD HYNES & LERACH et al.

523 US —, 140 L Ed 2d 62, 118 S Ct 956

[No. 96-1482]

Argued November 10, 1997.

Decided March 3, 1998.

Decision: Federal District Court to which civil actions with common issues of fact are transferred under 28 USCS § 1407(a) for pretrial proceedings held not permitted to invoke 28 USCS § 1404(a) to assign transferred case to itself for trial.

SUMMARY

Under 28 USCS § 1407(a), (1) the Judicial Panel on Multidistrict Litigation may transfer civil actions with common questions of fact to any federal judicial district for coordinated or consolidated pretrial proceedings, and (2) each such action shall be remanded by the Panel at or before the conclusion of such pretrial proceedings to the district from which it was transferred. Under 28 USCS § 1404(a), a Federal District Court, in the interest of convenience and justice, may transfer a civil action to any other federal judicial district where it might have been brought. In addition, Rule 14(b) of the Rules of the Judicial Panel on Multidistrict Litigation authorizes a transferee court to assign an action to itself for trial. After class action claims against a law and economics consulting firm and one of its principals ("the consultants") concerning allegedly inaccurate and misleading reports given to federal and state banking regulators about a failed savings and loan were dismissed, the consultants brought against two law firms a diversity action in the United States District Court for the Northern District of Illinois, alleging several torts, including defamation, arising from the firms' conduct as counsel for the class action plaintiffs. The Panel ordered a § 1407(a) transfer to the United States District Court for the District of Arizona. After the remaining parties to the class action reached a final settlement and the only claim by the consultants that remained was the defamation claim against one of the firms, the Arizona District Court invoked § 1404(a) to assign the case to itself for trial and entered a judgment for the firm (884 F Supp 1388). The United States Court of Appeals for the Ninth Circuit, in affirming, expressed the view that permitting the transferee court to assign a case to itself upon completion of its pretrial work was not only consistent with the statutory language, but also conducive to efficiency (102 F3d 1524).

On certiorari, the United States Supreme Court reversed and remanded. In an opinion by SOUTER, J., joined by REHNQUIST, Ch. J., and STEVENS, O'CONNOR, KENNEDY, THOMAS, GINSBURG, and BREYER, JJ., and joined in pertinent part by SCALIA, J., it was held that (1) a District Court conducting the pretrial proceedings referred to in § 1407(a) could not properly invoke § 1404(a) to transfer a case to itself for trial, because the straightforward language of § 1407(a) precluded a transferee court from granting any motion, including one for self-transfer, under § 1404(a); and (2) thus, Rule 14(b) was invalid.

COUNSEL

Michael K. Kellogg argued the cause for petitioners.
Jerold S. Solovy argued the cause for respondents.

———————

DANIEL BOGAN and MARILYN RODERICK, Petitioners

v

JANET SCOTT-HARRIS

523 US —, 140 L Ed 2d 79, 118 S Ct 966

[No. 96-1569]

Argued December 3, 1997.
Decided March 3, 1998.

Decision: Legislative actions of city's mayor and city council's vice president in enacting ordinance that eliminated position of city administrator held protected by absolute immunity from liability under 42 USCS § 1983.

SUMMARY

In 1990, a city agency administrator in Fall River, Massachusetts, received a complaint that an employee had made racial and ethnic slurs. The administrator prepared termination charges against the employee, who allegedly pressed her case with several state and local officials, including the vice president of the city council. The council held a hearing on the charges and ultimately accepted a settlement proposal under which the employee was to be suspended without pay for 60 days. The mayor of Fall River subsequently reduced the punishment. While the charges against the employee were pending, the mayor (1) prepared his budget proposal for the 1992 fiscal year, and (2) proposed eliminating 135 city positions, including that of the administrator. The council's ordinance committee, chaired by the vice president, approved an ordinance eliminating the administrator's agency. The council adopted the ordinance by a vote of 6 to 2, with the vice president among those voting in favor. The mayor signed the ordinance into law. The administrator filed suit under 42 USCS § 1983 in the United States District Court for the District of Massachusetts against the city, the mayor, the vice president, and several other city officials, in which suit it was alleged that the elimination of the administrator's position was motivated by racial animus and a desire to retaliate against the administrator for exercising her rights under the Federal Constitution's First Amendment in filing the complaint against the employee. The District Court denied motions by the mayor and the vice president to dismiss on the basis of legislative immunity, and the case proceeded to trial. The jury found defendants including the mayor and the vice president liable on the First Amendment claim. On a motion for judgment notwithstanding the verdict, the District Court again denied the mayor's and the vice president's immunity claims, on the ground that the ordinance was an individually targeted administrative act, rather than a neutral and legislative elimination of a position that incidentally resulted in the administrator's termination. The United States Court of Appeals for the First Circuit, affirming the District Court's judgment in pertinent part, reasoned that (1) constitutionally sheltered speech was a substantial or motivating factor underlying the mayor's and the vice president's conduct, and (2) such conduct was administrative rather than legislative in nature (1997 US App LEXIS 594).

On certiorari, the United States Supreme Court reversed. In an opinion by THOMAS, J., expressing the unanimous view of the court, it was held that (1) local legislators are absolutely immune from suit under § 1983 for their legislative activities; and (2) the actions of the mayor and the vice president were protected by such immunity, regardless of the subjective intent motivating such actions, as (a) the actions were legislative in form, and (b) the ordinance was legislative in substance.

COUNSEL

Charles Rothfeld argued the cause for petitioners.
Harvey A. Schwartz argued the cause for respondent.

———————

MARGARET KAWAAUHAU, et vir, Petitioners

v

PAUL W. GEIGER

523 US —, 140 L Ed 2d 90, 118 S Ct 974

[No. 97-115]

Argued January 21, 1998.
Decided March 3, 1998.

Decision: Debt arising from medical malpractice judgment, attributable to negligent or reckless conduct, held not to be debt for willful and malicious injury that was excepted from discharge in bankruptcy under 11 USCS § 523(a)(6).

SUMMARY

After a jury had found a physician, who carried no malpractice insurance, liable for malpractice with respect to treatment of a patient's foot injury and had awarded damages to the patient and her husband, the physician petitioned for bankruptcy. The United States Bankruptcy Court for the Eastern District of Missouri entered a judgment to the effect that the malpractice damages constituted a debt that, under the 11 USCS § 523(a)(6) exception from discharge for any debt for willful and malicious injury, was nondischargeable (172 BR 916), and the United States District Court for the Eastern District of Missouri affirmed in an unpublished order. A three-judge panel of the United States Court of Appeals for the Eighth Circuit reversed (93 F3d 443), and an en banc court, adhering to the panel's position, expressed the view that (1) the § 523(a)(6) exemption was confined to debts based on intentional torts, and

(2) a debt for malpractice, being based on negligent or reckless conduct, thus was dischargeable (113 F3d 848).

On certiorari, the United States Supreme Court affirmed. In an opinion by GINSBURG, J., expressing the unanimous view of the court, it was held that debts arising from recklessly or negligently inflicted injuries did not fall within the compass of § 523(a), and thus the damages owed to the patient and her husband were dischargeable, where (1) the word "willful" in § 523(a)(6) modified the word "injury," indicating that nondischargeability required a deliberate or intentional injury, not merely a deliberate or intentional act that led to injury, and (2) the § 523(a)(6) formulation triggered in the lawyer's mind intentional torts, as distinguished from negligent or reckless torts.

COUNSEL

Norman W. Pressman argued the cause for petitioners.

Laura K. Grandy argued the cause for respondent.

_____

UNITED STATES, Petitioner

v

HERNAN RAMIREZ

523 US —, 140 L Ed 2d 191, 118 S Ct 992

[No. 96-1469]

Argued January 13, 1998.

Decided March 4, 1998.

Decision: As to police officers' no-knock entry resulting in property damage, (1) Fourth Amendment held not to impose higher justification standard for entry, and (2) 18 USCS § 3109 held to include exigent circumstances exception to announcement requirement.

SUMMARY

After a prison inmate who had a violent past and had stated that he would "not do federal time" escaped, a reliable informant told a federal agent that the informant had seen a person who the informant thought was the inmate at the private residence of another individual, the agent and the informant drove to an area near the home, and the agent observed outside the home a man who resembled the inmate. Subsequently, police officers—who had obtained a no-knock warrant to enter and search the home and had been told by the informant that the resident might have guns and drugs hidden in his garage—executed the warrant by simultaneously (1) announcing that they had a search warrant, and (2) breaking a single garage window, through which the officers pointed a gun. The search resulted in the resident being indicted under 18 USCS § 922(g)(1) for being a felon in possession of firearms. The United States District for the District of Oregon, granting the resident's motion to suppress evidence regarding his possession of the firearms, expressed the view that the police officers had violated the Federal Constitution's Fourth Amendment and 18 USCS § 3109—which provides that a police officer may break a door or window of a house, or any part of a house, or anything therein, to execute a search warrant, if, after notice of the officer's authority and purpose, the officer is refused admittance or when necessary to liberate the officer or a person aiding the officer in the execution of the warrant—because there were insufficient exigent circumstances to justify the officers' destruction of property in their execution of the warrant. The United States Court of Appeals for the Ninth Circuit, affirming, expressed the view that the standard for justification of a no-knock entry was heightened when property was destroyed (91 F3d 1297).

On certiorari, the United States Supreme Court reversed and remanded. In an opinion by REHNQUIST, Ch. J., expressing the unanimous view of the court, it was held that (1) the Fourth Amendment did not hold police officers to a higher standard than the test articulated in Richards v Wisconsin (1997) 520 US ——, 137 L Ed 2d 615, 117 S Ct 1416—that a no-knock entry was justified if police had a reasonable suspicion that knocking and announcing would be dangerous or futile, or would inhibit the effective investigation of the crime—when a no-knock entry resulted in the destruction of property; (2) this same standard was the measure to determine the applicability of the knock-and-announce requirement's exigent circumstances exception codified in § 3109; and (3) the officers in the instant case did not violate the Fourth Amendment or § 3109.

96

COUNSEL

David C. Frederick argued the cause for petitioner.
Michael R. Levine argued the cause for respondent.

JOSEPH ONCALE, Petitioner

v

SUNDOWNER OFFSHORE SERVICES, INCORPO-
RATED, et al.

523 US —, 140 L Ed 2d 201, 118 S Ct 998

[No. 96-568]

Argued December 3, 1997.

Decided March 4, 1998.

Decision: Same-sex sexual harassment in workplace
held actionable as sex discrimination under provision of Title VII of Civil Rights Act of 1964 (42
USCS § 2000e-2(a)(1)).

SUMMARY

A man employed as a roustabout on an eight-man oil
platform crew alleged that (1) on several occasions, he
had been forcibly subjected to humiliating sex-related
actions against him by some male coworkers in the
presence of the rest of the crew, (2) a male co-worker
had physically assaulted him in a sexual manner and
had threatened him with rape; and (3) after the
employee's complaints to supervisory personnel had
produced no remedial action, he had quit his job in the
belief that otherwise he would have been raped or
forced to have sex. The employee, filing a complaint
against his former employer in the United States District Court for the Eastern District of Louisiana, alleged
that he had been discriminated against in his employment because of his sex, in violation of a provision of
Title VII of the Civil Rights Act of 1964 (42 USCS
§ 2000e-2(a)(1)). The District Court, in granting sum-

mary judgment for the employer, expressed the view that the employee had no cause of action under Title VII for harassment by male co-workers (1995 US Dist LEXIS 4119). On appeal, the United States Court of Appeals for the Fifth Circuit affirmed (83 F3d 118, 1996 US App LEXIS 11479).

On certiorari, the United States Supreme Court reversed and remanded. In an opinion by SCALIA, J., expressing the unanimous view of the court, it was held that (1) workplace sexual harassment is actionable as sex discrimination under Title VII where the harasser and the harassed employee are of the same sex; (2) harassing conduct need not be motivated by sexual desire to support an inference of employment discrimination on the basis of sex in violation of Title VII; (3) a plaintiff who brings a same-sex sexual harassment claim under Title VII must prove that the conduct at issue was not merely tinged with offensive sexual connotations, but actually constituted discrimination because of sex; and (4) in such cases—as in all Title VII sexual harassment cases—there must be careful consideration of the social context in which particular behavior occurs and is experienced by the target of the behavior.

THOMAS, J., concurring, expressed the view that the Supreme Court had properly stressed that in every sexual harassment case, the plaintiff must plead and ultimately prove Title VII's statutory requirement that there be discrimination because of sex.

COUNSEL

Nicholas Canaday, III argued the cause for petitioner.

Edwin S. Kneedler argued the cause for the United States, as amicus curiae, by special leave of court.

99

Harry M. Reasoner argued the cause for respondents.

STEEL COMPANY, aka CHICAGO STEEL AND
PICKLING COMPANY, Petitioner

v

CITIZENS FOR A BETTER ENVIRONMENT

523 US —, 140 L Ed 2d 210, 118 S Ct 1003

[No. 96-643]

Argued October 6, 1997.
Decided March 4, 1998.

Decision: Environmental organization held to lack
standing to maintain suit under Emergency Planning and Community Right-To-Know Act provision
(42 USCS § 11046(a)(1)), where no relief sought
was likely to remedy organization's alleged injury.

SUMMARY

An environmental protection organization that assertedly sought, used, and acquired data reported
under the Emergency Planning and Community Right-
To-Know Act of 1986 (EPCRA) (42 USCS §§ 11001 et
seq.) brought suit in the United States District Court
for the Northern District of Illinois under EPCRA's
citizen-suit provision (42 USCS § 11046(a)(1)) against
a manufacturing company in Chicago. The complaint
(1) alleged that the manufacturer had failed in the past
to file timely reports as to hazardous and toxic chemi-
cals as required under EPCRA; (2) did not allege a
continuing EPCRA violation or the imminence of a
future violation; (3) asserted that the manufacturer's
failure to provide EPCRA information in a timely
fashion and the lingering effects of that failure constituted injury in fact to the organization and its mem-

101

bers; and (4) asked for (a) a declaratory judgment that the manufacturer had violated EPCRA, (b) various forms of injunctive relief, (c) an order requiring the manufacturer to pay civil penalties of $25,000 per day, as authorized by an EPCRA provision (42 USCS § 11045(c)), for each EPCRA violation, (d) an award, under another EPCRA provision (42 USCS § 11046(f)), of all the organization's costs in connection with the investigation and prosecution of the case at hand, and (e) any such further relief as the court might deem appropriate. The District Court granted the manufacturer's motion to dismiss on the grounds that (1) because the manufacturer's filings had been up to date when the complaint was filed, the court had no jurisdiction to entertain a suit for a present violation; and (2) EPCRA did not allow suit for a purely historical violation (1995 US Dist LEXIS 18948). The United States Court of Appeals, in reversing, concluding that EPCRA authorized citizen suits for purely past violations (90 F3d 1237, 1996 US App LEXIS 18262).

On certiorari, the United States Supreme Court (1) vacated the Court of Appeals' judgment, and (2) remanded the case with instructions to direct that the complaint be dismissed. In an opinion by SCALIA, J., joined by REHNQUIST, Ch. J., and O'CONNOR, KENNEDY, and THOMAS, JJ., and joined in part (as to holding 2 below) by BREYER, J., it was held that (1) the issue of the organization's standing to maintain the suit was a threshold jurisdictional question that had to be resolved in the organization's favor before the Supreme Court could proceed to the merits question whether 42 USCS § 11046(a) authorized a cause of action for purely past violations of EPCRA; and (2) the organization did not have such standing, as none of the relief sought was likely to remedy the organization's alleged injury in fact.

O'CONNOR, J., joined by KENNEDY, J., concurring, (1) agreed that (a) the organization lacked standing, and (b) federal courts ought to be certain of their jurisdiction before reaching the merits of a case; and (2) expressed the view that the Supreme Court's opinion ought not to be read as an exhaustive list of circumstances under which federal courts might properly exercise judgment in reserving difficult questions of jurisdiction when the case alternatively could be resolved on the merits in favor of the same party.

BREYER, J., concurring in part and concurring in the judgment, expressed the view that (1) the organization lacked standing, and (2) federal courts often and typically should decide standing questions at the outset of a case, but (3) federal courts may properly reserve difficult questions of jurisdiction when the case alternatively could be resolved on the merits in favor of the same party.

STEVENS, J., joined in part (as to points 1 and 3 below) by SOUTER, J., and joined in part (as to point 3 below) by GINSBURG, J., concurring in the judgment, expressed the view that (1) the question whether § 11046(a) authorized a suit for purely past violations of EPCRA could and ought to have been addressed first, regardless of whether the question was properly characterized as whether EPCRA (a) conferred "jurisdiction" over such suits, or (b) created such a "cause of action"; (2) the Supreme Court ought not to have passed on the standing question; and (3) Congress did not intend to confer jurisdiction over EPCRA citizen suits for wholly past violations.

GINSBURG, J., concurring in the judgment, expressed the view that EPCRA did not permit citizen suits for wholly past violations.

COUNSEL

Sanford M. Stein argued the cause for petitioner.

Mr. David A. Strauss argued the cause for respondent.

Irving L. Gornstein argued the cause for the United States, as amicus curiae, by special leave of court.

———————

QUALITY KING DISTRIBUTORS, INC., Petitioner

v

L'ANZA RESEARCH INTERNATIONAL, INC.

523 US —, 140 L Ed 2d 254, 118 S Ct 1125

[No. 96-1470]

Argued December 8, 1997.

Decided March 9, 1998.

Decision: Copyright owner's right under 17 USCS § 602(a) to prohibit unauthorized importation of copies of copyrighted works held subject to 17 USCS § 109(a) limitation, on exclusive right to vend, to first sales of works.

SUMMARY

A California manufacturer of hair care products whose labels were copyrighted in the United States sold its products to domestic distributors, who agreed to resell the products within limited geographical areas and to only authorized retailers. The manufacturer also sold its products to foreign distributors at prices lower than the prices charged to domestic distributors. After the manufacturer's distributor in the United Kingdom arranged the sale of some of the manufacturer's products—with copyrighted labels affixed—to a distributor in Malta, a domestic distributor, without the manufacturer's permission, allegedly imported the products and sold them to unauthorized retailers who resold the products in California. The manufacturer (1) brought in the United States District Court for the Central District of California an action against the domestic distributor, the retailers, and the Malta dis-

105

tributor; and (2) alleged that such importation and distribution of the products bearing copyrighted labels was, under 17 USCS § 602, an infringement of the manufacturer's exclusive domestic distribution right under 17 USCS § 106, actionable under 17 USCS § 501. After the claims against the retailers were settled and a default judgment was entered against the Malta distributor, the District Court, rejecting the domestic distributor's defense—based on the 17 USCS § 109(a) limitation, on the exclusive right to vend, to first sales of copies of works—entered a summary judgment in favor of the manufacturer. The United States Court of Appeals for the Ninth Circuit affirmed (98 F3d 1109).

On certiorari, the United States Supreme Court reversed. In an opinion by STEVENS, J., expressing the unanimous view of the court, it was held that the domestic distributor's alleged importation and resale of the products was not an infringement, under 17 USCS § 602(a), of the manufacturer's exclusive right to distribute the copyrighted labels in the United States, because § 602(a) was subject to 109(a)'s limitation, on a copyright owner's exclusive right to vend, to first sales of copies of works, where (1) § 109(a) unambiguously stated that after the first sale of a copy of a lawfully made copyrighted work, the owner of the work was entitled, without the authority of the copyright owner to sell the copy, and (2) a copyright owner's exclusive distribution right "under section 106" referred to in § 602(a) did not encompass resales by lawful owners.

GINSBURG, J., concurring, expressed the view that the court in the instant case did not resolve cases in which the allegedly infringing imports were manufactured abroad.

COUNSEL

Allen R. Snyder argued the cause for petitioner.

Raymond H. Goettsch argued the cause for respondent.

Lawrence G. Wallace argued the cause for the United States, as amicus curiae, by special leave of court.

———————

DEBRA FAYE LEWIS, Petitioner

v

UNITED STATES

523 US —, 140 L Ed 2d 271, 118 S Ct 1135

[No. 96-7151]

Argued November 12, 1997.

Decided March 9, 1998.

Decision: Assimilative Crimes Act provision (18 USCS § 13(a)) held not to make Louisiana's first-degree murder statute applicable in federal prosecution involving killing of child on federal army base in Louisiana.

SUMMARY

A provision of the Assimilative Crimes Act (ACA) (18 USCS § 13(a)) makes state criminal statutes applicable to a wrongful "act or omission" of a person within a federal enclave in the state, where such an act or omission is "not made punishable by any enactment of Congress." A husband and wife allegedly beat and killed the husband's 4-year-old daughter while all three lived on a federal army base in Louisiana. A federal indictment, relying on the ACA, charged the husband and wife with first-degree murder under a Louisiana statute that (1) defined first-degree murder to include a killing in which the offender had the specific intent to kill or harm a victim under the age of 12, and (2) required a punishment of death or life imprisonment. After a trial in the United States District Court for the Western District of Louisiana, the wife was convicted of Louisiana first-degree murder and sentenced to life

108

imprisonment without parole (848 F Supp 692, 1994 US Dist LEXIS 4531). The United States Court of Appeals for the Fifth Circuit, in affirming in part and reversing in part, (1) expressed the view that the ACA did not permit the application of the Louisiana statute to the wife's acts, as (a) Congress had made those acts punishable as federal second-degree murder under 18 USCS § 1111, and (b) the federal and state laws were directed at roughly the same sort of conduct; (2) affirmed the wife's conviction, on the ground that the jury had found all of the requisite elements of federal second-degree murder; and (3) affirmed the sentence, on the ground that the sentence was no greater than the maximum sentence permitted by § 1111 (92 F3d 1371, 1996 US App LEXIS 20700).

On certiorari, the United States Supreme Court (1) vacated the Court of Appeals' judgment, and (2) remanded the case for resentencing. In an opinion by BREYER, J., joined by REHNQUIST, Ch. J., and STEVENS, O'CONNOR, SOUTER, and GINSBURG, JJ., it was held that (1) a court, in determining whether the ACA assimilates a particular state statute, must ask (a) whether the accused's act or omission is made punishable by any enactment of Congress, and (b) if so, whether the federal statutes that apply to the act or omission preclude application of the state statute; (2) pursuant to such principles, the ACA did not make Louisiana's first-degree murder statute applicable to the crime at issue, which was thus governed by § 1111; and (3) the Court of Appeals had (a) correctly affirmed the conviction, but (b) wrongly affirmed the life sentence.

SCALIA, J., joined by THOMAS, J., concurring in the judgment, (1) agreed that the ACA did not incorporate Louisiana's first-degree murder statute into the criminal law governing federal enclaves in that state; and (2) expressed the view that (a) in determining whether the

ACA assimilates a particular state statute, courts must decide whether the state offense is "the same" as some crime defined by federal law, and (b) the focus of this inquiry ought to be on the way that crimes were traditionally defined and categorized at common law.

KENNEDY, J., dissenting, expressed the view that (1) in determining whether the ACA assimilates a particular state statute, courts must examine whether the state offense and a federal offense require proof of the same elements; and (2) assimilation of the state offense would have been proper in the case at hand, because (a) Congress did not take a victim's age into account in defining first-degree murder in § 1111, and (b) the state offense thus included a substantive element missing from the federal statute.

COUNSEL

Frank Granger argued the cause for petitioner.
Malcolm L. Stewart argued the cause for respondent.

***

KEVIN D. GRAY, Petitioner

v

MARYLAND

523 US —, 140 L Ed 2d 294, 118 S Ct 1151

[No. 96-8653]

Argued December 8, 1997.
Decided March 9, 1998.

Decision: Use of nontestifying codefendant's redacted confession at joint trial, with defendant's name replaced with obvious indications of alteration, held to violate rule of Bruton v United States.

SUMMARY

In Bruton v United States (1968) 391 US 123, 20 L Ed 2d 476, 88 S Ct 1620, the United States Supreme Court held that a defendant's rights under the confrontation clause of the Sixth Amendment to the United States Constitution were violated by the introduction, at a joint criminal trial, of a nontestifying codefendant's confession which named and incriminated the defendant. However, the scope of Bruton v United States was limited by Richardson v Marsh (1987) 481 US 200, 95 L Ed 2d 176, 107 S Ct 1702, in which the Supreme Court held that the confrontation clause was not violated by the admission, at a joint criminal trial, of a nontestifying codefendant's confession, when (1) a proper limiting instruction was given to the jury, and (2) the confession was redacted to eliminate not only the nonconfessing defendant's name, but also any reference to his or her existence. In the case at hand, at a joint Maryland trial of two defendants for murder, the

111

trial judge (1) permitted the state to introduce a redacted version of a nontestifying codefendant's confession, with the nonconfessing defendant's name substituted with a blank space or the word "deleted"; and (2) gave a limiting instruction that the confession be used only against the codefendant. The jury convicted both defendants. Maryland's Court of Special Appeals held that Bruton v United States prohibited use of the confession and set aside the nonconfessing defendant's conviction. The Court of Appeals of Maryland disagreed and reinstated the conviction (344 Md 417, 687 A2d 660).

On certiorari, the Supreme Court vacated the Court of Appeals' judgment and remanded the case for further proceedings. In an opinion by BREYER, J., joined by STEVENS, O'CONNOR, SOUTER, and GINSBURG, JJ., it was held that, unlike Richardson v Marsh's redacted confession, a nontestifying codefendant's redacted confession fell within the class of statements protected by the Bruton rule, where, as in the case at hand, the nonconfessing defendant's name was replaced with an obvious blank space, a word such as "deleted," a symbol, or other similarly obvious symbols of alteration.

SCALIA, J., joined by REHNQUIST, Ch. J., and KENNEDY and THOMAS, JJ., dissenting, expressed the view that (1) the line drawn by Richardson v Marsh should not be changed, and (2) the confession in the case at hand could constitutionally have been admitted with a limiting instruction to the jury.

COUNSEL

Arthur A. Delano, Jr. argued the cause for petitioner.

Carmen M. Shepard argued the cause for respondent.

Roy W. McLeese, III argued the cause for the United States, as amicus curiae, by special leave of court.

———————

GLENDORA, Petitioner

v

JOHN PORZIO et al.

523 US —, 140 L Ed 2d 310, 118 S Ct 1124

[No. 97-7300]

Decided March 9, 1998.

Decision: Person denied leave to proceed in forma pauperis on (1) petition for certiorari to review Federal Court of Appeals' dismissal of appeal concerning dispute with landlord as frivolous, and (2) future petitions for certiorari in noncriminal matters.

SUMMARY

An individual sought leave to proceed in forma pauperis in the United States Supreme Court with respect to a petition for certiorari to review a United States Court of Appeals for the Second Circuit decision that dismissed as frivolous the individual's appeal of a Federal District Court's dismissal of the individual's claims—based on purported "sewer service" used by her landlord's lawyers and acceptance of the affidavits of service by a state court trial judge—brought under 42 USCS §§ 1983 and 1985, which claims alleged violations concerning due process. The individual had filed in the Supreme Court 14 petitions within approximately the preceding 4 years, and the Supreme Court had (1) denied all the petitions without recorded dissent, and (2) in one instance, denied the individual leave to proceed in forma pauperis by invoking Supreme Court Rule 39.8, which authorizes the Supreme Court to deny such leave with respect to frivolous petitions.

In a per curiam opinion expressing the view of REHNQUIST, Ch. J., and O'CONNOR, SCALIA, KENNEDY, SOUTER, THOMAS, GINSBURG, and BREYER, JJ., the Supreme Court (1) indicating that the instant petition was frivolous, (a) denied the individual leave to proceed in forma pauperis, and (b) allowed the individual a specified period within which to pay the docketing fee required by Supreme Court Rule 38 and to submit her petition in compliance with Supreme Court Rule 33.1; and (2) directed the Clerk of the Supreme Court not to accept any further petitions for certiorari in noncriminal matters from the individual unless she first complied with Rules 33.1 and 38.

STEVENS, J., dissented for the reasons expressed in a previous Supreme Court case involving some similar issues.

JANICE E. HETZEL, Petitioner

v

PRINCE WILLIAM COUNTY, VIRGINIA, and CHAR-
LIE T. DEANE

523 US —, 140 L Ed 2d 336, 118 S Ct 1210

[No. 97-954]

Decided March 23, 1998.

Decision: Writ of mandamus which required Federal
District Court to enter judgment for lesser amount
than that determined by jury without allowing
option of new trial held to be violation of Seventh
Amendment right to jury trial.

SUMMARY

In a civil rights suit under 42 USCS § 1983 and Title
VII of the Civil Rights Act of 1964 (42 USCS §§ 2000e et
seq.), where a jury found for an individual on her
claims against defendants including a Virginia county, a
Federal District Court in Virginia reduced the damages
from $750,000 to $500,000, on the grounds that one of
the claims supporting the award was legally insufficient.
The United States Court of Appeals for the Fourth
Circuit affirmed the finding of liability, but also (1) set
aside the damage award as grossly excessive because it
was unsupported by the limited evidence of harm
presented at trial, and (2) remanded the case to the
District Court for recalculation (89 F3d 169). On
remand, the District Court recalculated the damages
and reduced the individual's award to $50,000. The
individual filed a motion for a new trial in which she
declined the award and argued that (1) in reducing her
116

damages, the Court of Appeals in effect had offered her a remittitur, and (2) she was entitled to a new trial under the Seventh Amendment of the United States Constitution. In a memorandum opinion, the District Court granted the individual's motion for a new trial and expressed the view that the Court of Appeals' mandate clearly did not address the Seventh Amendment issue. The defendants petitioned the Court of Appeals for a writ of mandamus. The Court of Appeals, in an unpublished order, granted the petition and stayed the scheduled retrial.

Granting certiorari, the United States Supreme Court reversed. In a per curiam opinion expressing the unanimous view of the court, it was held that (1) the District Court correctly afforded the individual the option of a new trial when the District Court entered judgment for the reduced damages; and (2) the Court of Appeals' writ of mandamus, which required the District Court to enter judgment for a lesser amount than that determined by the jury without allowing petitioner the option of a new trial, was a violation of the right to a jury trial under the Seventh Amendment.

EDWARD S. COHEN, Petitioner

v

HILDA de la CRUZ et al.

523 US —, 140 L Ed 2d 341, 118 S Ct 1212

[No. 96-1923]

Argued January 20, 1998.
Decided March 24, 1998.

Decision: 11 USCS § 523(a)(2)(A) held to except from discharge in bankruptcy all liability arising from fraud, including award of treble damages (plus attorneys' fees and costs).

SUMMARY

A landlord/debtor who had been charging rents above the levels permitted by a local rent control ordinance in New Jersey was ordered by a rent control administrator to refund the affected tenants $31,382.50 in excess of rents charged. The landlord/debtor did not comply with this order and subsequently filed for bankruptcy under Chapter 7 of the Bankruptcy Code (11 USCS §§ 701 et seq.), seeking to discharge his debts. The tenants filed an adversary proceeding and argued that (1) the monies owed to them arose from rent payments obtained by actual fraud, and (2) the debt of the landlord/debtor was, therefore, nondischargeable under 11 USCS § 523(a)(2)(A). The tenants also sought treble damages, plus attorneys' fees and costs. A Federal Bankruptcy Court ruled in the tenants' favor and awarded treble damages of $94,147.50 (plus attorneys' fees and costs) and found that the landlord/debtor committed actual fraud
118

within the meaning of § 523(a)(2)(A) (185 BR 171; 185 BR 180). A Federal District Court affirmed (191 BR 599). The United States Court of Appeals for the Third Circuit affirmed and concluded that the treble damages award of $94,147.50 (plus attorneys' fees and costs) resulted from the money obtained through fraud and was, therefore, nondischargeable (106 F3d 52).

On certiorari, the United States Supreme Court affirmed. In an opinion by O'CONNOR, J., expressing the unanimous view of the court, it was held that § 523(a)(2)(A) excepted from discharge "any debt" respecting "money, property, services, or . . . credit" that a debtor had fraudulently obtained, including an award of treble damages (plus attorneys' fees and costs).

COUNSEL

Donald B. Ayer argued the cause for petitioner.

Gregory G. Diebold argued the cause for respondents.

Jeffrey A. Lamken argued the cause for the United States, as amicus curiae, by special leave of court.

HUGO ROMAN ALMENDAREZ-TORRES, Petitioner

v

UNITED STATES

523 US —, 140 L Ed 2d 350, 118 S Ct 1219

[No. 96-6839]

Argued October 14, 1997.

Decided March 24, 1998.

Decision: Provision of 8 USCS § 1326(b)(2) authoriz-
ing increased sentence for deported alien's illegal
return if deportation was subsequent to aggravated
felony conviction held to be penalty provision, so
that aggravated felony need not be charged in
indictment.

SUMMARY

At the time pertinent to the case at hand, (1) under
8 USCS § 1326(a), a deported alien, who returned to
the United States without special permission, committed a crime for which the alien might be sentenced to
a prison term of up to 2 years; and (2) under 8 USCS
§ 1326(b)(2), any alien described in § 1326(a) whose
initial deportation was subsequent to a conviction for
an aggravated felony might be sentenced to a prison
term of up to 20 years. After an alien was indicted for
returning to the United States in violation of 8 USCS
§ 1326, the alien, in pleading guilty at a hearing before
the United States District Court for the Northern
District of Texas, admitted that (1) the alien had been
deported, (2) he had unlawfully returned to the United
States, and (3) the deportation had taken place pursuant to three "convictions" for aggravated felonies. The
120

District Court, rejecting the argument that the failure of the indictment to mention the aggravated felony convictions limited the alien's maximum prison sentence to 2 years, imposed an 85-month sentence. The United States Court of Appeals for the Fifth Circuit affirmed (113 F3d 515).

On certiorari, the United States Supreme Court affirmed. In an opinion by BREYER, J., joined by REHNQUIST, Ch. J., and O'CONNOR, KENNEDY, and THOMAS, JJ., it was held that (1) rather than defining a separate crime of which a prior aggravated felony conviction was an element, § 1326(b)(2) was a penalty provision which simply authorized a court to increase the sentence for a recidivist; and (2) therefore, neither § 1326(b)(2) nor the due process clause of the Federal Constitution's Fifth Amendment required, for imposition of a sentence greater than 2 years, that the government charge a prior aggravated felony conviction in the alien's indictment.

SCALIA, J., joined by STEVENS, SOUTER, and GINSBURG, JJ., dissenting, expressed the view that the alien's sentence ought to be set aside, because (1) illegal re-entry described in § 1326(a) and illegal re-entry, after conviction of an aggravated felony, described in § 1326(b)(2) were separate criminal offenses, and (2) prior conviction of an aggravated felony, being an element of an offense under § 1326(b)(2), had to be charged in the indictment.

COUNSEL

Peter M. Fleury argued the cause for petitioner.

Beth S. Brinkmann argued the cause for respondent.

OHIO ADULT PAROLE AUTHORITY, et al., Petitioners

v

EUGENE WOODARD

523 US —, 140 L Ed 2d 387, 118 S Ct 1244

[No. 96-1769]

Argued December 10, 1997.
Decided March 25, 1998.

Decision: Ohio's clemency procedures for state prison
inmates under death sentences held not to violate
(1) due process under Federal Constitution's Fourteenth Amendment, or (2) right to remain silent
under Fifth Amendment.

SUMMARY

With respect to Ohio state prison inmates under
death sentences, Ohio law (1) gave the governor the
power to grant clemency, (2) provided that the state's
parole authority was required to conduct a clemency
hearing within 45 days of an inmate's scheduled date of
execution, (3) allowed the inmate to request an interview with one or more parole authority members prior
to the hearing, and (4) did not allow counsel at that
interview. After an Ohio inmate who had been sentenced to death for aggravated murder failed to obtain
a stay of execution more than 45 days before his
scheduled execution date, the parole authority commenced a clemency investigation. The inmate, rather
than requesting an interview, (1) objected to the short
notice that he had been given of the opportunity for an
interview, and (2) requested assurances that counsel
122

could attend and participate in the interview and hearing. After the authority failed to respond to these requests, the inmate filed suit in the United States District Court for the Southern District of Ohio under 42 USCS § 1983 against the parole authority and other parties, in which suit it was alleged that Ohio's clemency process violated the inmate's right to due process under the Federal Constitution's Fourteenth Amendment and the right to remain silent under the Constitution's Fifth Amendment. With respect to due process, the inmate specifically contended that (1) 3 days' notice of the interview and 10 days' notice of the hearing were inadequate; (2) the inmate had not had a meaningful opportunity to prepare his clemency application, as postconviction proceedings had been pending; (3) his counsel had improperly been excluded from the interview and permitted to participate in the hearing only at the discretion of the parole authority chair; and (4) the inmate had been precluded from testifying or submitting documentary evidence at the hearing. The District Court granted the defendants' motion for judgment on the pleadings. The United States Court of Appeals for the Sixth Circuit—in affirming in part, vacating in part, and remanding the case for further proceedings—expressed the view that (1) under a "first strand" of due process analysis, the inmate had failed to establish a protected life or liberty interest; but (2) under a "second strand" of due process analysis, (a) clemency was a significant and traditionally available remedy that was an integral part of the adjudicatory system, and (b) a minimal due process was thus required in clemency procedures; and (3) it was for the District Court to decide (a) what that process ought to be, and (b) whether the nature of the parole authority's procedures was such that the inmate had to risk self-incrimination to participate in the clemency interview (107 F3d 1178, 1997 US App LEXIS 3693).

On certiorari, the United States Supreme Court reversed. All of the members of the court joined in an opinion holding that the inmate's Fifth and Fourteenth Amendment privilege against compelled self-incrimination had not been violated. Although unable to agree on an opinion as to the due process issue, eight members of the court (REHNQUIST, Ch. J., and SCALIA, KENNEDY, THOMAS, O'CONNOR, SOUTER, GINSBURG, and BREYER, JJ.) agreed that the inmate's due process claim would be rejected.

REHNQUIST, Ch. J., announced the judgment of the court, and in a part of his opinion which constituted the opinion of the court and which expressed the unanimous view of the court, it was held that Ohio had not violated the inmate's privilege against compelled self-incrimination by giving the inmate the option of voluntarily participating in a clemency interview without the benefit of counsel or a grant of immunity for any statements made by the inmate, for even if it was assumed that the parole authority would draw adverse inferences from the inmate's refusal to answer questions, such pressure on the inmate to speak did not make the inmate's testimony "compelled" within the meaning of the Fifth Amendment. Also, REHNQUIST, Ch. J., joined by SCALIA, KENNEDY, and THOMAS, JJ., expressed the view that Ohio's clemency procedures did not violate due process, as (1) clemency proceedings were not an integral part of the system for finally adjudicating the guilt or innocence of a defendant, and (2) the process that the inmate sought would have been inconsistent with the heart of executive clemency, which was to grant clemency as a matter of grace.

O'Connor, J., joined by Souter, Ginsburg, and Breyer, JJ., concurring in part and concurring in the judgment, expressed the view that (1) some minimal due process safeguards apply to clemency proceedings, but (2) a remand to permit the District Court to address the inmate's specific allegations of due process violations was not required, as none of those allegations amounted to a due process violation.

Stevens, J., concurring in part and dissenting in part, expressed the view that (1) if a state adopts a clemency procedure as an integral part of the system for finally determining whether to deprive a person of life, then that procedure must comport with the Fourteenth Amendment's due process clause; and (2) the case ought to have been remanded to the District Court for a determination whether Ohio's procedures met the minimum requirements of due process.

COUNSEL

William A. Klatt argued the cause for petitioners.
S. Adele Shank argued the cause for respondent.

TEXAS, Appellant

v

UNITED STATES et al.

523 US —, 140 L Ed 2d 406, 118 S Ct 1257

[No. 97-29]

Argued January 14, 1998.

Decided March 31, 1998.

Decision: Texas' claim seeking declaration that sanctions which could be applied against school districts were not subject to federal preclearance requirement of § 5 of Voting Rights Act (42 USCS § 1973c) held not ripe for adjudication.

In 1995, the Texas legislature enacted a comprehensive statutory scheme holding local school boards accountable to the state for student achievement. Under the scheme, the state's commissioner of education was authorized to select various sanctions against school districts that failed to satisfy the state's accreditation criteria. Among these sanctions were (1) appointing a master to oversee a district's operations, (2) appointing a management team to direct a district's operations in areas of unacceptable performance, and (3) requiring a district to contract for services from another person. Because Texas was a covered jurisdiction under § 5 of the Voting Rights Act of 1965 (42 USCS § 1973c) and thus had to obtain federal preclearance before implementing changes affecting voting, Texas submitted the statutory scheme to the United States Attorney General for preclearance. An assistant attorney general, in
126

reviewing the scheme, expressed the view that under some foreseeable circumstances, the implementation of the sanctions in question might result in a violation of § 5 that would require preclearance. Texas, in a complaint filed in the United States District Court for the District of Columbia, sought a declaration that § 5 did not apply to the sanctions in question. A three-judge panel of the District Court (1) concluded that Texas' claim was not ripe for adjudication, and (2) thus granted the United States' motion to dismiss without reaching the merits of the case (1997 US Dist LEXIS 3138).

On direct appeal, the United States Supreme Court affirmed. In an opinion by SCALIA, J., expressing the unanimous view of the court, it was held that Texas' claim was not ripe, as (1) Texas had not pointed to any particular district in which the application of such sanctions was currently foreseen or likely; (2) it could not be affirmed that the imposition of these sanctions would not constitute a change affecting voting—so as to require § 5 preclearance—under any circumstances; (3) Texas was not required to engage in or refrain from any conduct unless and until the state chose to implement one of the sanctions at issue; (4) there was no reason to doubt that a Federal District Court would deny a preliminary injunction against the imposition of one of the sanctions if the state went ahead with such a sanction without preclearance; and (5) Texas' asserted immediate hardship of a "threat to federalism" was inadequate to support the claim.

COUNSEL

Javier Aguilar argued the cause for appellant.
Paul R. Q. Wolfson argued the cause for appellees.

UNITED STATES, Petitioner

v

EDWARD G. SCHEFFER

523 US —, 140 L Ed 2d 413, 118 S Ct 1261

[No. 96-1133]

Argued November 3, 1997.

Decided March 31, 1998.

Decision: Military Rule of Evidence 707, which made polygraph evidence inadmissible in court-martial proceedings, held not to abridge accused's right, under Federal Constitution, to present defense.

SUMMARY

A United States Air Force airman who, as a voluntary informant on Air Force drug investigations, had submitted to a urinalysis and a polygraph test, was tried by a general court-martial on a number of charges, which included using methamphetamine, after the airman was absent without leave and Air Force agents learned that the urinalysis had revealed the presence of methamphetamine. The airman entered a motion to introduce, in support of his testimony that he had not knowingly used drugs, polygraph evidence, where in the opinion of the examiner who had administered the airman's polygraph test, the test had indicated no deception when the airman had denied using drugs. A military judge, relying on Military Rule of Evidence 707—which made inadmissible in court-martial proceedings (1) the results of a polygraph test, (2) the opinion of a polygraph examiner, or (3) any reference to an offer to take, failure to take, of taking of a

129

polygraph test—denied the motion. After the airman was convicted on all charges, the Air Force Court of Criminal Appeals affirmed in all material respects (41 MJ 683). The United States Court of Appeals for the Armed Forces, reversing, expressed the view that a per se exclusion of polygraph evidence offered by an accused to rebut an attack on the accused's credibility violated the accused's right, under the Federal Constitution's Sixth Amendment, to present a defense (44 MJ 442).

On certiorari, the United States Supreme Court reversed. In that portion of the opinion of THOMAS, J., that constituted the opinion of the court and was joined by REHNQUIST, Ch. J., and O'CONNOR, SCALIA, KENNEDY, SOUTER, GINSBURG, and BREYER, JJ., it was held that Rule 707 (1) did not abridge the airman's constitutional right to present a defense; (2) served the legitimate governmental interest in insuring that only reliable evidence was presented at a criminal trial; and (3) did not implicate any significant interest of the airman, where Rule 707 did not prohibit the airman from (a) introducing any factual evidence or testimony about the crime itself, or (b) testifying on his own behalf. In addition, THOMAS, J., joined by REHNQUIST, Ch. J., and SCALIA and SOUTER, JJ., expressed the view that Rule 707 also served the legitimate governmental interests in (1) preserving the jury's core function of making credibility determinations in criminal trials, and (2) avoiding litigation over issues other than the guilt or innocence of an accused.

KENNEDY, J., joined by O'CONNOR, GINSBURG, and BREYER, JJ., concurring in part and concurring in the judgment, (1) agreed that Rule 707 was not so arbitrary or disproportionate that it was unconstitutional, but (2) expressed the view that (a) some later case might present a more compelling case for introduction of

130

testimony concerning a polygraph test than did the instant case, and (b) neither in the federal system nor in the military courts was it convincing to say that polygraph test results should be excluded because of some lingering concern about usurping the jury's responsibility to decide ultimate issues.

STEVENS, J., dissenting, expressed the view that Rule 707 violated (1) 10 USCS § 836(a), which authorized the President to promulgate, for military courts, rules of evidence that, so far as practicable, applied the evidence rules generally recognized in criminal trials in Federal District Courts; and (2) the Constitution, as the government's interests concerning exclusion were insufficient to support a categorical prohibition of admission of polygraph evidence in all cases.

COUNSEL

Michael R. Dreeben argued the cause for petitioner. Kim L. Sheffield argued the cause for respondent.

────────────

C. ELVIN FELTNER, JR., Petitioner

v

COLUMBIA PICTURES TELEVISION, INC.

523 US —, 140 L Ed 2d 438, 118 S Ct 1279

[No. 96-1768]

Argued January 21, 1998.
Decided March 31, 1998.

Decision: Seventh Amendment held to provide right to jury trial on issues pertinent to award when copyright owner elected to recover statutory damages under 17 USCS § 504(c).

SUMMARY

A broadcast company terminated several television series' licensing agreements with three television stations owned by one individual after the television stations' royalty payments became delinquent. When the stations continued broadcasting the series, the broadcast company sued defendants, including the stations' owner, for copyright infringement under § 504(c) of the Copyright Act of 1976 (17 USCS § 504(c)). On the broadcasting company's motion, the District Court (1) entered partial summary judgment for the broadcasting company, (2) awarded statutory damages to the broadcasting company, (3) denied the station owner's request for a jury trial on statutory damages, and (4) instead ruled that such issues would be determined at a bench trial. At the bench trial, the trial judge determined that the station owner's acts of infringement totaled 440 and fixed statutory damages at $20,000 per act, which entitled the broadcasting
132

company to $8,800,000 in statutory damages, plus costs and attorneys' fees. The United States Court of Appeals for the Ninth Circuit affirmed in all relevant respects and expressed the view that (1) § 504(c) did not grant a right to a jury determination of statutory damages, and (2) the Seventh Amendment of the United States Constitution did not provide a right to a jury trial on the issue of statutory damages, as an award of such damages was equitable in nature (106 F3d 284).

On certiorari, the United States Supreme Court reversed the Court of Appeals' judgment and remanded the case for further proceedings. In an opinion by THOMAS, J., joined by REHNQUIST, Ch. J., and STEVENS, O'CONNOR, KENNEDY, SOUTER, GINSBURG, and BREYER, JJ., it was held that (1) there was no statutory right to a jury trial when a copyright owner elected to recover statutory damages; (2) therefore, the question of the right to a jury trial under the Seventh Amendment had to be addressed; and (3) in view of factors including the historical evidence, the Seventh Amendment provided a right to a jury trial on all issues pertinent to an award of statutory damages under § 504(c), including the amount itself.

SCALIA, J., concurring in the judgment, expressed the view that § 504(c) could have been read in a broader meaning to have authorized jury determination on the amount of statutory damages and, therefore, have avoided the Seventh Amendment question.

COUNSEL

John G. Roberts, Jr. argued the cause for petitioner.
Henry J. Tashman argued the cause for respondent.

UNITED STATES, Petitioner

v

UNITED STATES SHOE CORPORATION

523 US —, 140 L Ed 2d 453, 118 S Ct 1290

[No. 97-372]

Argued March 4, 1998.
Decided March 31, 1998.

Decision: Harbor Maintenance Tax (26 USCS § 4461(a)), as applied to goods loaded at United States ports for export, held to violate Federal Constitution's export clause (Art I, § 9, cl 5), as such tax did not qualify as user fee.

SUMMARY

The Harbor Maintenance Tax (HMT) (26 USCS § 4461(a)) obligated exporters, importers, and domestic shippers to pay a uniform percentage of the value of shipments of commercial cargo through the nation's ports. The tax was imposed on exports at the time of loading. HMT monies were deposited in a fund from which Congress could appropriate amounts to pay for harbor maintenance and development projects and related expenses. An exporter, after paying the HMT for articles exported during a portion of 1994, filed a protest with the United States Customs Service, in which protest it was alleged that the HMT, as applied to exports, violated the Federal Constitution's export clause (Art I, § 9, cl 5), which provided that no tax or duty was to be laid on articles exported from any state. The Customs Service responded with a letter stating that the HMT was merely a statutorily mandated fee assessment on port users. The exporter, seeking a refund, brought an action against the Federal Government in the United States Court of International Trade (CIT). The CIT, in entering summary judgment for the exporter, concluded that the HMT, as applied, was a tax rather than a user fee—and was thus invalid under the export clause—as the HMT was assessed directly upon the value of the cargo itself and not upon any services rendered for the cargo (907 F Supp 408, 1995 Ct Intl Trade LEXIS 220). On appeal, the United States Court of Appeals for the Federal Circuit affirmed (114 F3d 1564, 1997 US App LEXIS 13032).

On certiorari, the United States Supreme Court affirmed. In an opinion by GINSBURG, J., expressing the unanimous view of the court, it was held that the HMT, as applied to exports, violated the export clause, as (1) the HMT was determined entirely on an ad valorem basis, (2) the value of export cargo did not correlate reliably with the federal harbor services used or usable by the exporter, and (3) thus, the HMT did not qualify as a permissible user fee.

COUNSEL

Lawrence G. Wallace argued the cause for petitioner. James R. Atwood argued the cause for respondent.

ANGEL FRANCISCO BREARD, Petitioner

v

FRED W. GREENE, Warden (No. 97-8214 (A-732))

———

THE REPUBLIC OF PARAGUAY et al., Petitioners

v

JAMES S. GILMORE, Governor of Virginia, et al.
(No. 97-1390 (A-738))

———

IN RE ANGEL FRANCISCO BREARD, Petitioner
(No. 97-8660 (A-767))

———

REPUBLIC OF PARAGUAY et al., Plaintiffs

v

JAMES GILMORE, III, Governor of Virginia, et al.
(No. 125, Orig. (A-771))

523 US —, 140 L Ed 2d 529, 118 S Ct 1352

[Nos. 97-8214 (A-732), 97-1390 (A-738), 97-8660 (A-767), and 125 Orig. (A-771)]

Decided April 14, 1998.

Decision: Stay and other relief—requested by Paraguay citizen under Virginia death sentence and by Paraguay diplomats—based on alleged violation of rights under Vienna Convention (21 UST 77, TIAS No. 6820), denied per curiam.

SUMMARY

A citizen of Paraguay residing in the United States was arrested in Virginia and charged with attempted rape and capital murder. Following a 1993 jury trial in the Circuit Court of Arlington County, Virginia, the accused was convicted of both charges and sentenced to death. On appeal, the Supreme Court of Virginia affirmed the convictions and sentences (248 Va 68, 445 SE2d 670), and the United States Supreme Court denied certiorari (513 US 971, 130 L Ed 2d 353, 115 S Ct 442). State collateral relief was subsequently denied as well. In 1996, the accused filed a motion in the United States District Court for the Eastern District of Virginia for federal habeas corpus relief, in which motion the accused argued for the first time that (1) the Vienna Convention on Consular Relations (21 UST 77, TIAS No. 6820) conferred on foreign nationals the right to consular assistance following arrest; and (2) at the time of the accused's arrest, the arresting authorities had failed to inform him that he had the right, as a foreign national, to contact his nation's consulate. The District Court, in dismissing the habeas corpus petition, concluded that the accused (1) had procedurally defaulted the Vienna Convention claim when he failed to raise the claim in state court, and (2) could not demonstrate cause and prejudice for this default (949 F Supp 1255, 1996 US Dist LEXIS 19005). The United States Court of Appeals for the Fourth Circuit affirmed (134 F3d 615, 1998 US App LEXIS 892). In a separate action in the District Court, (1) the Republic of Paraguay, Paraguay's ambassador to the United States, and Paraguay's consul general to the United States brought suit against some Virginia officials for the alleged violation of Paraguay's rights under the Vienna Convention, and (2) the consul general, alleging a denial of

137

his own rights under the Vienna Convention, asserted a claim under 42 USCS § 1983. The District Court dismissed the action for lack of subject matter jurisdiction (949 F Supp 1269, 1996 US Dist LEXIS 19006), and the Court of Appeals affirmed (134 F3d 622, 1998 US App LEXIS 895). In 1998, Paraguay pursued the Vienna Convention claim by instituting proceedings against the United States in the International Court of Justice (ICJ), which issued an order requesting that the United States take measures to insure that the accused not be executed pending the final decision in the ICJ proceedings. In addition, in the United States Supreme Court, (1) the accused filed a petition for habeas corpus as an original matter; (2) Paraguay, invoking the Supreme Court's original jurisdiction over cases affecting ambassadors and consuls, filed a motion for leave to file a bill of complaint; and (3) the accused and Paraguay filed applications for a stay of execution.

The Supreme Court denied (1) the petition for an original writ of habeas corpus, (2) the motion for leave to file a bill of complaint, (3) petitions filed by the accused and Paraguay for certiorari to the Court of Appeals, and (4) the stay applications. In a per curiam opinion expressing the views of REHNQUIST, Ch. J., and O'CONNOR, SCALIA, KENNEDY, and THOMAS, JJ., it was held that (1) the accused could not raise the Vienna Convention claim on federal habeas corpus review, as he had procedurally defaulted the claim; (2) no showing could have been made that the alleged violation had an effect on the trial that ought to have resulted in the overturning of the judgment of conviction; (3) Paraguay's actions against Virginia officials could not succeed, for (a) the Vienna Convention did not clearly provide a foreign nation with a private right of action in United States courts, and (b) the alleged violation had no continuing effect, and thus Virginia was immune

138

from suit under the Federal Constitution's Eleventh Amendment; (4) the consul general's § 1983 claim was not cognizable; and (5) the Supreme Court could not make, for the governor of Virginia, the choice to stay the execution pending the ICJ's decision.

SOUTER, J., in a separate statement, (1) agreed that the lack of any reasonably arguable causal connection between the alleged Vienna Convention violations and the accused's conviction and sentence disentitled the accused to relief on any theory offered; (2) expressed the view that it was doubtful that (a) either Paraguay or any official acting for Paraguay was a "person" within the meaning of § 1983, or (b) the Vienna Convention was enforceable in any judicial proceeding currently underway; and (3) concluded that (a) the stay requests ought to be denied, and (b) Paraguay's claims were thus moot.

STEVENS, J., dissenting, expressed the view that the Supreme Court ought to have granted the stay applications and considered the merits of the accused's certiorari petition.

GINSBURG, J., dissenting, expressed the view that the Supreme Court ought to have granted the stay of execution and considered in the ordinary course the accused's first federal habeas corpus petition.

BREYER, J., dissenting, expressed the view that (1) the Supreme Court ought to have granted the stay of execution and considered the certiorari petitions in the ordinary course; and (2) the accused's arguments as to cause and prejudice could not be said, without further examination, to be obviously without merit.

ATLANTIC MUTUAL INSURANCE COMPANY, Petitioner

v

COMMISSIONER OF INTERNAL REVENUE

523 US —, 140 L Ed 2d 542, 118 S Ct 1413

[No. 97-147]

Argued March 2, 1998.
Decided April 21, 1998.

Decision: Interpretation, under 26 CFR § 1.846-3(c), of "reserve strengthening" as generally including any increase in property and casualty insurers' loss reserves—for purpose of exception from one-time federal income tax exclusion—held to be reasonable.

SUMMARY

With respect to the fact that the Tax Reform Act of 1986, 26 USCS §§ 1 et seq., changed property and casualty insurers' method of calculating federal income tax deduction for loss reserves—by replacing the use of current dollars with the use of discounted present value to calculate the amounts of deductible future loss payments—the Act included, for tax years beginning in 1986 only, a transitional provision (note following 26 USCS § 846) under which the difference between undiscounted and discounted yearend 1986 loss reserves was excluded from taxable income. The Act excepted "reserve strengthening" from the exclusion, but did not define reserve strengthening, which was defined, under a Treasury Regulation (26 CFR § 1.846-3(c)) to generally include any net additions to loss
140

reserves. After a determination by the Commissioner of Internal Revenue that a property and casualty insurer had strengthened its reserves resulted in a tax deficiency for the insurer, the United States Tax Court (1) expressed the view that reserve strengthening referred to only increases in reserves that resulted from any changes in the methods or assumptions used to compute reserves; and (2) concluded that the insurer, whose reserve increases had not resulted from any such changes, had not strengthened its reserves. The United States Court of Appeals for the Third Circuit, reversing the Tax Court judgment, expressed the view that the § 1.846-3(c) interpretation of reserve strengthening to include any net additions to reserves was permissible (111 F3d 1056).

On certiorari, the United States Supreme Court affirmed. In an opinion by SCALIA, J., expressing the unanimous view of the court, it was held that the § 1.846-3(c) interpretation of reserve strengthening to include any net additions to loss reserves was reasonable, where (1) neither prior legislation nor industry use established that the term meant only reserve increases attributable to changes in insurers' computation methods or assumptions, (2) the term was broad enough to embrace any reserve amount increases, and (3) the interpretation seemed to be a reasonable accommodation of the competing interests of fairness, administrability, and avoidance of abuse.

COUNSEL

George R. Abramowitz argued the cause for petitioner.

Kent L. Jones argued the cause for respondent.

TERRY CAMPBELL, Petitioner

v

LOUISIANA

523 US —, 140 L Ed 2d 551, 118 S Ct 1419

[No. 96-1584]

Argued January 20, 1998.

Decided April 21, 1998.

Decision: White accused held to have standing to raise, under Federal Constitution's Fourteenth Amendment, equal protection and due process claims alleging discrimination against blacks in selection of Louisiana grand jury forepersons.

SUMMARY

A white accused, who had been indicted by a Louisiana grand jury for second-degree murder of another white person, filed a pretrial motion to quash the indictment on the grounds that the grand jury was constituted in violation of the Federal Constitution's (1) Fourteenth Amendment equal protection and due process provisions, and (2) Sixth Amendment fair-cross-section requirement. The claims were based on alleged discrimination against blacks in the selection of grand jury forepersons in the parish in which the accused had been indicted, which selection had been done in accordance with Louisiana law under which the judge selected the foreperson from the grand jury venire before the remaining grand jury members were chosen by lot. The state did not dispute the accused's evidence that no black person had served as a grand jury foreperson in the parish during the prior approxi-
142

mately 17 years. However, the trial judge—expressing the view that the accused, being a white person accused of killing another white person, lacked standing to complain where all the forepersons were white—refused to quash the indictment. The accused, after a mistrial, was retried and convicted of second-degree murder. The Louisiana Court of Appeals, reversing and remanding for an evidentiary hearing, expressed the view that the accused had standing to object to the alleged discrimination (651 So 2d 412). The Louisiana Supreme Court reversed with respect to the standing issue and remanded with respect to other claims by the accused (661 So 2d 1321). After the Court of Appeals rejected these other claims (673 So 2d 1061), the Louisiana Supreme Court refused to reconsider its ruling on the standing issue (685 So 2d 140).

On certiorari, the United States Supreme Court reversed and remanded. In an opinion by KENNEDY, J., joined by REHNQUIST, Ch. J., and STEVENS, O'CONNOR, SOUTER, GINSBURG, and BREYER, JJ., with respect to holding 1(a) below, and expressing the unanimous view of the court with respect to holdings 1(b) and 2 below, it was held that (1) the accused had standing to assert (a) the equal protection rights of black persons not to be excluded from grand jury service on the basis of their race—where the court had previously held, in Powers v Ohio (1991) 499 US 400, 113 L Ed 2d 411, 111 S Ct 1364, that a white accused had standing to challenge discrimination against black persons in the use of peremptory challenges—and (b) the accused's claim that his conviction had been procured by means or procedures which contravened his own due process rights; and (2) the United States Supreme Court would decline to address the accused's Sixth Amendment fair-cross-section claim, where it appeared that neither the Louisiana Supreme Court nor the Louisiana Court of Appeals had discussed this contention.

THOMAS, J., joined by SCALIA, J., concurring in part and dissenting in part, (1) agreed that (a) the accused had standing to raise the claim asserting his own due process rights, and (b) the court ought not address the fair-cross-section claim; but (2) expressed the view that the accused lacked standing to raise the equal protection rights of black members of the grand jury venire excluded from serving as forepersons, as the Powers decision both (a) ought to be overruled, and (b) was inapposite to the case at hand.

COUNSEL

Dmitrc I. Burnes argued the cause for petitioner.

Richard P. Ieyoub argued the cause for respondent.

DAVID R. BEACH, et ux., Petitioners

v

OCWEN FEDERAL BANK

523 US —, 140 L Ed 2d 566, 118 S Ct 1408

[No. 97-5310]

Argued March 2, 1998.
Decided April 21, 1998.

Decision: 15 USCS § 1635(f) held completely to extinguish right to rescind home loan transaction after 3 years, and borrowers held, therefore, unable to assert right of rescission as affirmative defense in lender's collection action brought more than 3 years after transaction's consummation.

SUMMARY

Two borrowers refinanced their house in Florida in 1986 with a loan from a bank. In 1991, the borrowers stopped making mortgage payments, and in 1992, the bank began a foreclosure proceeding. The borrowers acknowledged their default but raised affirmative defenses, alleging that the bank's failure to make disclosures required by the Truth in Lending Act (15 USCS §§ 1601 et seq.) gave them rights under 15 USCS §§ 1635 and 1640 to rescind the mortgage agreement and to reduce the bank's claim by the amount of their actual and statutory damages. The Circuit Court of the 15th Judicial Circuit of Florida agreed that under § 1640, the borrowers were entitled to offset the amount owed to the bank in actual and statutory damages because the bank had overstated the monthly mortgage payment and finance charge. But the court, rejecting the borrowers' effort to rescind the mortgage, expressed the view that the loan at issue was immune to rescission because under § 1635, the right to rescind had expired after 3 years, in 1989. The Florida Fourth District Court of Appeals affirmed (670 So 2d 986). The Supreme Court of Florida also affirmed, remarking that the plain language of § 1635(f) was evidence of the unconditional congressional intent to limit the right of rescission to 3 years (692 So 2d 146).

On certiorari, the United States Supreme Court affirmed the Florida Supreme Court's decision. In an opinion by SOUTER, J., expressing the unanimous view of the court, it was held that because 15 USCS § 1635(f) completely extinguishes the right to rescind a home loan transaction after 3 years, a borrower may not assert the right of rescission as an affirmative defense in the lender's collection action brought more than 3 years after the transaction's consummation.

COUNSEL

Bruce S. Rogow argued the cause for petitioners.

Carter G. Phillips argued the cause for respondent.

LORELYN PENERO MILLER, Petitioner

v

MADELEINE K. ALBRIGHT, Secretary of State

523 US —, 140 L Ed 2d 575, 118 S Ct 1428

[No. 96-1060]

Argued November 4, 1997.

Decided April 22, 1998.

Decision: Federal Court of Appeals' judgment affirmed, where court had upheld dismissal of equal protection challenge to 8 USCS § 1409(a)(4)'s proof-of-paternity requirement for citizenship for some foreign-born out-of-wedlock children.

SUMMARY

An out-of-wedlock daughter of a Filipino-national mother was born in 1970 in the Philippines and grew up in that country. In November 1991, the daughter filed an application with the United States State Department for registration as a United States citizen. After the application was denied in 1992, a man who was a United States citizen residing in Texas—and who had (1) apparently served in the United States Air Force in the Philippines at the time of the daughter's conception, but (2) never married the mother—filed an unopposed petition in a Texas court to establish his relationship with the daughter. The court entered a "voluntary paternity decree" which found him to be the daughter's "biological and legal father." The daughter subsequently reapplied for United States citizenship, but the reapplication was denied on the ground that the Texas decree did not satisfy the re-

147

quirements of § 309(a)(4) of the Immigration and Nationality Act (INA) (8 USCS § 1409(a)(4)), which effectively provided that children born abroad and out of wedlock to citizen fathers and alien mothers had to obtain formal proof of paternity by age 18 in order to acquire United States citizenship by birth. In 1993, in a suit filed against the Secretary of State in the United States District Court for the Eastern District of Texas, the daughter and father (1) sought, among other matters, a declaratory judgment that the daughter was a United States citizen; and (2) alleged that the INA's different treatment of citizen fathers and citizen mothers—in that § 1409(a)(4)'s proof-of-paternity requirement applied to children born to citizen fathers but not to those born to citizen mothers—was an unjustified gender classification that violated the father's federal constitutional right to equal protection. The father was dismissed as a party for lack of standing, and the case was transferred to the United States District Court for the District of Columbia, which (1) concluded that even though the daughter had suffered an injury caused by the Secretary's refusal to register her as a citizen, the injury was not redressable, as federal courts did not have the power to grant citizenship; and (2) accordingly dismissed the suit (870 F Supp 1, 1994 US Dist LEXIS 14448). The United States Court of Appeals for the District of Columbia Circuit, in affirming, expressed the view that (1) the daughter had standing to challenge the constitutionality of § 1409(a)(4); but (2) the requirements imposed on the child of a citizen father but not on the child of a citizen mother were justified by the interest in fostering the child's ties with the United States (321 US App DC 19, 96 F3d 1467, 1996 US App LEXIS 26361).

On certiorari, the United States Supreme Court affirmed. Although unable to agree on an opinion, six members of the court agreed that the daughter was not entitled to relief.

STEVENS, J., announced the judgment of the court and, in an opinion joined by REHNQUIST, Ch. J., expressed the view that (1) the daughter had standing to invoke the jurisdiction of the federal courts; and (2) it was appropriate for the Supreme Court to evaluate the alleged discrimination against the father as well as the impact of such alleged discrimination upon the daughter; but (3) even under the heightened scrutiny that normally governed gender discrimination claims, § 1409(a)(4)'s proof-of-paternity requirement for children born abroad and out of wedlock to citizen fathers did not violate the equal protection guarantee of the Federal Constitution's Fifth Amendment, as (a) the requirement was justified by important government interests in (i) insuring reliable proof that a person born out of wedlock who claims citizenship by birth actually shares a blood relationship with a United States citizen, (ii) encouraging the development of a healthy relationship between the citizen parent and the child while the child is a minor, and (iii) fostering ties between the child and the United States, (b) the particular means used in § 1409(a)(4) were well tailored to serve those interests, and (c) § 1409(a)(4) was not a stereotypical gender-based classification, for the biological differences between single men and single women provided a relevant basis for differing rules governing such persons' ability to confer citizenship on children born in foreign lands.

O'CONNOR, J., joined by KENNEDY, J., concurring in the judgment, expressed the view that (1) the daughter (a) did not have standing to raise the father's gender discrimination claim, (b) could not herself invoke a gender discrimination claim that would trigger heightened scrutiny, for 8 USCS § 1409 drew a distinction based on the gender of the parent, not that of the child, and (c) could argue only that § 1409 irrationally discriminated between illegitimate children of citizen fathers and those of citizen mothers; (2) the daughter's own constitutional challenge triggered only rational basis scrutiny; and (3) even though § 1409 could not withstand heightened scrutiny, § 1409 was sustainable under rational basis scrutiny.

SCALIA, J., joined by THOMAS, J., concurring in the judgment, expressed the view that (1) the daughter had third-party standing to make the father's equal protection claim; but (2) regardless of whether 8 USCS § 1409(a) passed heightened scrutiny or any other test, the daughter's complaint had to be dismissed, because the Supreme Court had no power to provide the relief requested, that is, conferral of citizenship on an alien on a basis other than that prescribed by Congress.

GINSBURG, J., joined by SOUTER and BREYER, JJ., dissenting, expressed the view that § 1409 classified unconstitutionally on the basis of gender in determining the capacity of a parent to qualify a child for citizenship.

BREYER, J., joined by SOUTER and GINSBURG, JJ., dissenting, expressed the view that (1) the daughter had standing to assert the father's constitutional rights; (2) § 1409 was subject to heightened scrutiny; (3) under heightened scrutiny, § 1409 violated the equal protection guarantee as (a) depending upon the generalization that mothers were significantly more likely than fathers to care for or develop caring relationships with their children, and (b) not fitting the governmental interests that were assertedly served; and (4) the remedy was to strike from § 1409 the provisions that offended the equal protection guarantee, with the results that (a) the statute granted citizenship automatically and at birth, and (b) the Supreme Court needed only to declare that this was so.

COUNSEL

Donald R. Patterson argued the cause for petitioner. Edwin S. Kneedler argued the cause for respondent.

CALIFORNIA and STATE LANDS COMMISSION,
Petitioners

v

DEEP SEA RESEARCH, INC., et al.

523 US —, 140 L Ed 2d 626, 118 S Ct 1464

[No. 96-1400]

Argued December 1, 1998.
Decided April 22, 1998.

Decision: Eleventh Amendment held not to bar Federal
District Court's adjudication, in in rem admiralty
action filed by company, of competing claims by
company and California to wreck of sunken vessel
located several miles off state's coast.

SUMMARY

A vessel was shipwrecked in 1865 while reportedly
carrying valuable cargo. In 1991, a company filed, in
the United States District Court for the Northern
District of California, an action under the court's in
rem admiralty jurisdiction with respect to the sunken
vessel. The District Court initially dismissed the action
without prejudice at the company's initiative. The case
was reinstated in 1994, after the company had actually
located the sunken vessel several miles off the coast of
California. The company (1) sought either an award of
title to the ship and its cargo or a salvage award on the
basis of the company's efforts in recovering the vessel,
and (2) in addition, claimed a right of ownership on
the basis of a purchase of subrogation interests from
some insurers that had paid claims on the cargo. In
response, the state of California entered an appearance
152

for the limited purpose of filing a motion to dismiss the company's complaint for lack of jurisdiction. The state asserted that (1) it possessed title to the vessel under either (a) the Abandoned Shipwreck Act of 1987 (ASA) (43 USCS §§ 2101-2106), or (b) a California statute which apparently operated to transfer title of abandoned shipwrecks not covered by the ASA to the state; and (2) therefore, the company's in rem action against the vessel was an action against the state in violation of the Federal Constitution's Eleventh Amendment, which restricted the jurisdiction of the federal courts. Eventually, the District Court denied the state's motion and issued some admiralty orders in favor of the company, as the court expressed the view that (1) the state had not established that the vessel was abandoned, for purposes of establishing the state's title under the ASA; (2) the ASA pre-empted the state statute; and (3) since the state failed to demonstrate a colorable claim to the vessel under federal or state law, the state could not invoke the Eleventh Amendment, and the court had subject matter jurisdiction (883 F Supp 1343, 1995 US Dist LEXIS 9237). On appeal, the United States Court of Appeals for the Ninth Circuit, in affirming, expressed the view that (1) the state statute was pre-empted to the extent that it gave the state title to shipwrecks that did not meet the ASA's requirements, and (2) the District Court properly ruled that the state did not have a colorable claim to the vessel and therefore was not entitled to Eleventh Amendment immunity from suit (102 F3d 379, 1996 US App LEXIS 31082, as amended on denial of rehearing and suggestion for rehearing en banc).

On certiorari, the United States Supreme Court affirmed the Court of Appeals' judgment assuming jurisdiction over the case at hand, vacated the Court of Appeals' judgment in all other respects, and remanded the case for further proceedings. In an opinion by O'CONNOR, J., expressing the unanimous view of the court, it was held that (1) in the case at hand, the District Court could properly adjudicate the competing claims of the company and the state of California to the shipwreck, because the Eleventh Amendment did not bar the jurisdiction of a federal court over an in rem admiralty action where the res was not within the state's possession; (2) under the circumstances, the Supreme Court would (a) decline to determine whether the sunken vessel was "abandoned" within the meaning of the ASA, and (b) leave that issue for consideration on remand, with the clarification that the meaning of "abandoned" under the ASA conformed with the word's meaning under admiralty law; and (3) the District Court's full consideration, on remand, of the ASA's application might negate the need to address the issue whether the ASA pre-empted the state statute.

STEVENS, J., concurring, expressed the view that—upon further consideration of factors including the special characteristics of in rem admiralty actions—he and some other Justices had erred in concluding, in a prior Supreme Court case involving such an action, that the District Court in the prior case had lacked the power to adjudicate a state's interest in property without the state's consent.

KENNEDY, J., joined by GINSBURG and BREYER, JJ., concurring, expressed the view that the distinction, for purposes of Eleventh Amendment analysis in admiralty cases, between a state's possession or nonpossession of property was open to reconsideration.

COUNSEL

Joseph C. Rusconi argued the cause for petitioners.

David C. Frederick argued the cause for the United States, as amicus curiae, by special leave of court.

Fletcher C. Alford argued the cause for respondents.

VINCENT EDWARDS, REYNOLDS A. WINTER-
SMITH, HORACE JOINER, KARL V. FORT, and JO-
SEPH TIDWELL, Petitioners

v

UNITED STATES

523 US —, 140 L Ed 2d 703, 118 S Ct 1475

[No. 96-8732]

Argued February 23, 1998.
Decided April 28, 1998.

Decision: Federal judge held authorized under Federal
Sentencing Guidelines (18 USCS Appx) to determine for sentencing purposes whether crack as
well as cocaine was involved in controlled-
substances conspiracy.

SUMMARY

Various criminal defendants were tried in the United
States District Court for the Northern District of Illinois
under 21 USCS §§ 841 and 846 for conspiring to
possess with intent to distribute mixtures containing
cocaine and cocaine base ("crack"). The record
showed a series of interrelated drug transactions involving both cocaine and crack. The jury, having been
instructed that the prosecution had to prove that the
conspiracy involved measurable amounts of "cocaine
or cocaine base," returned a general verdict of guilty.
The judge imposed sentences based on his finding that
each defendant's illegal conduct involved both cocaine
and crack. On appeal in the United States Court of
Appeals for the Seventh Circuit, the defendants argued
for the first time that the sentences were unlawful

insofar as the sentences were based upon crack, because the word "or" in the jury instruction meant that
the judge had to assume that the conspiracy involved
only cocaine, which was treated more leniently than
crack under the Federal Sentencing Guidelines (18
USCS Appx). However, the Court of Appeals, in affirming, reasoned that the judge did not have to assume
that only cocaine was involved, as (1) the Guidelines
required the sentencing judge, not the jury, to determine both the kind and the amount of the drugs at
issue in a drug conspiracy; and (2) the jury's belief
about which drugs were involved—cocaine, crack, or
both—was therefore beside the point (105 F3d 1179,
1997 US App LEXIS 1737).

On certiorari, the United States Supreme Court
affirmed. In an opinion by BREYER, J., expressing the
unanimous view of the court, it was held that under the
circumstances presented, (1) the judge was authorized
under the Guidelines to determine for sentencing
purposes whether crack, as well as cocaine, was involved
in the offense-related activities; and (2) there was no
need to consider the merits of the defendants' claim
that the judge was required by §§ 841 and 846 or by the
Federal Constitution to assume that the jury convicted
the defendants of a conspiracy involving only cocaine.

COUNSEL

Steven Shobat argued the cause for petitioners.
Edward C. DuMont argued the cause for respondent.

UNITED STATES, Petitioner

v

ESTATE OF FRANCIS J. ROMANI et al.

523 US —, 140 L Ed 2d 710, 118 S Ct 1478

[No. 96-1613]

Argued January 12, 1998.

Decided April 29, 1998.

Decision: Federal priority statute, 31 USCS § 3713(a), held not to require that federal tax claim be given preference over judgment creditor's perfected lien on real property.

SUMMARY

After a $400,000 judgment, which had been entered in favor of a corporation against an individual by the Court of Common Pleas of Cambria County, Pennsylvania, was recorded and became, under Pennsylvania law, a perfected lien on all of the individual's real property in the county, the Internal Revenue Service filed a series of notices of tax liens, which amounted to approximately $490,000, on the individual's property. The individual subsequently died with an estate that consisted entirely of real estate worth $53,001, and the estate's administrator sought to transfer the property to the corporation in lieu of execution. The Court of Common Pleas, rejecting the Federal Government's contention that such a transfer would violate the federal priority statute (31 USCS § 3713)—which provided in § 3713(a) that a claim of the United States had to be paid first when a decedent's estate could not pay all of its debts—authorized the transfer. The Superior Court of Pennsylvania affirmed, and the Supreme Court of Pennsylvania, also affirming, expressed the view that the Tax Lien Act of 1966, 26 USCS §§ 6321 et seq.—which provided in 26 USCS § 6323(a) that a federal tax lien was not valid until a prescribed notice had been given—limited the operation of § 3713 as to tax debts (547 Pa 41, 688 A2d 703).

On certiorari, the United States Supreme Court affirmed. In an opinion by STEVENS, J., joined by REHNQUIST, Ch. J., and O'CONNOR, KENNEDY, SOUTER, THOMAS, GINSBURG, and BREYER, JJ., it was held that § 3713(a) did not require that a federal tax claim be given preference over a judgment creditor's perfected lien on real property, as (1) each time Congress had revisited the federal tax lien, Congress had ameliorated the lien's original harsh impact on other secured creditors of a delinquent taxpayer; (2) the parties agreed that under § 6323(a) the Federal Government's liens were not valid as against the lien concerning the corporation's judgment; (3) § 3713 itself did not create a lien in favor of the United States; and (4) the Tax Lien Act (a) was the later and more specific statute, (b) contained comprehensive provisions reflecting an attempt to accommodate policy objections to the enforcement of secret liens, and (c) represented Congress' judgment as to when federal claims for unpaid taxes ought to yield to different interests in different types of property.

SCALIA, J., concurring in part and concurring in the judgment, expressed the view that the court should not have considered the Federal Government's contention that § 3713(a) had priority over the Tax Lien Act because Congress had twice "failed to enact" a proposal put forward by the American Bar Association that would have subordinated § 3713(a) to the Tax Lien Act.

159

COUNSEL

Kent L. Jones argued the cause for petitioner.

Patrick F. McCartan argued the cause for respondents.

ARTHUR CALDERON, Warden, Petitioner

v

THOMAS THOMPSON

523 US —, 140 L Ed 2d 728, 118 S Ct 1489

[No. 97-215]

Argued December 9, 1997.
Decided April 29, 1998.

Decision: Federal Court of Appeals held to have abused its discretion when, 2 days before scheduled execution of accused under California death sentence, court recalled mandate which had denied all habeas corpus relief to accused.

SUMMARY

In 1983, in a California trial court, a jury (1) convicted an accused of the rape and first-degree murder of a victim; and (2) found the special circumstance, making the accused eligible for the death penalty, of murder during the commission of rape. The jury then recommended a death sentence, which the trial judge imposed. The accused was unsuccessful on direct review and in three attempts at state habeas corpus relief. In addition, the accused filed, in the United States District Court for the Central District of California, his first federal habeas corpus petition. In 1995, the District Court (1) denied relief as to the murder conviction; but (2) granted relief as to the rape conviction and the rape special circumstance, on the theory that the accused's attorney had rendered ineffective assistance as to the rape charge; and (3) ruled that the accused's death sentence was invalid. In 1996, a panel of the United

161

States Court of Appeals for the Ninth Circuit (1) affirmed the denial of relief as to the murder conviction; (2) reversed the grant of relief as to the rape conviction and rape special circumstance, for the panel expressed the view that the accused could not demonstrate prejudice from his attorney's performance; and (3) reinstated the death sentence. The accused filed a petition for rehearing and suggestion for rehearing en banc, which circulated to each active judge of the Court of Appeals. On March 9, 1997, the panel (1) denied the rehearing petition; (2) rejected the en banc suggestion, as the panel indicated that no judge in active service had requested a vote to rehear the matter en banc; and (3) reissued the panel's 1996 opinion with minor changes (109 F3d 1358, 1996 US App LEXIS 38503). On June 2, 1997, the United States Supreme Court denied certiorari (520 US ——, 138 L Ed 2d 188, 117 S Ct 2426). On June 11, the Court of Appeals issued a mandate denying all habeas corpus relief. The state scheduled the accused's execution for August 5. The accused filed a fourth state habeas corpus petition, a District Court motion for relief from judgment, and a motion for the Court of Appeals to recall its mandate, all of which efforts claimed that there was new evidence that the accused and the victim had engaged in consensual sex. The state petition was denied on July 16, the District Court motion was denied on July 25, and the Court of Appeals panel (122 F3d 28, 1997 US App LEXIS 20009) denied the recall motion on July 28. Moreover, on July 31, the governor of California denied clemency to the accused. However, on August 3—2 days before the accused's scheduled execution—the Court of Appeals, acting en banc, issued a decision which recalled the June 11 mandate, affirmed the District Court's grant of relief as to the accused's rape conviction and rape special circumstance, vacated the death sentence, and ordered a remand, as the en banc court expressed the view that (1) the recall was on the court's own motion and on the basis of the claims and evidence presented in the accused's first federal habeas corpus petition; (2) the court had considered whether to recall the mandate sooner, but had chosen to wait until the conclusion of the state judicial proceedings; (3) in the absence of some procedural misunderstandings—apparently including a mishandled law clerk transition in one judge's chambers and the failure of another judge to notice the panel's proposed rejection of the en banc suggestion—the court would have called for en banc review of the underlying decision before issuing the mandate denying relief; (4) the panel decision would lead to a miscarriage of justice; and (5) the accused's attorney had rendered ineffective assistance as to the rape conviction and rape special circumstance, to the accused's prejudice (120 F3d 1045, 1997 US App LEXIS 24912).

On certiorari, the Supreme Court reversed the Court of Appeals' judgment and remanded the case with instructions to reinstate the June 11, 1997, mandate denying habeas corpus relief to the accused. In an opinion by KENNEDY, J., joined by REHNQUIST, Ch. J., and O'CONNOR, SCALIA, and THOMAS, JJ., it was held that (1) even though the Court of Appeals' recall of the mandate did not contravene the letter of the restrictions in 28 USCS § 2244(b) concerning second or successive federal habeas corpus applications, the Court of Appeals had (a) to exercise its discretion in a manner consistent with the objects of the statute, and (b) to be guided by the general principles underlying the Supreme Court's habeas corpus jurisprudence; (2) where a Court of Appeals, on its own motion, recalls its mandate in order to revisit the merits of an earlier decision denying habeas corpus relief to a state prisoner, the court abuses its discretion unless it acts to avoid a miscarriage of justice, as defined by the Supreme Court's habeas corpus jurisprudence with respect to the prisoner's actual innocence; and (3) in the case at hand, the recall action was a grave abuse of discretion, where (a) even by standards of general application, the recall decision rested on the most doubtful of grounds, and (b) the state's judgment would not result in a miscarriage of justice, in that (i) the accused made no appreciable effort to assert his innocence of the murder, and (ii) on the basis of the record of his first federal habeas corpus petition, the accused's evidence supporting his actual innocence of rape did not meet the "more likely than not" showing necessary to vacate his rape conviction, much less the "clear and convincing" showing necessary to vacate his sentence of death.

SOUTER, J., joined by STEVENS, GINSBURG, and BREYER, JJ., dissenting, expressed the view that—on the assumption that the en banc Court of Appeals, in recalling the June 11 mandate, acted on the court's own and in the interest of the integrity of the court's appellate process—(1) while the timing of the en banc court's actions was a matter for regret, that was not the ground on which the Supreme Court based its reversal; (2) the Supreme Court instead employed a new and erroneous standard to review the recall; and (3) under the traditional and flexible standard of reviewing for an abuse of discretion, the en banc Court of Appeals did not abuse its discretion in recalling the June 11 mandate.

COUNSEL

Holly D. Wilkens argued the cause for petitioner.
Gregory A. Long argued the cause for respondent.

LEONARD ROLLON CRAWFORD-EL, Petitioner

v

PATRICIA BRITTON

523 US —, 140 L Ed 2d 759, 118 S Ct 1584

[No. 96-827]

Argued December 1, 1997.
Decided May 4, 1998.

Decision: Prisoner alleging that corrections officer retaliated for prisoner's exercise of First Amendment free speech rights held not required to adduce clear and convincing evidence of improper motive in order to defeat summary judgment motion.

SUMMARY

A litigious and outspoken prisoner in the District of Columbia's correctional system was transferred among a number of facilities, including a Washington state prison and ultimately a federal prison in Florida. When the District of Columbia department of corrections received the prisoner's belongings from the Washington state prison, a District of Columbia corrections officer, rather than sending the belongings directly to the prisoner's next destination, had the prisoner's brother-in-law pick up the belongings, which were not recovered by the prisoner until several months after he reached Florida. The prisoner (1) filed against defendants including the corrections officer a suit under 42 USCS § 1983, and (2) alleged that the officer had diverted the prisoner's belongings, which included legal materials, in order to interfere with the prisoner's federal constitutional right of access to the courts. After the United States District Court for the District of Columbia denied the officer's motion for summary judgment or dismissal, the United States Court of Appeals for the District of Columbia Circuit, reversing and remanding, expressed the view that (1) the prisoner's allegations were insufficient to avoid dismissal, but (2) he ought to be allowed to replead (951 F2d 1314). On remand, the prisoner amended his complaint to include, in addition to the court access claim, a due process claim and a claim that the officer's alleged diversion of the prisoner's belongings had been motivated by an intent to retaliate for the prisoner's exercise of his free speech rights under the Federal Constitution's First Amendment. After the District Court dismissed the amended complaint (844 F Supp 795), a panel of the Court of Appeals affirmed the dismissal of the court access and due process claims but suggested that the entire Court of Appeals ought to review the dismissal of the First Amendment retaliation claim (72 F3d 919). The Court of Appeals, en banc, in vacating and remanding, expressed, among other views, the view that in order to avoid summary judgment against a party alleging that a government official had acted with an unconstitutional motive, the party had to offer clear and convincing evidence on the motive issue (93 F3d 813).

On certiorari, the United States Supreme Court vacated and remanded. In an opinion by STEVENS, J., joined by KENNEDY, SOUTER, GINSBURG, and BREYER, JJ., it was held that the prisoner was not required to adduce clear and convincing evidence of improper motive in order to defeat the officer's summary judgment motion with respect to the First Amendment retaliation claim, as (1) it would not be unfair to hold the officer accountable for actions that she knew, or should have known, violated the prisoner's constitutional rights; (2) the proper balance did not justify a judicial revision of the law to bar claims that depended on proof of an official's motive, where, without precedential grounding, a change in the burden of proof for an entire category of claims would stray from the traditional limits on judicial authority; and (3) given the wide variety of civil rights and "constitutional tort" claims that trial judges confronted, broad discretion in the management of factfinding might be more useful and equitable to all parties than a categorical "clear-and-convincing" requirement.

KENNEDY, J., concurring, expressed the view, with respect to prisoner suits under § 1983, that disdain for the judicial system had to be guarded against.

REHNQUIST, Ch. J., joined by O'CONNOR, J., dissenting, expressed the view that (1) a government official was entitled to immunity from a motive-based tort suit if (a) the official could offer a legitimate reason for the challenged action, and (b) the plaintiff was unable to establish, by reliance on objective evidence, that the offered reason was a pretext; and (2) in the instant case, there was (a) a legitimate reason for the officer's action, and (b) no evidence of pretext.

SCALIA, J., joined by THOMAS, J., dissenting, expressed the view that in a § 1983 case involving a government official's alleged constitutional violation that was based on improper motive, the rule ought to be that once the trial court found that the asserted grounds for the official's action were objectively valid, the court would not admit any proof that something other than those reasonable grounds was the genuine motive.

COUNSEL

Daniel M. Schember argued the cause for petitioner.
Walter A. Smith, Jr. argued the cause for respondent.
Jeffrey P. Minear argued the cause for the United
States, as amicus curiae, by special leave of court.

KENNETH EUGENE BOUSLEY, Petitioner

v

UNITED STATES

523 US —, 140 L Ed 2d 828, 118 S Ct 1604

[No. 96-8516]

Argued March 3, 1998.

Decided May 18, 1998.

Decision: Convicted person held entitled to hearing on merits of collateral claim contesting validity of his guilty plea to federal firearms charge, if, on remand, he makes necessary showing to relieve his prior procedural default in raising claim.

SUMMARY

After police officers found some drugs and guns in an accused's Minnesota home, the accused was charged with (1) a federal drug offense; and (2) using firearms in relation to a drug trafficking crime, in violation of 18 USCS § 924(c)(1). In 1990, the accused pleaded guilty to both charges, while reserving the right to challenge one aspect of his sentence. The United States District Court for the District of Minnesota (1) accepted the guilty pleas, as the court found that (a) the accused was competent to enter the pleas, (b) they were knowingly entered, and (c) there was a factual basis for the pleas; and (2) sentenced the accused to a prison term. On appeal—where the accused appealed his sentence, but did not challenge the validity of his guilty pleas—the United States Court of Appeals for the Eighth Circuit affirmed (950 F2d 727, 1991 US App LEXIS 25267). Later, in 1994, the accused filed a challenge which

contested the factual basis for his guilty plea to the
§ 924(c)(1) charge. However, the District Court ordered a dismissal of the challenge, as the court adopted
the recommendation of a magistrate judge that the
challenge be (1) treated as a motion for collateral relief
under 28 USCS § 2255, and (2) dismissed on the
merits. While the accused's appeal was pending, the
United States Supreme Court held in Bailey v United
States (1995) 516 US 137, 133 L Ed 2d 472, 116 S Ct
501, that a § 924(c)(1) conviction for use of a firearm
required the government to show active employment of
the firearm. The accused then argued that his conviction under § 924(c)(1) ought to be vacated, on the
theory that (1) the Bailey decision ought to be applied
to the case at hand; (2) the accused's guilty plea to the
§ 924(c)(1) charge had been involuntary, since he had
been misinformed by the District Court as to the nature
of the charged crime; and (3) this claim had not been
waived by the guilty plea. Nevertheless, the Court of
Appeals affirmed the dismissal, as the court expressed
the view that (1) the accused, by failing in his prior
appeal to challenge his § 924(c)(1) guilty plea, had
procedurally defaulted that challenge; (2) the Bailey
decision did not "resurrect" the challenge; and (3) the
accused had not shown the requisite cause to excuse his
procedural default (97 F3d 284, 1996 US App LEXIS
26008).

On certiorari, the Supreme Court reversed and remanded. In an opinion by REHNQUIST, Ch. J., joined by
O'CONNOR, KENNEDY, SOUTER, GINSBURG, and BREYER,
JJ., it was held that the accused will be entitled to a
hearing on the merits of his misinformation claim, if,
on remand, the accused makes the necessary showing
of actual innocence to relieve his procedural default in
failing to contest his § 924(c)(1) guilty plea in his prior
direct appeal, as (1) if the record disclosed that at the

time of the plea, neither the accused, nor his counsel, nor the District Court correctly understood the essential elements of the crime with which he was charged, then the plea was invalid under the Federal Constitution; (2) the accused was not precluded from relying on Bailey v United States in support of his claim; and (3) even though the accused had failed to establish cause to relieve his procedural default, it was appropriate to remand the case to permit him to attempt to make a showing of actual innocence to relieve the default.

STEVENS, J., concurring in part and dissenting in part, expressed agreement that the accused's collateral attack on his conviction under § 924(c)(1) was not foreclosed, but expressed the view that because the record in the case at hand already established that the accused's plea of guilty to the § 924(c)(1) charge was constitutionally invalid, the case ought to be remanded with directions to vacate the accused's § 924(c)(1) conviction and to allow him to plead anew.

SCALIA, J., joined by THOMAS, J., dissenting, expressed the view that (1) the accused had not demonstrated cause for his failing, on direct review, to challenge the validity of his guilty plea to the § 924(c)(1) charge; (2) the Supreme Court had previously applied the actual innocence exception—to the rule that required cause and prejudice to excuse a procedural default—in only the context of a criminal defendant who had been convicted by a jury; and (3) the actual innocence exception ought not to be extended to the guilty-plea context of the case at hand.

COUNSEL

I. Marshall Smith argued the cause for petitioner.

Michael R. Dreeben argued the cause for respondent.

Thomas C. Walsh argued the cause, as amicus curiae, by special leave of court.

TERRY STEWART, Director, Arizona Department of
Correction, et al., Petitioners

v

RAMON MARTINEZ-VILLAREAL

523 US —, 140 L Ed 2d 849, 118 S Ct 1618

[No. 97-300]

Argued February 25, 1998.
Decided May 18, 1998.

Decision: Accused's request for federal habeas corpus
relief from Arizona death sentence—on basis of
reopening claim which had been dismissed as
premature—held not subject to 28 USCS
§ 2244(b)'s restrictions on "second or successive"
applications.

SUMMARY

In Ford v Wainwright (1986) 477 US 399, 91 L Ed 2d
335, 106 S Ct 2595, the United States Supreme Court
held that the Federal Constitution's Eighth Amendment prohibits a state from inflicting the death penalty
upon a prisoner who is insane. An accused was convicted in an Arizona state court of first-degree murder
and sentenced to death. The accused was unsuccessful
on direct review and in a series of state habeas corpus
petitions. In addition, he filed three federal habeas
corpus petitions, all of which were dismissed for failure
to exhaust state remedies. In 1993, the accused (1)
filed, in the United States District Court for the District
of Arizona, his fourth federal habeas corpus petition;
and (2) included a Ford claim that he was incompetent
to be executed. The District Court dismissed the Ford

claim as premature, but granted a writ of habeas corpus on other grounds. The United States Court of Appeals for the Ninth Circuit reversed the grant, but explained that the court's instruction to enter a judgment denying the petition was not intended to affect any later litigation of the Ford claim (80 F3d 1301, 1996 US App LEXIS 6290). In 1997, the state obtained a warrant for the accused's execution. The accused, after unsuccessfully seeking state court relief, moved in the District Court to reopen his Ford claim. However, the District Court ruled that it lacked jurisdiction, under the restrictions in 28 USCS § 2244(b), as amended by the Antiterrorism and Effective Death Penalty Act of 1996 (AEDPA), on "second or successive" federal habeas corpus applications. The accused then sought relief in the Court of Appeals, which (1) expressed the view that § 2244(b) did not apply to a federal habeas corpus petition that raised only a Ford claim which had previously been dismissed as premature; and (2) ordered the case transferred back to the District Court (118 F3d 628, 1997 US App LEXIS 15347).

On certiorari, the Supreme Court affirmed. In an opinion by REHNQUIST, Ch. J., joined by STEVENS, O'CONNOR, KENNEDY, SOUTER, GINSBURG, and BREYER, JJ., it was held that the accused's 1997 request for federal habeas corpus relief on the basis of reopening his Ford claim was not subject to the restrictions in § 2244(b), as amended by AEDPA, on second or successive applications, for (1) even though the accused's 1997 request may have been the second time that he asked the federal courts to provide relief on his Ford claim, (a) there was only one application for federal habeas corpus relief, and (b) the accused was entitled to an adjudication of all of the claims presented in his 1993 application for relief; and (2) if the accused's 1997 request were to be considered a second or succes-

175

sive application, then the implications for federal habeas corpus practice would be far reaching and seemingly perverse.

SCALIA, J., joined by THOMAS, J., dissenting, expressed the view that (1) the language of § 2244(b), as amended by AEDPA, clearly precluded the accused's renewed Ford claim; and (2) there was nothing perverse about such a result, except that it contradicted pre-existing judge-made law, which it was AEDPA's purpose to change.

THOMAS, J., joined by SCALIA, J., dissenting, expressed the view that (1) the Supreme Court's concerns about perversity were not sufficient to override the plain meaning of § 2244(b), as amended by AEDPA; and (2) under the plain language of the statute, the accused's Ford claim that was presented in his 1997 request for relief should have been dismissed as a claim presented in a second or successive application.

COUNSEL

Bruce M. Ferg argued the cause for petitioners.
Denise L. Young argued the cause for respondent.

TEXTRON LYCOMING RECIPROCATING ENGINE
DIVISION, AVCO CORP., Petitioner

v

UNITED AUTOMOBILE, AEROSPACE AND AGRI-
CULTURAL IMPLEMENT WORKERS OF AMERICA,
INTERNATIONAL UNION and ITS LOCAL 787

523 US —, 140 L Ed 2d 863, 118 S Ct 1626

[No. 97-463]

Argued February 23, 1998.
Decided May 18, 1998.

Decision: Federal courts held to lack subject matter
jurisdiction under § 301(a) of Labor Management
Relations Act, 29 USCS § 185(a), over case in
which labor union alleged that employer fraudulently induced union to sign collective bargaining
agreement.

SUMMARY

At a time when an employer and a labor union were
parties to a collective bargaining agreement—which
prohibited the union from striking against the employer and, through a separate memorandum agreement, required the employer to notify the union before
agreeing to subcontract out work that otherwise would
be performed by union members he employer announced a plan to subcontract out work that would
cause approximately one-half of the union members to
lose their jobs. The union filed in the United States
Court for the Middle District of Pennsylvania a complaint (1) alleging that the employer—through its
failure, despite the union's repeated requests, to dis-

177

close the existence of a plan to subcontract out work that would otherwise be performed by union members—had fraudulently induced the union to sign the collective bargaining agreement, and (2) seeking compensatory and punitive damages, as well as a declaratory judgment that the agreement was voidable at the union's option. The union, which did not allege that either the union or the employer had violated the agreement, invoked, as the basis of federal subject matter jurisdiction, § 301(a) of the Labor Management Relations Act (29 USCS § 185(a)), which conferred federal subject matter jurisdiction over "suits for violation of contracts" between an employer and a labor organization. After the District Court dismissed the complaint for lack of subject matter jurisdiction, the United States Court of Appeals for the Third Circuit reversed the District Court's judgment (117 F3d 119).

On certiorari, the United States Supreme Court reversed the judgment of the Court of Appeals. In an opinion by SCALIA, J., joined by REHNQUIST, Ch. J., and STEVENS, O'CONNOR, KENNEDY, SOUTER, THOMAS, and GINSBURG, JJ., it was held that because the union's complaint alleged no violation of the collective bargaining agreement, neither the Supreme Court nor the federal courts below had subject matter jurisdiction over the case under § 301(a), since (1) suits for violation of contracts under § 301(a) are not suits that claim a contract is invalid, but suits that claim a contract has been violated, and (2) the fact that the fraud damages claim, if successful, would have established a voidability that, as far as appeared, no one cared about—where the union had never threatened to strike, and the employer had not asserted that a strike would violate the collective bargaining agreement—did not make the question of voidability a "case of actual controversy" under the

178

Declaratory Judgment Act, 28 USCS § 2201, over which the federal courts had § 301(a) jurisdiction.

STEVENS, J., concurring, expressed the view that the conclusion that the federal courts did not have § 301(a) jurisdiction over the union's suit comported with the goal of protecting the primary jurisdiction of the National Labor Relations Board in resolving disputes arising from the collective bargaining process.

BREYER, J., concurring in part and concurring in the judgment, (1) agreed that because the union had failed to demonstrate an actual controversy, the federal courts lacked subject matter jurisdiction over the case under § 301(a), but (2) expressed the view that § 2201 would have authorized the District Court to adjudicate the case if the union had shown that a strike and consequent employer breach-of-contract lawsuit were imminent.

COUNSEL

Timothy B. Dyk argued the cause for petitioner.
Stephen Yokich argued the cause for respondents.

———————

ARKANSAS EDUCATIONAL TELEVISION COMMIS-
SION, Petitioner

v

RALPH P. FORBES

523 US —, 140 L Ed 2d 875, 118 S Ct 1633

[No. 96-779]

Argued October 8, 1997.
Decided May 18, 1998.

Decision: Arkansas public television broadcaster's decision to exclude independent congressional candidate from televised debate held to be reasonable
exercise of journalistic discretion consistent with
Federal Constitution's First Amendment.

SUMMARY

The Arkansas Educational Television Commission
(AETC) is an Arkansas state agency owning and operating a network of noncommercial television stations.
In 1992, AETC's staff planned a televised debate among
candidates for Arkansas' Third Congressional District.
Because of time constraints, the staff decided to limit
participation in the debate to the major party candidates or any other candidate who had strong popular
support. An independent candidate who was certified
as qualified to appear on the ballot for the seat in
question requested permission to participate in the
debate. AETC's executive director, in denying the
request, asserted that AETC had made a bona fide
journalistic judgment that the viewers would be best
served by limiting the debate to the two major-party
candidates who had already been invited. In a suit filed
180

against AETC in the United States District Court for the Western District of Arkansas, the independent candidate (1) claimed, among other matters, that he was entitled to participate in the debate under the Federal Constitution's First Amendment; and (2) sought injunctive and declaratory relief as well as damages. The District Court dismissed the complaint, and the debate took place without the independent candidate's participation. The United States Court of Appeals for the Eighth Circuit, in reversing the District Court's judgment in pertinent part, (1) concluded that the First Amendment claim was sufficient to survive a motion for dismissal, (2) held that AETC was required to have a legitimate reason to exclude the independent candidate strong enough to survive First Amendment scrutiny, and (3) remanded the case for further proceedings (22 F3d 1423, 1994 US App LEXIS 8984, cert denied 513 US 995, 130 L Ed 2d 409, 115 S Ct 500). On remand, (1) the District Court determined that the debate was a nonpublic forum, (2) the jury found that AETC's decision to exclude the independent candidate had not been influenced by political pressure or disagreement with his views, and (3) judgment was entered for AETC. The Court of Appeals, in reversing, expressed the view that the debate was a public forum and that AETC's assessment of the independent candidate's "political viability" was not a compelling or narrowly tailored reason for excluding him from the debate (93 F3d 497, 1996 US App LEXIS 21152).

On certiorari, the United States Supreme Court reversed. In an opinion by KENNEDY, J., joined by REHNQUIST, Ch. J., and O'CONNOR, SCALIA, THOMAS, and BREYER, JJ., it was held that (1) for First Amendment purposes, the debate was a nonpublic forum with selective access for individual speakers; and (2) AETC's decision to exclude the independent candidate from the debate was a reasonable, viewpoint-neutral exercise of journalistic discretion consistent with the First Amendment, as there was ample support for the trial jury's finding that AETC's decision was reasonable and not based on objections or opposition to the independent candidate's views.

STEVENS, J., joined by SOUTER and GINSBURG, JJ., dissenting, expressed the view that even if a state-owned television network has no constitutional obligation to allow every candidate access to political debates that the network sponsors, (1) access to political debates planned and managed by state-owned entities ought to be governed by pre-established, objective criteria, and (2) the AETC staff's appraisal of the independent candidate's "political viability" was so subjective as to provide no secure basis for the exercise of governmental power consistent with the First Amendment.

COUNSEL

Richard D. Marks argued the cause for petitioner.

Lawrence G. Wallace argued the cause for the United States, as amicus curiae, by special leave of court.

Kelly J. Shackelford argued the cause for respondent.

MONTANA, et al., Petitioners

v

CROW TRIBE OF INDIANS et al.

523 US —, 140 L Ed 2d 898, 118 S Ct 1650

[No. 96-1829]

Argued February 24, 1998.
Decided May 18, 1998.

Decision: Restitution to Crow Tribe of all severance and gross proceeds taxes paid by non-Indian company to Montana and certain counties concerning coal mined—before tribe's severance tax became valid—on land for which tribe was entitled to mineral rights held not warranted.

SUMMARY

In 1972, with the approval of the United States Department of the Interior and pursuant to the Indian Mineral Leasing Act of 1938, 25 USCS §§ 396a et seq., a non-Indian company entered into a mining lease with the Crow Tribe of Indians for coal underlying a strip of land (1) that the tribe previously had ceded from its reservation to the United States for settlement by non-Indians, and (2) with respect to which rights to minerals underlying the land were held by the United States in trust for the tribe. In 1975, the state of Montana, in which the land was located, imposed a severance tax and a gross proceeds tax on all coal produced in the state. The Interior Department first approved a tribal severance tax in 1982 and a tribal gross proceeds tax in 1987, where the company had paid the state approximately $46.8 million in severance

183

taxes during the 1975-1982 period and had paid to certain of the state's counties approximately $11.4 million in gross proceeds taxes during the 1975-1987 period. The company, which had paid these taxes without timely pursuit of the procedures Montana law provided for protests and refunds, agreed to dismiss with prejudice any claims of entitlement to a refund of the taxes it had paid to the state and the counties, and the company paid into a United States District Court for the District of Montana registry the taxes incurred by the company after the relevant periods. Having secured for the tribe's benefit, through earlier litigation, the payments that had been held in the registry, the United States and the tribe sought restitution to the tribe of the $58.2 million that had been paid by the company to the state and the counties, but neither the United States nor the tribe requested, as additional or alternative relief, recovery for the tribe's actual financial losses attributable to the state taxes. After various proceedings in the District Court and the United States Court of Appeals for the Ninth Circuit, the District Court refused to order the requested restitution. The Ninth Circuit, in reversing the District Court judgment, expressed the view that the tribe was entitled to an order directing the state and the counties to disgorge the $58.2 million in coal taxes that had been paid to the state and the counties by the company (92 F3d 826, amended, 98 F3d 1194).

On certiorari, the United States Supreme Court reversed and remanded. In an opinion by GINSBURG, J., joined by REHNQUIST, Ch. J., and STEVENS, SCALIA, KENNEDY, THOMAS, and BREYER, JJ., it was held that the restitution sought for the tribe was not warranted, as the District Court had ignored no tenable law of the case and had not indulged in an abuse of discretion, where (1) the company had forfeited entitlement to a refund, (2) neither the state nor the tribe enjoyed authority to tax to the total exclusion of the other, (3) the tribe could not have taxed the company during the periods in question, for the Interior Department had withheld the essential permission, and (4) the tribe and the United States had argued for total disgorgement rather than developing a case for relief of a different kind and size.

SOUTER, J., joined by O'CONNOR, J., concurring in part and dissenting in part, (1) agreed that since Montana was free to levy and collect the portion of taxes below the threshold of excessiveness, the court properly had vacated the judgment and remanded for further proceedings, but (2) expressed the view that nothing in the record disentitled the tribe at least to press for disgorgement of some or all of Montana's pre-1983 excess tax revenues.

COUNSEL

Clay Riggs Smith argued the cause for petitioners.

Robert S. Pelcyger argued the cause for private respondent.

Jeffrey A. Lamken argued the cause for federal respondents.

OHIO FORESTRY ASSOCIATION, INC., Petitioner

v

SIERRA CLUB et al.

523 US —, 140 L Ed 2d 921, 118 S Ct 1665

[No. 97-16]

Argued February 25, 1998.
Decided May 18, 1998.

Decision: Federal suit by environmental organizations who challenged logging provisions of United States Forest Service's land and resource management plan for national forest held not justiciable.

SUMMARY

Pursuant to the National Forest Management Act of 1976 (16 USCS §§ 1601-1614) (NFMA), the United States Forest Service was required to develop land and resource management plans for units of the National Forest System. However, in order to authorize any specific logging project, the Forest Service was required, under certain NFMA provisions and regulations, to (1) propose a specific area and the harvesting method to be used, (2) insure that the project was consistent with the land and resource management plan, (3) provide those affected with notice and an opportunity to be heard, (4) conduct an environmental analysis to evaluate the project and to contemplate alternatives, and (5) make a final decision which could be challenged in an administrative appeal and in court. In 1988, the Forest Service adopted a 10-year plan for a 178,000-acre national forest in Ohio. The plan (1) designated 126,000 acres of the forest as areas from which timber could be cut; and (2) projected, based on a ceiling for the total amount of wood that could be cut, that (a) there would be logging on about 8,000 acres, and (b) there would be clearcutting or other forms of "even-aged" tree harvesting on 5,000 of the 8,000 acres. In 1992, after the Forest Service rejected attempts by two environmental advocacy organizations to modify the plan on administrative review, the organizations filed an action in the United States District Court for the Southern District of Ohio against the Forest Service. The organizations alleged that the plan's provisions for logging and clearcutting violated the NFMA and other laws. The District Court, determining that the Forest Service had acted lawfully, granted the Forest Service's motion for summary judgment (845 F Supp 485, 1994 US Dist LEXIS 2799). On appeal, the United States Court of Appeals for the Sixth Circuit, reversing and remanding, ruled that (1) the action was justiciable, and (2) the plan improperly favored clearcutting and therefore violated the NFMA (105 F3d 248, 1997 US App LEXIS 819).

On certiorari, the United States Supreme Court vacated and remanded. In an opinion by BREYER, J., expressing the unanimous view of the court, it was held that the organizations' action was not justiciable, as the dispute between the organizations and the Forest Service was not ripe for court review, because (1) delayed judicial review would not cause significant hardship to the parties, (2) immediate judicial intervention could hinder the Forest Service's efforts to refine its policies through both revision of the plan and application of the plan in practice, (3) the courts would benefit from further factual development of the issues presented, and (4) Congress had not provided for preimplementation judicial review of forest plans.

COUNSEL

Malcolm Stewart argued the cause for federal respondents supporting petitioner.

Steven P. Quarles argued the cause for petitioner.

Frederick M. Gittes argued the cause for private respondent.

ARTHUR CALDERON, Warden, et al., Petitioners

v

TROY A. ASHMUS, Individually and on Behalf of All
Others Similarly Situated

523 US —, 140 L Ed 2d 970, 118 S Ct 1694

[No. 97-391]

Argued March 24, 1998.
Decided May 26, 1998.

Decision: Federal class action by state death-row prisoner, who sought relief with respect to applicability
of expedited habeas corpus review under 28 USCS
§§ 2261-2266, held nonjusticiable under Article
III.

SUMMARY

Provisions of the Antiterrorism and Effective Death
Penalty Act of 1996, PL 104-132, which added to Title
28 of the United States Code a new Chapter 154 (28
USCS §§ 2261-2266), created an expedited review process, in federal habeas corpus proceedings brought by
prisoners who were subject to capital sentences, against
states that satisfied certain criteria with respect to the
appointment and compensation of counsel for petitioners in state postconviction proceedings. The generally
applicable provisions which governed federal habeas
corpus relief, Chapter 153 of Title 28 (28 USCS §§
2241-2255), lacked expedited review procedures. After
various California officials publicly indicated that they
thought that California qualified under Chapter 154
and that they intended to invoke such chapter's protections, a state prisoner who had been sentenced to

death filed a class action in the United States District Court for the Northern District of California against the officials. The class, consisting of capital prisoners in California whose convictions had been affirmed on direct appeal after a certain date, sought declaratory and injunctive relief with respect to the applicability of Chapter 154. The District Court issued (1) a declaratory judgment holding that California did not qualify for Chapter 154 and that such chapter did not apply to any class members, and (2) a preliminary injunction which enjoined the officials from seeking to obtain for California the benefits of Chapter 154's provisions in any state or federal proceedings involving any class member (935 F Supp 1048, 1996 US Dist LEXIS 10902). On appeal, the United States Court of Appeals for the Ninth Circuit, affirming, expressed the view that (1) the Federal Constitution's Eleventh Amendment did not bar the action; (2) the District Court had the authority to issue a declaratory judgment under the Declaratory Judgment Act (28 USCS §§ 2201, 2202), in that there was both an independent basis of federal jurisdiction under 28 USCS § 1331 and an actual case or controversy; and (3) the grant of injunctive relief did not interfere with the officials' rights to free speech under the Constitution's First Amendment (123 F3d 1199, 1997 US App LEXIS 21732).

On certiorari, the United States Supreme Court reversed and remanded. In an opinion by REHNQUIST, Ch. J., expressing the unanimous view of the court, it was held that (1) notwithstanding the Supreme Court's grant of certiorari on the First and Eleventh Amendment issues, the Supreme Court first had to address whether the prisoner's action was the sort of case or controversy, within the meaning of Article III of the Constitution, to which federal courts were limited; and (2) the action was not a justiciable case within the meaning of Article III, in part because (a) the underlying "controversy" between the prisoner and the officials was whether the officials were entitled to federal habeas corpus relief setting aside a sentence or conviction obtained in the state courts, but no such final or conclusive determination had been sought in the prisoner's federal court action in the case at hand, (b) use of the Declaratory Judgment Act for the purpose of having the question of whether, when the prisoner sought habeas corpus relief, the state would be governed in defending the action by Chapter 153 or by Chapter 154 was barred, and (c) any judgment in the case at hand would not resolve the entire case or controversy as to any one of the class members, but would merely determine a collateral legal issue governing certain aspects of their pending or future suits.

BREYER, J., joined by SOUTER, J., concurring, expressed the view that (1) it should prove possible for at least some habeas corpus petitioners to obtain a relatively expeditious judicial answer to the Chapter 154 compliance question and thereby provide legal guidance for others; and (2) a District Court's determination that turned on the legal answer to that question might qualify for interlocutory appeal under 28 USCS § 1292(b).

COUNSEL

Ronald S. Matthias argued the cause for petitioners.
Michael Laurence argued the cause for respondent.

KIOWA TRIBE OF OKLAHOMA, Petitioner

v

MANUFACTURING TECHNOLOGIES, INC.

523 US —, 140 L Ed 2d 981, 118 S Ct 1700

[No. 96-1037]

Argued January 12, 1998.
Decided May 26, 1998.

Decision: Indian tribes held immune from suits on contracts, regardless of whether contracts (1) involved governmental or commercial activities, and (2) were made on or off reservation.

SUMMARY

An Indian tribe's industrial development commission agreed to purchase certain stock from a corporation, and the chairman of the tribe's business committee signed a promissory note in the name of the tribe. Although the note recited on its face that it had been signed in an Oklahoma community where the tribe had a complex on land held for it in trust for the tribe by the United States, the corporation subsequently claimed that the note had been executed and delivered to it in Oklahoma City, beyond the tribe's lands. When the tribe defaulted, the corporation brought an action on the note in the Oklahoma state courts. The tribe's motion to dismiss the action for lack of jurisdiction, based partly on its asserted sovereign immunity from suit, was denied by an Oklahoma trial court, which rendered judgment in favor of the corporation. The Oklahoma Court of Appeals, affirming, held that Indian tribes were subject to suit in state court for breaches of contract involving off-reservation commercial conduct. The Supreme Court of Oklahoma declined to review the judgment.

On certiorari, the United States Supreme Court reversed. In an opinion by KENNEDY, J., joined by REHNQUIST, Ch. J., and O'CONNOR, SCALIA, SOUTER, and BREYER, JJ., it was held that (1) under Supreme Court precedents, Indian tribes enjoy immunity from suits on contracts, regardless of whether those contracts (a) involve governmental or commercial activities, and (b) were made on or off a reservation; and (2) although there are reasons to doubt the wisdom of perpetuating the doctrine of tribal immunity, the Supreme Court will defer to Congress, which has not abrogated this immunity.

STEVENS, J., joined by THOMAS and BREYER, JJ., dissented, expressing the view that (1) the Supreme Court has never considered whether an Indian tribe is immune from a suit which has no meaningful nexus to the tribe's land or sovereign functions, and (2) the doctrine of tribal immunity should not be extended beyond its present contours to include such cases.

COUNSEL

R. Brown Wallace argued the cause for petitioner.

Edward C. DuMont argued the cause for the United States, as amicus curiae, by special leave of court.

John E. Patterson, Jr. argued the cause for respondent.

STATE OF NEW JERSEY, Plaintiff

v

STATE OF NEW YORK

523 US —, 140 L Ed 2d 993, 118 S Ct 1726

[No. 120 Orig.]

Argued January 12, 1998.

Decided May 26, 1998.

Decision: State of New Jersey, not New York, held to have sovereign authority over about 24.5 acres of filled land that Federal Government had added around Ellis Island, former immigration station in New York Harbor.

SUMMARY

Ellis Island lies in New York Harbor about 1,300 feet from the New Jersey shore. There was a longstanding dispute between the states of New Jersey and New York concerning their boundary in the harbor area. Eventually, the two states entered into a boundary compact that was consented to by Congress in 1834 (4 Stat 708), pursuant to the Federal Constitution's compact clause (Art I, § 10, cl 3). At that time, Ellis Island comprised about 3 acres. The compact included provisions that (1) in Article First, established a general boundary line—as to which Ellis Island was later held to be on the New Jersey side—that applied except as otherwise mentioned in the compact; and (2) in Article Second, provided that New York would retain its "present jurisdiction" over Ellis Island. Meanwhile, New York had (1) in 1800, ceded, with a reservation for the service of judicial process, "jurisdiction" over Ellis

194

Island to the United States; and (2) in 1808, granted all of the state's property interest in the island to the United States. The Federal Government used Ellis Island for military purposes until the 1890's, when the location became a major immigration station. From about 1890 to 1934, the Federal Government, in connection with these immigration operations, enlarged the surface area by adding about 24.5 acres of filled land on the submerged lands around Ellis Island. Also, in 1904, New Jersey conveyed to the United States all of the state's property interest in about 48 acres that surrounded Ellis Island. The immigration station was closed in 1954, but the Federal Government retained control of the location and eventually developed it as a national historic site. However, for such purposes as taxation, zoning, environmental protection, and elections, both New Jersey and New York asserted rival claims of sovereign authority over the filled land which the Federal Government had added. In 1993, New Jersey (1) invoked the United States Supreme Court's original jurisdiction under Art III, § 2, cl 2 of the Constitution; and (2) sought leave to file a bill of complaint against New York concerning these rival claims to the filled land. The Supreme Court (1) granted New Jersey's petition (511 US 1080, 128 L Ed 2d 458, 114 S Ct 1828), and (2) appointed a special master (513 US 924, 130 L Ed 2d 273, 115 S Ct 309). In 1997, the special master submitted to the Supreme Court a final report and a supplement (520 US ——, 138 L Ed 2d 209, 117 S Ct 2451). The special master (1) concluded that the filled land was subject to the sovereign authority of New Jersey; (2) rejected New York's claims that (a) the state had obtained sovereign authority over the filled land by prescription and acquiescence, and (b) laches barred New Jersey's complaint; (3) determined that the original 1834 area of

Ellis Island followed the mean low-water mark; (4) recommended that the area covered by a particular pier which had existed in 1834 be treated as part of the original island; and (5) further recommended that the Supreme Court, in the interest of practicality, convenience, and fairness, adjust the boundary line between the two states so as to place all of the main immigration building and the land immediately surrounding it within New York.

On exceptions by both states to the report of the special master, the Supreme Court (1) sustained an exception by New Jersey to the portion concerning the Supreme Court's adjustment of the boundary line, (2) overruled New Jersey's other exceptions and all of New York's exceptions, and (3) recommitted the case to the special master for preparation of a proposal for a decree consistent with the Supreme Court's opinion. In an opinion by SOUTER, J., joined by REHNQUIST, Ch. J., and O'CONNOR, KENNEDY, GINSBURG, and BREYER, JJ., it was held that (1) New Jersey, not New York, had sovereign authority over the filled land that the Federal Government had added on the submerged lands around Ellis Island from about 1890 to 1934, as (a) New York did not have sovereign authority over the filled land under Article Second of the 1834 compact, (b) New York had not obtained sovereignty over the filled land through the exercise of prescriptive acts to which New Jersey had acquiesced, and (c) given that New York, with respect to laches, claimed prejudice only in presenting the state's affirmative defense of prescription and acquiescence, New York could not benefit from its asserted defense of laches; (2) New Jersey's sovereign authority extended to only the mean low-water mark of the original Ellis Island as it had existed in 1834, rather than to the mean high-water mark; (3) the special master had sufficient evidence to conclude

196

that the area covered by the pier in question was meant to fall within New York's authority as recognized in Article Second; and (4) the Supreme Court lacked the authority to adjust the boundary line in the manner recommended by the special master for reasons of practicality and convenience.

BREYER, J., joined by GINSBURG, J., concurring, expressed the view that the record showed that the filled portion of Ellis Island belonged to New Jersey, not New York, as (1) there was not "sufficient, relevant" ambiguity in the 1834 compact to allow evidence of custom, assumption, and late 19th century history to explain the alleged ambiguity; and (2) New Jersey did not lose through prescription what had once been rightfully the state's own.

STEVENS, J., dissenting, expressed the view that (1) a preponderance of the evidence supported a finding that for more than 60 years, all interested parties had shared the belief that the filled portions, as well as the original 3 acres, of Ellis Island were part of the state of New York; and (2) that finding supported the conclusion that New York had acquired the power to govern the entire island by prescription.

SCALIA, J., joined by THOMAS, J., dissenting, expressed the view that (1) the available evidence supported a finding that for more than 60 years, all interested parties had shared the belief that the filled portions, as well as the original 3 acres, of Ellis Island were part of the state of New York; and (2) thus, pursuant to the practical construction which had been given by the parties during that period to the 1834 compact, which was ambiguous on the point in question, New Jersey's claim to the filled portions of Ellis Island ought to be rejected.

COUNSEL

Joseph L. Yannotti argued the cause for plaintiff.

Jeffrey P. Minear argued the cause for the United States, as amicus curiae, by special leave of court.

Daniel Smirlock argued the cause for defendant.

COUNTY OF SACRAMENTO, et al., Petitioners

v

TERI LEWIS and THOMAS LEWIS, Personal Representative of the Estate of Philip Lewis, Deceased

523 US —, 140 L Ed 2d 1043, 118 S Ct 1708

[No. 96-1337]

Argued December 9, 1997.
Decided May 26, 1998.

Decision: Police officer held not to violate substantive due process guarantee of Federal Constitution's Fourteenth Amendment by causing death through deliberate or reckless indifference to life in high-speed automobile chase aimed at apprehending suspect.

SUMMARY

When a police officer who had responded to a call to break up a fight was returning to his patrol car, he saw a motorcycle carrying the operator and a passenger—neither of whom had anything to do with the fight—approaching at high speed. The officer turned on his car's overhead rotating lights, yelled for the motorcycle to stop, and, in an attempt to block the motorcycle, moved his car closer to the patrol car of a county sheriff's deputy, who also had responded to the call concerning the fight. The motorcycle operator maneuvered the motorcycle between the cars and sped off, and the deputy immediately switched on his emergency lights and siren and began a high-speed chase in a residential neighborhood. The motorcycle tipped over, and although the deputy slammed on the brakes

199

of his patrol car, the car struck and killed the motorcycle passenger. Representatives of the passenger's estate brought against the county, the sheriff's department, and the deputy an action under 42 USCS § 1983 alleging a deprivation of the passenger's substantive due process right to life under the Federal Constitution's Fourteenth Amendment. A Federal District Court, granting summary judgment for the deputy, expressed the view that the deputy was entitled to qualified immunity from the action. The United States Court of Appeals for the Ninth Circuit, reversing, expressed the view that the appropriate degree of fault to be applied to high-speed police pursuits is deliberate indifference to, or reckless disregard for, a person's right to life and personal security (98 F3d 434).

On certiorari, the United States Supreme Court reversed the judgment of the Court of Appeals. In an opinion by SOUTER, J., joined by REHNQUIST, Ch. J., and O'CONNOR, KENNEDY, GINSBURG, and BREYER, JJ., it was held that (1) the deputy did not violate the Fourteenth Amendment's guarantee of substantive due process by causing death through deliberate or reckless indifference to life in a high-speed automobile chase aimed at apprehending a suspected offender, (2) high-speed police chases with no intent to harm suspects physically or to worsen their legal plight do not give rise to liability under the Fourteenth Amendment, redressable by an action under § 1983, (3) in a due process challenge to executive action, the threshold question is whether the behavior of the governmental officer may be fairly said to shock the contemporary conscience, and (4) the deputy's instinctive and practically instantaneous response to the motorcycle driver's lawless behavior did not shock the conscience, where there was no reason to believe that the deputy had an improper or malicious motive.

200

REHNQUIST, Ch. J., concurring, expressed the view that the "shocks the conscience" standard (1) was the right choice among the alternatives posed in a question presented in the petition for certiorari, and (2) had not been met in this case.

KENNEDY, J., joined by O'CONNOR, J., concurring, expressed the view that neither legal traditions nor the present needs of law enforcement justified finding a due process violation when unintended injuries occurred after the police pursued a suspect who disobeyed their lawful order to stop.

BREYER, J., concurring, expressed the view that lower courts should not be denied flexibility, in appropriate cases, to decide § 1983 claims on the basis of qualified immunity and thereby avoid constitutional issues that were difficult or poorly presented.

STEVENS, J., concurring in the judgment, expressed the view that the constitutional question presented in the case (1) was difficult and, at the time of the chase, unresolved, and (2) therefore, should have been avoided, because the deputy was entitled to qualified immunity.

SCALIA, J., joined by THOMAS, J., concurring in the judgment, expressed the view that the deputy was entitled to a summary judgment not on the ground that the deputy's conduct failed to shock the conscience, but on the ground that the passenger's representatives offered no textual or historical support for the alleged due process right to be free from deliberate or reckless indifference to life in a high-speed automobile chase aimed at apprehending a suspected offender.

COUNSEL

Terrance J. Cassidy argued the cause for petitioners.
Paul J. Hedlund argued the cause for respondents.

AIR LINE PILOTS ASSOCIATION, Petitioner

v

ROBERT A. MILLER et al.

523 US —, 140 L Ed 2d 1070, 118 S Ct 1761

[No. 97-428]

Argued March 23, 1998.
Decided May 26, 1998.

Decision: Nonunion employees in agency shop who challenged union's calculation of agency fees and who had never agreed to submit fee disputes to arbitration held not required to exhaust arbitration remedy before suing in federal court.

SUMMARY

Pursuant to § 2, Eleventh, of the Railway Labor Act (45 USCS § 152, Eleventh), a collective bargaining agreement between an airline and a pilots' union included an "agency shop" clause that required nonunion employee pilots to pay the union a monthly service charge for representing those pilots. In 1991, some nonunion pilots, challenging the facial legality of the clause and seeking a preliminary injunction against the clause's implementation, filed an action in the United States District Court for the District of Columbia. The District Court denied the pilots' motion for a preliminary injunction (1992 US Dist LEXIS 579). For 1992, the union collected an agency fee that amounted to 81 percent of the amount that union members paid as dues. The plaintiff pilots, alleging that the union had overstated the percentage of union expenditures that were genuinely attributable to activities germane to

203

collective bargaining, amended the District Court complaint to add a count challenging the manner in which the union had calculated the fee. While the District Court action was pending, a group of pilots, including some who were plaintiffs in the District Court action, filed fee-calculation objections with the union. Pursuant to a union policy under which pilots who objected to a fee calculation could request arbitration by the American Arbitration Association (AAA), the union treated these objections as requests for arbitration and referred them to the AAA. Of the objecting pilots, those who preferred to pursue their claims in the context of the District Court action asked the AAA to suspend the arbitration. The AAA referred this request to the arbitrator, who declined to defer to the District Court litigation. After the District Court denied a motion to enjoin the arbitration, the arbitrator sustained the union's agency fee calculation in substantial part. The District Court, in sustaining the arbitrator's decision and granting a motion by the union for summary judgment, concluded that (1) pilots seeking to challenge the union's agency fee calculation had to exhaust arbitral remedies before proceeding in court, and (2) accordingly, the pilots who had not joined the arbitration were nonetheless bound by the arbitrator's decision (1993 US Dist LEXIS 10892). The United States Court of Appeals for the District of Columbia Circuit, in reversing, expressed the view that there was no legal basis for requiring objectors to arbitrate agency fee challenges unless the objectors had agreed to do so (323 US App DC 386, 108 F3d 1415, 1997 US App LEXIS 4718, rehearing en banc denied, 325 US App DC 154, 116 F3d 498, 1997 US App LEXIS 26928).

On certiorari, the United States Supreme Court affirmed. In an opinion by GINSBURG, J., joined by REHNQUIST, Ch. J., and O'CONNOR, SCALIA, KENNEDY,

SOUTER, and THOMAS, JJ., it was held that nonunion employees in an agency shop who challenged a union's calculation of agency fees and who never agreed to submit fee disputes to arbitration could not be required by the union to exhaust an arbitration remedy before bringing the claims in federal court, as (1) the requirement that a union must accord such employees a reasonably prompt opportunity to challenge the amount of the fee before an impartial decisionmaker weighed against exhaustion as a prerequisite to federal court consideration of such challenges; (2) although requiring objectors to proceed to arbitration first assertedly would have led to efficiency gains, the answer to the efficiency concern lay in conscientious management of the pretrial process to guard against abuse; (3) the degree to which an exhaustion requirement would reduce the burden on the courts was uncertain; (4) if the union's arbitration process in fact operated to provide a remedy for agency fee errors, then dissenting employees might avail themselves of that process even if not required to do so; and (5) the union's interest in avoiding multiple proceedings did not overwhelm objectors' (a) resistance to arbitration to which the objectors did not consent, and (b) election to proceed immediately to court.

BREYER, J., joined by STEVENS, J., dissenting, expressed the view that with respect to challenges to agency fee calculations, a union rule requiring initial participation in prompt but nonbinding arbitration was consistent with—and a reasonable extension of —Supreme Court precedent.

COUNSEL

Jerry S. Anker argued the cause for petitioner.

Raymond J. LaJeunesse, Jr. argued the cause for respondents.

———————

UNITED STATES, Petitioner

v

VICKIE S. CABRALES

524 US —, 141 L Ed 2d 1, 118 S Ct 1772

[No. 97-643]

Argued April 29, 1998.
Decided June 1, 1998.

Decision: Missouri held improper venue for trial of money laundering charges under 18 USCS §§ 1956(a)(1)(B)(ii) and 1957, where money allegedly derived from illegal acts by others in Missouri, but where alleged money laundering by defendant occurred entirely in Florida.

SUMMARY

A woman who allegedly had made deposits in and withdrawals from banks in Florida, involving money which was allegedly traceable to illegal cocaine sales in Missouri, was indicted in the United States District Court for the Western District of Missouri on charges of (1) conspiracy to avoid the transaction-reporting requirement of 18 USCS § 1956(a)(1)(B)(ii); (2) conducting a financial transaction to avoid that requirement; and (3) engaging in monetary transactions in criminally derived property in violation of 18 USCS § 1957. The woman moved to dismiss the indictment for improper venue, and the District Court, while denying the motion with respect to the conspiracy count on the ground that the woman had committed certain acts in furtherance of the conspiracy in Missouri, dismissed the two money laundering counts. In affirming the dismissal of the money-laundering counts, the United States Court of Appeals for the Eighth Circuit held that (1) both the Federal Constitution and Rule 18 of the Federal Rules of Criminal Procedure require that a person be tried for an offense where the offense is committed; and (2) since the counts in question alleged acts which occurred in only Florida and alleged no act committed by the woman in Missouri, and since it was not alleged that the woman transported the money from Missouri to Florida, the counts could not be tried in Missouri (109 F3d 471, 1997 US App LEXIS 5497). The government's petition for rehearing en banc was denied (115 F3d 621, 1997 US App LEXIS 14178).

On certiorari, the United States Supreme Court affirmed. In an opinion by GINSBURG, J., expressing the unanimous view of the court, it was held that although the money allegedly laundered allegedly derived from illegal sales of cocaine in Missouri, Missouri was not the appropriate venue for the trial of the money laundering counts, since those counts alleged acts occurring entirely in Florida.

COUNSEL

Malcolm L. Stewart argued the cause for petitioner. John W. Rogers argued the cause for respondent.

FEDERAL ELECTION COMMISSION, Petitioner

v

JAMES E. AKINS, RICHARD CURTISS, PAUL FIND-
LEY, ROBERT J. HANKS, ANDREW KILLGORE, and
ORIN PARKER

524 US —, 141 L Ed 2d 10, 118 S Ct 1777

[No. 96-1590]

Argued January 14, 1998.
Decided June 1, 1998.

Decision: Voters held to have standing to challenge
Federal Election Commission (FEC) decision that
organization was not political committee subject to
Federal Election Campaign Act, 2 USCS §§ 431 et
seq.; case remanded to await FEC decision on
political committee issue under new regulations.

SUMMARY

A group of voters filed a complaint requesting the
Federal Election Commission (FEC) to order an
organization—which lobbied elected officials, dissemi-
nated information about candidates for public office,
and had views that often were opposed by the
voters—to make disclosures regarding its membership,
contributions, and expenditures. Such disclosures are
required, under the Federal Election Campaign Act of
1971 (FECA), 2 USCS §§ 431 et seq., of a "political
committee" as defined by 2 USCS § 431(4). After the
FEC, expressing the view that the organization was not
a political committee, dismissed the voters' complaint,
the voters filed in the United States District Court for
the District of Columbia a petition seeking review of the

FEC decision. The District Court granted summary judgment for the FEC, and a divided panel of the United States Court of Appeals for District of Columbia Circuit affirmed the District Court judgment (66 F3d 348). The en banc Court of Appeals, reversing the District Court judgment, expressed the view that the FEC had improperly interpreted FECA's definition of a "political committee" (101 F3d 731).

On certiorari, the United States Supreme Court vacated the judgment of the Court of Appeals and remanded the case for further proceedings. In an opinion by BREYER, J., joined by REHNQUIST, Ch. J., and STEVENS, KENNEDY, SOUTER, and GINSBURG, JJ., it was held that (1) the voters had standing to challenge the FEC decision that the organization was not a political committee because (a) given the language of FECA and the nature of the voters' injury—the failure to obtain relevant information—the asserted injury was of a kind that FECA seeks to address, and the voters thus had prudential standing, and (b) the voters had standing under the Federal Constitution's Article III, since (i) the asserted injury was sufficiently concrete and specific to constitute an injury in fact, (ii) the injury in fact was fairly traceable to the FEC's decision not to issue a complaint against the organization, and (iii) the courts could redress the injury in fact; but (2) the Supreme Court would not determine whether the organization was a political committee, because (a) after the FEC decided not to issue a complaint against the organization, the Court of Appeals, in another case, had overturned certain FEC rules that were relevant to the issue whether the organization was a political committee, (b) the FEC had responded with proposed rules that could affect this issue, and (c) allowing the FEC to first address the issue, would allow the FEC to develop a more precise rule that might dispose of the case, or at

SUMMARIES   141 L Ed 2d 10

a minimum, would aid the Supreme Court in reaching a more informed conclusion.

SCALIA, J., joined by O'CONNOR, and THOMAS, JJ., dissenting, expressed the view that (1) FECA should not be interpreted to confer upon the entire electorate the power to invoke judicial direction of prosecutions, and (2) the court's entertainment of the case violated Article III.

COUNSEL

Seth P. Waxman argued the cause for petitioner.

Daniel M. Schember argued the cause for respondents.

UNITED STATES, Petitioner

v

CHRIS W. BEGGERLY et al.

524 US —, 141 L Ed 2d 32, 118 S Ct 1862

[No. 97-731]

Argued April 27, 1998.
Decided June 8, 1998.

Decision: Federal court held to lack jurisdiction over action to reopen settlement quieting land title in Federal Government, either (1) as independent action under Rule 60(b) of Federal Rules of Civil Procedure, or (2) under Quiet Title Act (28 USCS § 2409a).

SUMMARY

In 1979, the Federal Government brought an action in the United States District Court for the Southern District of Mississippi to quiet title in certain tracts of lands—which had been part of the territory encompassed by the Louisiana Purchase of 1803—in the belief that the supposed owners lacked clear title because the government had never patented the property. A settlement was reached in 1982 whereby title was quieted in the government in exchange for a payment of about $200,000. Subsequently, however, the former owners discovered records which allegedly showed that the property in question had been granted by Spanish authorities to a private party prior to 1803 and had therefore not passed to the United States as part of the Louisiana Purchase. In 1994, the former owners filed a complaint asking the District Court to set aside the
212

settlement and award them over $10 million in dam-
ages. The District Court dismissed the complaint for
lack of jurisdiction. However, the United States Court
of Appeals for the Fifth Circuit reversed and remanded
with instructions to enter a judgment quieting title in
favor of the former owners, as the court ruled that (1)
the suit satisfied the elements of an "independent
action" for obtaining relief from a judgment, under
Rule 60(b) of the Federal Rules of Civil Procedure, (2)
the Quiet Title Act (QTA) (28 USCS § 2409a) also
conferred jurisdiction over the suit, and its 12-year
statute of limitations was subject to equitable tolling in
this case, and (3) the government had no legitimate
claim to the property (114 F3d 484).

On certiorari, the United States Supreme Court
reversed. In an opinion by REHNQUIST, Ch. J., expressing the unanimous view of the court, it was held that
(1) the former owners' claim that the government had
failed to thoroughly research its records and make full
disclosure concerning the property did not allege the
grave miscarriage of justice required for an independent action under Rule 60(b), and (2) equitable tolling
was not available under the QTA.

STEVENS, J., joined by SOUTER, J., concurred, expressing the view that the case at hand did not present the
question whether doctrines such as fraudulent conceal-
ment or equitable estoppel might apply under the
QTA.

COUNSEL

Paul R. Q. Wolfson argued the cause for petitioner.
Ernest G. Taylor, Jr. argued the cause for respondents.

UNITED STATES, Petitioner

v

BESTFOODS et al.

524 US —, 141 L Ed 2d 43, 118 S Ct 1876

[No. 97-454]

Argued March 24, 1998.

Decided June 8, 1998.

Decision: Parent corporation held (1) not subject to derivative liability for environmental cleanup costs as to subsidiary's operations unless corporate veil is pierced, but (2) subject to direct liability for such costs as to parent's own operations.

SUMMARY

Under § 107(a)(2) of the Comprehensive Environmental Response, Compensation, and Liability Act of 1980 (CERCLA), 42 USCS § 9607(a)(2), the United States may bring suit to recover the costs of cleaning up hazardous waste at a facility against a party that at the time of disposal of the waste owned or operated the facility. The United States brought under § 107(a)(2) a suit against, among others, a parent corporation to recover the costs of cleaning up industrial waste generated at its subsidiary's chemical plant. The United States District Court for the Western District of Michigan concluded—at least in part on the basis of findings that the parent had selected the subsidiary's board of directors and had populated the subsidiary's executive ranks with officials of the parent, and that a particular official of the parent had played a significant role in shaping the subsidiary's environmental compliance policy—that the parent was directly liable under § 107(a)(2) as an operator of the facility (777 F Supp 549). After a panel of the United States Court of Appeals for the Sixth Circuit reversed in part the District Court judgment (59 F3d 584), the Court of Appeals granted rehearing en banc and vacated the panel decision (67 F3d 586). The Court of Appeals, again reversing in part the District Court judgment, expressed the view that although a parent conceivably might independently operate a facility in the stead of its subsidiary or as a sort of joint venturer operate the facility alongside the subsidiary, (1) liability based on the parent's control of the subsidiary would occur only when the requirements necessary to pierce the corporate veil under state law were met, and (2) such requirements were not met in this case (113 F 3d 572).

On certiorari, the United States Supreme Court vacated the judgment of the Court of Appeals and remanded the case with instructions to return it to the District Court for further proceedings. In an opinion by SOUTER, J., expressing the unanimous view of the court, it was held that under § 107(a)(2), (1) a parent corporation that actively participated in, and exercised control over, the operations of a subsidiary may not, without more, be held derivatively liable as an operator of a polluting facility owned or operated by the subsidiary, unless the corporate veil may be pierced, as nothing in CERCLA, 42 USCS §§ 9601 et seq., purports to reject the general principles of corporate law that (a) a parent corporation is not liable for the acts of its subsidiaries, and (b) the corporate veil may be pierced when the corporate form would otherwise be misused to accomplish certain wrongful purposes; and (2) a parent that actively participated in, and exercised control over, the operations of the facility itself may be held directly liable in its own right as operator of the facility, as CERCLA does not bar a parent from direct liability for its own actions in operating a facility owned by its subsidiary.

COUNSEL

Lois J. Schiffer argued the cause for petitioner.

Kenneth S. Geller argued the cause for respondents.

BONNIE L. GEISSAL, Beneficiary and Representative
of the Estate of James W. Geissal, Deceased, Petitioner

v

MOORE MEDICAL CORPORATION et al.

524 US —, 141 L Ed 2d 64, 118 S Ct 1869

[No. 97-689]

Argued April 29, 1998.
Decided June 8, 1998.

Decision: 29 USCS § 1162(2)(D)(i) held not to allow
employer to deny continuation coverage, under
employer's group health plan, to qualified beneficiary who was covered under another group health
plan at time that beneficiary made election to
continue coverage.

SUMMARY

Under some provisions (29 USCS §§ 1161 et seq.) of
the Employee Retirement Income Security Act of 1974
as amended by the Consolidated Omnibus Budget
Reconciliation Act of 1985 (COBRA), a qualified beneficiary of an employer's group health plan is authorized to obtain continued coverage under the plan
when the beneficiary might otherwise lose that benefit
for certain reasons, such as the termination of employment. At the time pertinent to the case at hand, 29
USCS § 1162(2)(D)(i) (later amended) provided that
an employer might cancel COBRA continuation coverage as of the date on which the qualified beneficiary
first became, "after the date of the election . . .
covered under any other group health plan (as an

217

employee or otherwise)'' that did not contain any exclusion or limitation with respect to any pre-existing condition of the beneficiary. In 1993, a medical corporation fired an individual who had cancer and who had been covered, while employed, under both (1) the corporation's group health plan, and (2) a group health plan provided by his wife's employer. According to the individual, the corporation told him that he had a right to elect COBRA continuation coverage under the corporation's plan. The individual so elected and made the necessary premium payments until, in 1994, the corporation informed the individual that he was not actually entitled to COBRA benefits, as on the date of his COBRA election he had already been covered by another group health plan. The individual then brought suit in the United States District Court for the Eastern District of Missouri against defendants including the corporation. The individual's first two counts claimed that the defendants (1) had violated COBRA by renouncing an obligation to provide continuing coverage, and (2) were estopped to deny him COBRA continuation coverage. The parties agreed to have a magistrate judge conduct all proceedings. The individual (1) moved for partial summary judgment on the first two counts, and (2) included an argument that the defendants' reliance upon § 1162(2)(D)(i) to deny him continuation coverage was misplaced, as he had first been covered under his wife's plan before he had elected continuation coverage. While the motion was pending, the individual died and his wife, who was also the personal representative of his estate, replaced him as plaintiff. The magistrate judge granted partial summary judgment in favor of the defendants on the two counts, as the magistrate judge expressed the view that under § 1162(2)(D)(i), an employee with coverage under another group health plan as of the date on which the employee elected COBRA continuation coverage was ineligible for such coverage (927 F Supp 352, 1996 US Dist LEXIS 7145). On appeal, the United States Court of Appeals for the Eighth Circuit, in affirming, expressed the view that (1) under § 1162(2)(D)(i), it was within the defendants' rights to cancel the individual's COBRA benefits unless there was a "significant gap" between the coverage afforded under the corporation's plan and that afforded under his wife's plan; and (2) the wife had failed to carry her burden of showing that such a significant gap existed (114 F3d 1458, 1997 US App LEXIS 13589).

On certiorari, the United States Supreme Court vacated the Court of Appeals' judgment and remanded the case for further proceedings. In an opinion by SOUTER, J., expressing the unanimous view of the court, it was held that § 1162(2)(D)(i) did not allow an employer to deny COBRA continuation coverage to a qualified beneficiary who was covered under another group health plan at the time that the beneficiary made a COBRA election, as (1) under the plain meaning of § 1162(2)(D)(i) as it read at the time pertinent to the case at hand, the medical corporation could not cut off the individual's COBRA continuation coverage, where the individual (a) was covered under his wife's plan before he made his COBRA election, and (b) so did not first become covered under his wife's plan after the date of election; and (2) there was no justification for disparaging the clarity of § 1162(2)(D)(i).

COUNSEL

Sheldon Weinhaus argued the cause for petitioner.

James A. Feldman argued the cause for the United States, as amicus curiae, by special leave of court.

Bradley J. Washington argued the cause for respondents.

―――――――――

FRANK X. HOPKINS, Warden, Petitioner

v

RANDOLPH K. REEVES

524 US —, 141 L Ed 2d 76, 118 S Ct 1895

[No. 96-1693]

Argued February 23, 1998.

Decided June 8, 1998.

Decision: In capital felony murder case, Nebraska court held not to have erred in failing to give jury instructions as to second-degree murder and manslaughter, where such offenses were not lesser included offenses of felony murder under state law.

SUMMARY

A person accused of committing two murders in the perpetration of a rape was prosecuted in a Nebraska trial court for felony murder, a form of first-degree murder under Nebraska law. At trial, the accused requested that the jury be instructed on murder in the second degree and manslaughter. The trial court refused, on the ground that the Supreme Court of Nebraska had consistently held that second-degree murder and manslaughter were not lesser included offenses of felony murder. The accused was convicted on two felony murder counts, and a three-judge sentencing panel sentenced him to death on both convictions. After the Nebraska Supreme Court affirmed the convictions and sentences (216 Neb 206, 344 NW2d 433, cert den 469 US 1028, 83 L Ed 2d 372, 105 S Ct 447) and the accused unsuccessfully pursued state

221

collateral relief (234 Neb 711, 453 NW2d 359), the United States Supreme Court vacated the Nebraska Supreme Court's judgment and remanded the case for further consideration with respect to an issue unrelated to the jury instructions (498 US 964, 112 L Ed 2d 409, 111 S Ct 425). On remand, the Nebraska Supreme Court reaffirmed the accused's sentences (239 Neb 419, 476 NW2d 829, cert den 506 US 837, 121 L Ed 2d 71, 113 S Ct 114). The accused, in filing a petition for a federal writ of habeas corpus in the United States District Court for the District of Nebraska, raised a claim that the trial court's failure to give his requested instructions violated the Federal Constitution. The District Court ultimately granted the petition on other grounds (928 F Supp 941, 1996 US Dist LEXIS 6857), but the United States Court of Appeals for the Eighth Circuit, in affirming in part and reversing in part, (1) upheld the accused's claim as to the jury instructions, (2) granted the accused a conditional writ of habeas corpus, and (3) gave the state the option of retrying the accused or agreeing to modify his sentence to life imprisonment (102 F3d 977, 1996 US App LEXIS 33412, reh, en banc, den 1997 US App LEXIS 3761).

On certiorari, the United States Supreme Court reversed. In an opinion by THOMAS, J., joined by REHNQUIST, Ch. J., and O'CONNOR, SCALIA, KENNEDY, SOUTER, GINSBURG, and BREYER, JJ., it was held that (1) in capital cases, a state trial court is not required, under the Constitution, to instruct the jury on offenses that are not lesser included offenses of the charged crime under state law; and (2) the Nebraska trial court did not commit federal constitutional error in failing to give the requested jury instructions as to second-degree murder and manslaughter.

STEVENS, J., joined by BREYER, J., dissenting, expressed the view that the accused was entitled to the

222

requested instruction as to second-degree murder, because (1) the rationale for Nebraska's general rule that second-degree murder was not a lesser included offense of felony murder did not apply in the case at hand, and (2) it appeared that Nebraska law might have been in flux on the question whether second-degree murder was a lesser included offense of felony murder.

COUNSEL

Donald B. Stenberg argued the cause for petitioner.

Roy W. McLeese, III argued the cause for the United States, as amicus curiae, by special leave of court.

Paula Hutchinson argued the cause for respondent.

CASS COUNTY, MINNESOTA, et al., Petitioners

v

LEECH LAKE BAND OF CHIPPEWA INDIANS

524 US —, 141 L Ed 2d 90, 118 S Ct 1904

[No. 97-174]

Argued February 24, 1998.
Decided June 9, 1998.

Decision: Indian tribe's reservation lands that had been sold by Federal Government to non-Indians and subsequently repurchased by tribe held subject to county's ad valorem property taxes.

SUMMARY

The Leech Lake Reservation in northern Minnesota was set aside for the Leech Lake Band of Chippewa Indians by federal treaty in 1855. Under the Nelson Act of 1889 (25 Stat 642), reservation lands were alienated from the Band's ownership by (1) allotment of parcels to individual Indians, (2) sale of "pine lands" at public auction to non-Indians, and (3) sale of agricultural lands to non-Indian settlers as homesteads. By 1977, the Band and individual Band members owned less than 5 percent of the reservation's land. Subsequently, the Band began purchasing back parcels of reservation land that had been allotted to individual Indians or sold to non-Indians. In 1993, a Minnesota county began assessing ad valorem property taxes on 21 parcels that had been reacquired by the Band. Under protest, the Band paid more than $64,000 in taxes, interest, and penalties. In 1995, the Band, filing suit in the United States District Court for the District of Minnesota, sought a declaratory judgment that the county could not tax the 21 parcels. Also in 1995, the Band successfully applied, pursuant to § 465 of the Indian Reorganization Act (25 USCS § 465), to restore 11 of the parcels to federal trust status. The District Court, in granting summary judgment in the county's favor, concluded that all of the 21 parcels were taxable (908 F Supp 689, 1995 US Dist LEXIS 19466). The United States Court of Appeals for the Eighth Circuit, in affirming in part and reversing in part, expressed the view that of the 21 parcels, (1) 13 parcels, which had been allotted to individual Indians under the Nelson Act, could be taxed so long as the District Court confirmed, on remand, that those parcels had been patented after passage of a 1906 federal statutory proviso that manifested Congress' "unmistakably clear" intent to subject such lands to state or local taxation, but (2) 8 parcels, which had been sold as pine lands or homestead lands under the Nelson Act, could not be taxed (108 F3d 820, 1997 US App LEXIS 3879). The United States Supreme Court granted certiorari to review the Court of Appeals' judgment solely with respect to the 8 parcels.

On certiorari, the Supreme Court reversed the Court of Appeals' judgment in pertinent part. In an opinion by THOMAS, J., expressing the unanimous view of the court, it was held that (1) with respect to an Indian tribe's reservation land that has been made alienable by Congress and sold to non-Indians by the Federal Government, the subsequent repurchase of the land by the tribe does not cause the land to reassume the status of exemption from state taxation; and (2) the 8 parcels that had been sold as pine lands or homestead lands were subject to the county's ad valorem property taxes unless and until such parcels were restored to federal trust protection under § 465, because (a) Congress, by

225

providing for the public sale of such lands to non-Indians under the Nelson Act, removed such lands from federal protection and made the lands fully alienable and thus taxable, and (b) the tribe's reacquisition of the lands in fee did not render the lands nontaxable once again.

COUNSEL

Earl Edwin Maus argued the cause for petitioners.

James M. Schoessler argued the cause for respondent.

Barbara B. McDowell argued the cause for the United States, as amicus curiae, by special leave of court.

PHILOMENA DOOLEY, Personal Representative of
the Estate of Cecelio Chuapoco, et al., Petitioners

v

KOREAN AIR LINES CO., LTD.

524 US —, 141 L Ed 2d 102, 118 S Ct 1890

[No. 97-704]

Argued April 27, 1998.
Decided June 8, 1998.

Decision: Survival action under general maritime law
for decedent's pain and suffering, with respect to
death on high seas, held precluded by Death on
the High Seas Act (46 USCS Appx §§ 761 et seq.).

SUMMARY

The Death on the High Seas Act (DOHSA) (46 USCS
Appx §§ 761 et seq.) provides that (1) where a wrongful
death has occurred on the high seas, the personal
representative of the decedent may maintain a suit for
damages in Federal District Court for the exclusive
benefit of the decedent's wife, husband, parent, child
or dependent relative (46 USCS Appx § 761); and (2)
the recovery in such suit is to be a fair and just
compensation for the pecuniary loss sustained by the
persons for whose benefit the action is brought (46
USCS Appx § 762). In 1983, an air carrier's passenger
flight en route from Anchorage, Alaska, to Seoul, South
Korea, strayed into air space of the then Soviet Union
and was shot down over the Sea of Japan. All passengers
on board the flight were killed. Personal representatives of three of the passengers brought actions in the
United States District Court for the District of Colum-

bia against the carrier. The District Court jury, after a trial, found that the carrier had committed willful misconduct and awarded punitive damages. However, the United States Court of Appeals for the District of Columbia Circuit vacated the punitive damages award on the ground that the Warsaw Convention did not permit the recovery of punitive damages. The United States Supreme Court denied certiorari. Following remand to the District Court, while the representatives' cases were awaiting trial, the Supreme Court held in Zicherman v Korean Air Lines Co. (1996) 516 US 217, 133 L Ed 2d 596, 116 S Ct 629, that DOHSA supplied the substantive law where an airplane crash occurred on the high seas. Thereafter, the carrier moved to dismiss the representatives' claims for nonpecuniary damages, and the District Court granted the motion (935 F Supp 10, 1996 US Dist LEXIS 7957). On appeal, the Court of Appeals, affirming, expressed the view that assuming that there was a survival cause of action under general maritime law which allowed a decedent's estate to recover for injuries sustained by the decedent—including predeath pain and suffering—such an action was unavailable when the death was on the high seas (117 F3d 1477, 1997 US App LEXIS 17372).

On certiorari, the Supreme Court affirmed. In an opinion by THOMAS, J., expressing the unanimous view of the court, it was held that the decedent's relatives in the case at hand could not recover damages for the decedent's predeath pain and suffering through a survival action under general maritime law, because (1) DOHSA expressed Congress' judgment that survival actions for decedents' predeath pain and suffering should not be available in cases of deaths that occur on the high seas; (2) accordingly, Congress has precluded the judiciary from enlarging either the class of beneficiaries or the recoverable damages under DOHSA; and (3) in 1920, Congress chose to adopt a more limited survival provision in DOHSA than it did in the same year in the Jones Act (46 USCS Appx § 688), into which Congress incorporated a survival action.

COUNSEL

Juanita Madole argued the cause for petitioners.

Andrew J. Harakas argued the cause for respondent.

Jeffrey P. Minear argued the cause for the United States, as amicus curiae, by special leave of court.

FRANK J. MUSCARELLO, Petitioner

v

UNITED STATES (No. 96-1654)

———

DONALD E. CLEVELAND and ENRIQUE GRAY-
SANTANA, Petitioners

v

UNITED STATES (No. 96-8837)

524 US —, 141 L Ed 2d 111, 118 S Ct 1911

[Nos. 96-1654 and 96-8837]

Argued March 23, 1998.
Decided June 8, 1998.

Decision: Phrase "carries a firearm" in 18 USCS
§ 924(c)(1), which imposes mandatory sentence
for person carrying firearm during drug trafficking crime, held to apply to person who knowingly
possesses and conveys firearm in vehicle, including
in locked glove compartment or trunk of car,
which person accompanies.

SUMMARY

These two consolidated cases presented a question
concerning the definition of the term "carries a firearm" in 18 USCS § 924(c)(1), which imposes a 5-year
mandatory prison term on a person who uses or carries
a firearm during and in relation to any drug trafficking
crime, which sentence is in addition to the punishment
provided for the predicate offense. In the first case (No.
96-1654), in which a defendant who was convicted

concerning marijuana trafficking had carried the marijuana to the place of sale in his truck, in which the
police had found a handgun locked in the glove
compartment, the United States Court of Appeals for
the Fifth Circuit determined that the defendant had
"carried" the gun (106 F3d 636). In the second case
(No. 96-8837), the United States Court of Appeals for
the First Circuit determined that two defendants who
were convicted concerning cocaine trafficking had
"carried" guns, where the two defendants had placed
several guns in a bag, put the bag in the trunk of a car,
and traveled in the car to a proposed drug-sale point
with the intent to steal drugs from the seller (106 F3d
1056).

On certiorari, the United States Supreme Court
affirmed the judgments of the Courts of Appeals. In an
opinion by BREYER, J., joined by STEVENS, O'CONNOR,
KENNEDY, and THOMAS, JJ., it was held that the phrase
"carries a firearm" in § 924(c)(1) applies to a person
who knowingly possesses and conveys a firearm in a
vehicle, including in the locked glove compartment or
trunk of car, which the person accompanies, as (1)
under the primary meaning of "carry," one can, as a
matter of ordinary English, "carry firearms" in a
wagon, car, truck, or other vehicle that one accompanies, (2) there is no linguistic reason to think that
Congress intended to limit "carries" in the statute to its
secondary meaning, which suggests support rather
than movement or transportation, and (3) neither the
statute's basic purpose to combat the dangerous combination of drugs and guns nor its legislative history
supports circumscribing "carry" by applying an "on
the person" limitation.

GINSBURG, J., joined by REHNQUIST, Ch. J., and SCA-
LIA, and SOUTER, JJ., dissenting, expressed the view that
for purposes of § 924(a)(1), "carries a firearm" indi-

cates not merely keeping arms on one's premises or in one's vehicle, but bearing them in such a manner as to be ready for use as a weapon.

COUNSEL

Robert H. Klonoff argued the cause for petitioner in No. 96-1654.

Norman S. Zalkind argued the cause for petitioners in No. 96-8837.

James A. Feldman argued the cause for respondent in both cases.

NEW MEXICO, ex rel. MANUEL ORTIZ, Petitioner

v

TIMOTHY REED

524 US —, 141 L Ed 2d 131, 118 S Ct 1860

[No. 97-1217]

Decided June 8, 1998.

Decision: Supreme Court of New Mexico held to have gone beyond scope of permissible inquiry in upholding grant of state habeas corpus relief to parolee whom state of Ohio sought to extradite from New Mexico as alleged fugitive from justice.

SUMMARY

The Federal Constitution's extradition clause (Art IV, § 2, cl 2) is implemented by the Extradition Act (18 USCS § 3182) and provides for the extradition from one state—often referred to as the asylum state—of a fugitive from justice when a demand for the fugitive's extradition is made by another state. A parolee from the Ohio correctional system fled to New Mexico after he was told by Ohio prison officials that they planned to revoke his parole status. Upon a demand by Ohio, the governor of New Mexico issued a warrant directing the parolee's extradition, but the parolee sought habeas corpus relief in the District Court of Taos County, New Mexico, which directed his release from custody. On appeal, the Supreme Court of New Mexico, in affirming the grant of habeas corpus relief, expressed the view that (1) the parolee was a refugee from injustice, rather than a fugitive from justice, as he had fled Ohio because of fear that (a) his parole would be revoked

233

without due process, and (b) he would thereafter be returned to prison, where he would face a threat of bodily injury; and (2) a provision in the New Mexico constitution that guaranteed the right of seeking and obtaining safety prevailed over the state's duty under the extradition clause (124 NM 129, 947 P2d 86, 1997 NM LEXIS 409).

The United States Supreme Court granted a motion by an association of extradition officials for leave to file an amicus curiae brief, granted a petition for certiorari by the state of New Mexico, reversed the judgment of the Supreme Court of New Mexico, and remanded the case for further proceedings. In a per curiam opinion expressing the unanimous view of the court, it was held that the Supreme Court of New Mexico had (1) gone beyond the scope of permissible inquiry in an extradition case, and (2) allowed the litigation of issues not open in the asylum state.

———————

THOMAS R. PHILLIPS, et al., Petitioners

v

WASHINGTON LEGAL FOUNDATION et al.

524 US —, 141 L Ed 2d 174, 118 S Ct 1925

[No. 96-1578]

Argued January 13, 1998.
Decided June 15, 1998.

Decision: Interest earned on client funds held by
lawyers in trust accounts pursuant to Texas IOLTA
program held to be client's private property for
purposes of takings clause of Federal Constitution's Fifth Amendment.

SUMMARY

Under Texas' Interest on Lawyers Trust Account
(IOLTA) program, an attorney who receives client
funds must place such funds in a separate, interest-
bearing, federally authorized Negotiable Order of
Withdrawal (NOW) account upon determining that
(1) the funds cannot not reasonably be expected to
earn interest for the client, or (2) the interest which
might be earned is not likely to be sufficient to offset
various costs and charges. IOLTA interest income is
paid to the Texas Equal Access to Justice Foundation
(TEAJF)—a nonprofit corporation established by the
Supreme Court of Texas—which finances legal services
for low-income persons. In 1994, a suit was filed in the
United States District Court for the Western District of
Texas against TEAJF, the chairman of TEAJF, and the
justices of the Texas Supreme Court by (1) a public-
interest law and policy center with members in Texas

235

who were opposed to the Texas IOLTA program, (2) an Texas attorney who maintained an IOLTA account, and (3) a Texas citizen whose retainer deposited with his attorney was being held in an IOLTA account. Among the plaintiffs' allegations was that the Texas IOLTA program violated the plaintiffs' rights under the takings clause of the Federal Constitution's Fifth Amendment by taking their property without just compensation. The District Court, among other matters, granted summary judgment to the defendants on the ground that the plaintiffs had no property interest in the interest proceeds generated by the funds held in IOLTA accounts (873 F Supp 1, 1995 US Dist LEXIS 960). The United States Court of Appeals for the Fifth Circuit, although affirming the District Court's judgment in part on other grounds, (1) concluded that attorneys' clients had a cognizable property interest in the interest proceeds, (2) vacated the award of summary judgment for the defendants and denial of summary judgment for the plaintiffs, and (3) remanded the case for further consideration (94 F3d 996, 1996 US App LEXIS 24158, reh en banc den 106 F3d 640, 1997 US App LEXIS 2813).

On certiorari, the United States Supreme Court affirmed. In an opinion by REHNQUIST, Ch. J., joined by O'CONNOR, SCALIA, KENNEDY, and THOMAS, JJ., it was held that for purposes of the takings clause, (1) interest earned on client funds held in IOLTA accounts was private property, because (a) the owner's possession, control, and disposition were valuable property rights that inhered in such interest income, (b) the value of such interest income was created by the owners' funds and was not "government-created value," and (c) the state's confiscation of such interest income did not amount to a fee for services performed; and (2) such interest income was the property of the client for whom the principal was being held, as (a) it was agreed that under Texas law, the principal was the client's property, (b) no background principles of Texas property law would lead to the conclusion that the owner of a fund that was temporarily deposited in an attorney trust account could be deprived of the interest that the fund generated, and (c) regardless of whether the owner of the principal had a constitutionally cognizable interest in the anticipated generation of interest income by the owner's funds, any interest income that did accrue attached as a property right incident to the ownership of the underlying principal.

SOUTER, J., joined by STEVENS, GINSBURG, and BREYER, JJ., dissenting, expressed the view that the Court of Appeals' judgment ought to have been vacated and the case ought to have been remanded for a determination of whether, for purposes of the takings clause, (1) the government had taken the property at issue, and (2) just compensation for the taking had been denied.

BREYER, J., joined by STEVENS, SOUTER, and GINSBURG, JJ., dissenting, expressed the view that interest earned on client funds held in IOLTA accounts was not the client's private property for purposes of the takings clause, as no such interest could have been earned absent the IOLTA program.

COUNSEL

Darrell E. Jordan argued the cause for petitioners.

Edwin S. Kneedler argued the cause for the United States, as amicus curiae, by special leave of court.

Richard A. Samp argued the cause for respondents.

SILLASSE BRYAN, Petitioner

v

UNITED STATES

524 US —, 141 L Ed 2d 197, 118 S Ct 1939

[No. 96-8422]

Argued March 31, 1998.
Decided June 15, 1998.

Decision: Term "willfully" in 18 USCS § 924(a)
(1)(D)—imposing penalty for violation of 18
USCS § 922(a)(1)(A), which forbids firearms dealing without federal license—requires proof only
that accused knew conduct was unlawful, not that
accused also knew of licensing requirement.

SUMMARY

Under 18 USCS § 924(a)(1)(D), a fine, imprisonment not more than 5 years, or both, may be imposed
against anyone who "willfully" violates certain provisions of the Firearms Owners' Protection Act, 18 USCS
§§ 921 et seq., including 18 USCS § 922(a)(1)(A),
which forbids dealing in firearms without a federal
license. At an accused's trial in the United States
District Court for the Eastern District of New York for
violating 18 USCS § 922(a)(1)(A), there was adequate
evidence that the accused was dealing in firearms and
knew that his conduct was unlawful, but there was no
evidence that he was aware of the federal licensing
requirement. After the trial judge instructed the jury
that "willfully" in § 924(a)(1)(D) required only the
intent to do something unlawful, the accused was
convicted. The United States Court of Appeals for the
238

Second Circuit, expressing the view that the jury instructions were proper, affirmed the District Court judgment (122 F3d 90).

On certiorari, the United States Supreme Court affirmed the judgment of the Court of Appeals. In an opinion by SC Stevens, J., joined by O'CONNOR, KENNEDY, SOUTER, THOMAS, and BREYER, JJ., it was held that (1) the term "willfully" in § 924(a)(1)(A) requires proof only that the accused knew that the accused's conduct was unlawful, not that the accused also knew of the federal licensing requirement, because (a) the willfulness requirement of § 924(a)(1)(D) does not carve out an exception to the traditional rule that ignorance of the law is no excuse, as generally, when used in a criminal context, a willful act is one undertaken with a bad purpose, and (b) the accused's additional arguments concerning congressional intent were not persuasive; and (2) a misstatement of law in one sentence of the jury instructions—indicating that proof of the accused's knowledge that he was breaking the law was not required—did not provide a basis for reversal.

SOUTER, J., concurring, expressed the view that if the accused had raised and preserved a specific objection to the erroneous statement in the jury instructions, then the accused's conviction ought to have been vacated.

SCALIA, J., joined by REHNQUIST, Ch. J., and GINS-BURG, JJ., dissenting, expressed the view that § 924(a)(1)(D)'s ambiguity concerning the precise contours of the awareness of the law required for conviction should be resolved in favor of lenity.

COUNSEL

Roger B. Adler argued the cause for petitioner.
Kent L. Jones argued the cause for respondent.

————

PENNSYLVANIA DEPARTMENT OF CORRECTIONS,
et al., Petitioners

v

RONALD R. YESKEY

524 US —, 141 L Ed 2d 215, 118 S Ct 1952

[No. 97-634]

Argued April 28, 1998.
Decided June 15, 1998.

Decision: Title II of Americans with Disabilities Act (42
USCS §§ 12131 et seq.) held applicable to inmates
in state prisons.

SUMMARY

An inmate in a Pennsylvania correctional facility,
having been denied admission to a motivational boot
camp for first-time offenders because of his history of
hypertension, filed an action against state officials in
Federal District Court and alleged therein that his
exclusion from the boot camp violated Title II of the
Americans with Disabilities Act (ADA) (42 USCS §§
12131 et seq.), which prohibits public entities from
discriminating against qualified individuals with disabilities. The United States District Court for the
Middle District of Pennsylvania, holding that the ADA
was inapplicable to state prisons, dismissed the inmate's
complaint. The United States Court of Appeals for the
Third Circuit, holding that the ADA was applicable to
state and locally operated correctional facilities reversed the District Court's judgment and remanded for
further proceedings (118 F3d 168, 1997 US App LEXIS
17364).

On certiorari, the United States Supreme Court affirmed. In an opinion by SCALIA, J., expressing the unanimous view of the court, it was held that the ADA was applicable to state prisons, because (1) the plain language of the ADA unambigously extended to state prison inmates; and thus (2) even assuming that the "plain statement" rule, which required an unmistakably clear expression of legislative intent before a statute would be interpreted as destroying a state's substantial sovereign powers, was applicable in this context, the ADA met that requirement.

COUNSEL

Paul A. Tufano argued the cause for petitioners.

Donald Specter argued the cause for respondent.

Irving L. Gornstein argued the cause for the United States, as amicus curiae, by special leave of court.

AMERICAN TELEPHONE AND TELEGRAPH COMPANY, Petitioner

v

CENTRAL OFFICE TELEPHONE, INC.

524 US —, 141 L Ed 2d 222, 118 S Ct 1956

[No. 97-679]

Argued March 23, 1998.
Decided June 15, 1998.

Decision: In dispute between providers of long-distance communications services, state-law claims for breach of contract and tortious interference held pre-empted by filed rate doctrine of § 203 of Communications Act of 1934 (47 USCS § 203).

SUMMARY

Common carriers, as defined under the Communications Act of 1934 (47 USCS §§ 151 et seq.), are required by § 203(a) of the Act (47 USCS § 203(a)) to file with the Federal Communications Commission (FCC) tariffs containing (1) all charges for interstate services, and (2) all classifications, practices, and regulations affecting such charges. Section 203(c) of the Act (47 USCS § 203(c)) makes it unlawful for a carrier to extend to any person any privileges or facilities, or to employ or enforce any classifications, regulations, or practices affecting such charges, except as specified in the tariff. In 1989, a provider of long-distance communications services contracted to sell a long-distance service to a reseller of volume-discounted communications services. The parties agreed in writing that the service was to be governed by the rates, terms, and
243

conditions in the long-distance provider's appropriate tariff. The reseller experienced problems with the service and ultimately withdrew from the contract before the expiration date. In 1991, the reseller filed suit in the United States District Court for the District of Oregon against the long-distance provider on a variety of claims, including state-law claims for breach of contract and tortious interference with contractual relations. The reseller alleged that (1) the reseller's contracts with the long-distance provider were not limited by the tariff in question, but also included various understandings that the reseller's president had derived from the long-distance provider's representatives and sales brochures; and (2) the long-distance provider had (a) promised the reseller various service, provisioning, and billing options in addition to those set forth in the tariff, and (b) provided such options without charge to other customers. The long-distance provider argued that the reseller's state-law contract and tort claims were pre-empted by the filed tariff requirements of § 203. A District Court magistrate judge, rejecting this argument, instructed the jury to consider not only the parties' written subscription agreements, but also any statements made or documents furnished before the parties signed the agreements. The jury found for the reseller on the state-law claims and awarded the reseller $13 million in lost profits. The magistrate judge reduced the judgment to $1.154 million. The United States Court of Appeals for the Ninth Circuit affirmed in pertinent part (108 F3d 981, 1997 US App LEXIS 3395).

On certiorari, the United States Supreme Court reversed. In an opinion by SCALIA, J., joined by REHNQUIST, Ch. J., and KENNEDY, SOUTER, THOMAS, GINSBURG, and BREYER, JJ., it was held that (1) the reseller's state-law claim for breach of contract was pre-empted

244

by the filed rate doctrine of § 203, under which doctrine a carrier's filed tariff rate is the only lawful charge, because all of the additional services and guarantees to which the reseller claimed to be entitled pertained to subjects that were specifically addressed by the tariff; and (2) the claim for tortious interference with contractual relations was also pre-empted as wholly derivative of the breach of contract claim.

REHNQUIST, Ch. J., concurring, (1) agreed that the tortious interference claim was wholly derivative of the contract claim and was thus barred by the filed rate doctrine; and (2) expressed the view that this finding was necessary to the conclusion that the reseller's state-law tort claim could not proceed, as the filed rate doctrine pre-empted only those state-law suits that sought to alter the terms and conditions provided for in the tariff.

STEVENS, Ch. J., dissenting, expressed the view that (1) the tort claim was not pre-empted by the filed rate doctrine, as the jury's verdict on the tort claim was supported by evidence that went well beyond, and differed in nature from, the contract claim; and (2) the Supreme Court thus ought to have remanded the case for a new trial rather than ordering judgment outright for the long-distance provider.

O'CONNOR, Ch. J., did not participate.

COUNSEL

David W. Carpenter argued the cause for petitioner. Bruce M. Hall argued the cause for respondent.

ARNOLD F. HOHN, Petitioner

v

UNITED STATES

524 US —, 141 L Ed 2d 242, 118 S Ct 1969

[No. 96-8986]

Argued March 3, 1998.

Decided June 15, 1998.

Decision: Supreme Court held to have jurisdiction to review Federal Court of Appeals' denial of certificate of appealability concerning Federal District Court's denial of accused's motion under 28 USCS § 2255 to vacate federal conviction.

SUMMARY

Under 28 USCS § 1254(1), the United States Supreme Court has jurisdiction to review, on certiorari, "[c]ases in" the Federal Courts of Appeals. In House v Mayo (1945) 324 US 42, 89 L Ed 739, 65 S Ct 517—which involved a Federal District Court's refusal, after denying habeas corpus relief to a state prisoner, to issue a certificate of probable cause for an appeal to a Court of Appeals—the Supreme Court held that it lacked statutory certiorari jurisdiction to review refusals to issue certificates of probable cause, because under a predecessor of § 1254(1), such cases were never "in" the Courts of Appeals. A similar jurisdictional issue later arose with respect to an accused who had been convicted of the use or carrying of a firearm in violation of 18 USCS § 924(c)(1). After the accused was unsuccessful on direct review, the Supreme Court held in Bailey v United States (1995) 516 US 137, 133 L Ed

2d 472, 116 S Ct 501, that the term "use" in § 924(c)(1) required active employment of a firearm. The accused then filed a motion under 28 USCS § 2255 to vacate his § 924(c)(1) conviction in light of the Bailey decision. While this motion was pending before the United States District Court for the District of Nebraska, the Antiterrorism and Effective Death Penalty Act of 1996 (AEDPA) amended 28 USCS § 2253—which had referred to certificates of probable cause—so as instead to include provisions in 28 USCS § 2253(c) that (1) unless a "circuit justice or judge" issued a certificate of appealability, an appeal could not be taken to a Court of Appeals from a final order in (a) a habeas corpus proceeding involving a state prisoner, or (b) a § 2255 proceeding, and (2) a certificate of appealability could issue only if an applicant made a substantial showing of the denial of a constitutional right. The District Court denied the accused § 2255 relief, as the court expressed the view that he had waived his claim by failing, on direct review, to challenge a jury instruction which had defined use for purposes of § 924(c)(1). A panel of the United States Court of Appeals for the Eighth Circuit then denied the accused a certificate of appealability, as the panel expressed the view that his § 2255 claim was statutory, not constitutional, in nature (99 F3d 892, 1996 US App LEXIS 28504). After the accused filed a petition for certiorari, a responsive brief for the United States (1) conceded, in agreement with the accused on this point, that his § 2255 claim was constitutional in nature; and (2) asked the Supreme Court to vacate the judgment below and to remand the case so that the Court of Appeals could reconsider in light of this concession.

On certiorari, the Supreme Court, in light of the position asserted in the responsive brief for the United States, vacated the Court of Appeals' decision and remanded the case for further consideration. In an opinion by KENNEDY, J., joined by STEVENS, SOUTER, GINSBURG, and BREYER, JJ., it was held that while the Supreme Court could not vacate and remand unless the court first had jurisdiction over the case, the court had jurisdiction over the case under § 1254(1), as (1) an application for a § 2253(c) certificate of appealability—such as the application involving the accused's § 2255 claim at issue—met the § 1254(1) description which confined the Supreme Court's certiorari jurisdiction under § 1254(1) to cases in the Courts of Appeals; and (2) the Supreme Court would overrule the portion of House v Mayo in which the court held that it lacked statutory certiorari jurisdiction to review refusals to issue certificates of probable cause, for (a) this portion was erroneous and should not be followed, and (b) stare decisis concerns did not require the Supreme Court to adhere to this portion of House v Mayo.

Souter, J., concurring, expressed the view that while he might have decided the case at hand on another ground involving the availability of a common-law writ of certiorari, he was persuaded to join the Supreme Court's opinion by (1) the weakness of the House v Mayo precedent concerning the statutory writ of certiorari, and (2) the advantage of having a clear majority for a rule governing the Supreme Court's jurisdiction.

SCALIA, J., joined by REHNQUIST, Ch. J., and O'CONNOR and THOMAS, JJ., dissenting, expressed the view that (1) with respect to the statutory writ of certiorari, the Supreme Court's opinion permitted review where Congress had clearly denied it; (2) in order to reach this result, the Supreme Court (a) ignored AEDPA's obvious intent, (b) distorted the meaning of § 1254(1), and (c) inappropriately overruled House v Mayo; and (3) the accused had failed to establish that he met the requirements for the Supreme Court's issuance of a common-law writ of certiorari.

COUNSEL

Eileen Penner argued the cause for petitioner.

Matthew D. Roberts argued the cause for respondent.

Jeffrey S. Sutton argued the cause, as amicus curiae, by special leave of court.

SANDRA K. FORNEY, Petitioner

v

KENNETH S. APFEL, Commissioner of Social Security

524 US —, 141 L Ed 2d 269, 118 S Ct 1984

[No. 97-5737]

Argued April 22, 1998.
Decided June 15, 1998.

Decision: Federal District Court's order, remanding case in which Social Security Administration denied claim for disability benefits, held appealable by claimant under 28 USCS § 1291 and 42 USCS § 405(g).

SUMMARY

An individual applied to the Social Security Administration (SSA) for disability benefits under § 223 of the Social Security Act (42 USCS § 423). The individual's claim was denied by an administrative law judge, and the SSA's Appeals Council denied the individual's request for review. Thereafter, the individual filed an action in the United States District Court for the District of Oregon, in which action the individual sought judicial review of the SSA's determination pursuant to 42 USCS § 405(g), which provides (1) in its fourth sentence, that Federal District Courts have power to enter a judgment affirming, modifying, or reversing the SSA's decision with or without remanding the case for a rehearing, and (2) in its eighth sentence, that the judgment of the court is final except that such judgment was subject to review in the same manner as a judgment in other civil actions. The District Court, remanding the case to the SSA for further proceedings pursuant to the fourth sentence of § 405(g), ruled that the SSA's final determination that the individual could hold other jobs was inadequately supported by the record. The individual, contending that the SSA's denial of benefits should have been reversed outright, filed an appeal in the United States Court of Appeals for the Ninth Circuit. The Court of Appeals, dismissing the individual's appeal, expressed the view that (1) the District Court's remand order had terminated the individual's civil action favorably to the individual, and (2) because the individual could secure all the relief that the individual sought on remand, the individual was a prevailing party who could not appeal the District Court's order (108 F3d 228, 1997 US App LEXIS 3752).

On certiorari—following the appointment of an amicus curiae to defend the Court of Appeals' decision, after the individual and the Solicitor General of the United States agreed that the individual had the legal right to appeal from the District Court's judgment—the United States Supreme Court reversed and remanded. In an opinion by BREYER, J., expressing the unanimous view of the court, it was held that the individual could appeal the District Court's order, because (1) such appeal fell within the scope of the jurisdictional grant of 28 USCS § 1291, which provides that the Courts of Appeals have jurisdiction of appeals from all final decisions of the District Courts, in that the District Court had entered its judgment under the authority of the fourth and eighth sentences of § 405(g); (2) nothing in the language of either § 405(g) or a prior Supreme Court opinion which interpreted § 405(g) suggested that a District Court judgment remanding a Social Security disability benefit case could be "final" for purposes of appeal only when the Federal Government sought to appeal, but not when the claimant sought to do so; and (3) the individual was not a prevailing party who, as such, could not appeal the District Court's order.

COUNSEL

Ralph Wilborn argued the cause for petitioner.

Lisa S. Blatt argued the cause for respondent.

Allen R. Snyder argued the cause, as amicus curiae, in support of the judgment below.

_____

ALIDA STAR GEBSER and ALIDA JEAN Mc-
CULLOUGH, Petitioners

v

LAGO VISTA INDEPENDENT SCHOOL DISTRICT

524 US —, 141 L Ed 2d 277, 118 S Ct 1989

[No. 96-1866]

Argued March 25, 1998.
Decided June 22, 1998.

Decision: In action under Title IX of Education
Amendments of 1972 (20 USCS §§ 1681 et seq.)
for teacher's sexual harassment of student, damages held not recoverable from school district
absent official's actual notice and deliberate indifference.

SUMMARY

A public high school student in Texas had a sexual
relationship with one of her teachers and did not
report the relationship to school officials. During the
time of the relationship, the public school district did
not fulfill a federal regulatory requirement to distribute
an official grievance procedure for lodging sexual
harassment complaints and a formal antiharassment
policy. Also during this time, the parents of two other
students complained to the high school's principal
about the teacher's alleged sexually suggestive comments in class. The principal arranged a meeting and
advised the teacher to be careful about classroom
comments, but the principal did not report the parents'
complaint to the school district's superintendent. In
1993, after a police officer discovered the teacher and

the student engaging in sexual intercourse and arrested the teacher, the school district terminated the teacher's employment. The student and her mother filed suit in Texas state court against the school district and the teacher. Among the claims raised in the suit was a damages claim against the school district for sexual harassment under Title IX of the Education Amendments of 1972 (20 USCS §§ 1681 et seq.). After the case was removed to the United States District Court for the Western District of Texas, the District Court granted summary judgment in favor of the school district on all claims. On appeal of the Title IX claim, the United States Court of Appeals for the Fifth Circuit affirmed, on the grounds that (1) the school district could not be liable on the basis of strict liability, vicarious liability, or constructive notice; (2) school districts generally were not liable in tort for teacher-student sexual harassment under Title IX unless an employee with supervisory power over the offending employee actually knew of the abuse, had the power to end the abuse, and failed to do so; and (3) that standard could not be satisfied in the case at hand (106 F3d 1223; 1997 US App LEXIS 3273).

On certiorari, the United States Supreme Court affirmed. In an opinion by O'CONNOR, J., joined by REHNQUIST, Ch. J., and SCALIA, KENNEDY, and THOMAS, JJ., it was held that (1) in a private action against a school district by a student under Title IX for the sexual harassment of the student by one of the district's teachers, damages may not be recovered unless an official of the district who, at a minimum, has authority to institute corrective measures on the district's behalf has actual notice of, and is deliberately indifferent to, the teacher's misconduct; and (2) damages could not be recovered in the case at hand, as (a) the only information about the teacher's misconduct that the

254

principal allegedly had was plainly insufficient to alert the principal to the possibility that the teacher was involved in a sexual relationship with a student, (b) the school district's alleged failure to fulfill a federal regulatory requirement to promulgate and publicize an effective policy and grievance procedure for sexual harassment claims did not establish the requisite actual notice and deliberate indifference on the part of the school district, and (c) such an alleged failure did not itself constitute sex discrimination under Title IX.

STEVENS, J., joined by SOUTER, GINSBURG, and BREYER, JJ., dissenting, expressed the view that (1) the Supreme Court's holding thwarted Title IX's purposes and was at odds with settled principles of agency law, and (2) reliance on Title IX's administrative enforcement scheme to limit the availability of a damages remedy was inappropriate and led to the adoption of an exceedingly high standard under which few Title IX plaintiffs who have been victims of intentional sexual harassment would be able to recover damages.

GINSBURG, J., joined by SOUTER and BREYER, JJ., dissenting, expressed the view that a school district's effective policy for reporting and redressing sexual harassment ought to be recognized as an affirmative defense to a Title IX sexual harassment charge.

COUNSEL

Terry L. Weldon argued the cause for petitioners.

Beth Ann Brinkmann argued the cause for the United States, as amicus curiae, by special leave of court.

Wallace B. Jefferson argued the cause for respondent.

GERALD R. CARON, Petitioner

v

UNITED STATES

524 US —, 141 L Ed 2d 303, 118 S Ct 2007

[No. 97-6270]

Argued April 21, 1998.

Decided June 22, 1998.

Decision: Prior felony conviction held predicate for subsequent federal conviction and enhanced sentence involving possession of rifles and shotguns, where state law had restricted possession of handguns in connection with restoration of felon's civil rights.

SUMMARY

Federal statutes (1) prohibit persons who have been convicted of crimes punishable by more than a year in prison from possessing any firearm (18 USCS § 922(g)(1)); (2) provide that persons violating § 922(g)(1) must receive enhanced sentences if they also have three violent felony convictions (18 USCS § 924(e)); and (3) state that a previous conviction does not provide the predicate for either the substantive offense or a sentence enhancement if the person's civil rights have been restored, "unless such . . . restoration of civil rights expressly provides that the person may not . . . possess . . . firearms" (18 USCS § 921(a)(20)). An individual who had several previous felony convictions, including three convictions in Massachusetts state courts, was convicted in the United States District Court for the District of Massachusetts of violating § 922(g)(1) on the basis of possession of several rifles and shotguns which were found at his home. The District Court initially imposed an enhanced sentence under § 921(a)(20) based on the three Massachusetts convictions and one other felony conviction, but the court subsequently ruled that the Massachusetts convictions did not count because (1) the individual's civil rights had been restored by operation of Massachusetts law, under statutes which allowed him to possess rifles and shotguns but prohibited his possession of handguns outside his home or business, and (2) the fact that the present case involved rifles and shotguns made the restriction as to handguns irrelevant (941 F Supp 238, 1996 US Dist LEXIS 13540). The United States Court of Appeals for the First Circuit reversed, holding that the Massachusetts convictions could be counted under § 921(a)(20) because the individual, though not prohibited by the state from possessing the particular firearms found in his possession, remained subject to significant firearms restrictions.

On certiorari, the United States Supreme Court affirmed. In an opinion by KENNEDY, J., joined by REHNQUIST, Ch. J., and STEVENS, O'CONNOR, GINSBURG, and BREYER, JJ., it was held that the class of criminals who "may not . . . possess . . . firearms" under § 921(a)(20) includes those who are forbidden to possess some firearms but not others, even if the firearms which they are charged with possessing are ones which the state allows them to possess, since (1) Massachusetts has treated certain offenders as more dangerous than law-abiding citizens and as not to be trusted with handguns, and (2) federal law uses this state determination of dangerousness to impose its own broader stricture and to forbid such offenders to possess any firearms.

THOMAS, J., joined by SCALIA and SOUTER, JJ., dissented, expressing the view that Massachusetts law, by prohibiting the individual from possessing only certain firearms in certain places, did not expressly provide that the individual could not possess firearms within the meaning of § 921(a)(20).

COUNSEL

Owen S. Walker argued the cause for petitioner.

Jonathan Nuechterlein argued the cause for respondent.

UNITED STATES, Petitioner

v

HOSEP KRIKOR BAJAKAJIAN

524 US —, 141 L Ed 2d 314, 118 S Ct 2028

[No. 96-1487]

Argued November 4, 1997.
Decided June 22, 1998.

Decision: With respect to accused's federal conviction for willfully failing to report that he was transporting more than $10,000 out of United States, punitive forfeiture of full $357,144 involved held to violate Eighth Amendment's excessive fines clause.

SUMMARY

The excessive fines clause of the Federal Constitution's Eighth Amendment provides that excessive fines shall not be imposed. At a California airport, an individual, who was preparing to leave the United States with his family, indicated to a federal customs inspector that he had $8,000 and his wife had another $7,000. However, customs officials found a total of $357,144. A federal grand jury indicted the individual on three counts, which (1) charged him with violating 31 USCS §§ 5316(a)(1)(A) and 5322(a) by willfully failing to report that he was transporting more than $10,000 outside the United States; (2) charged him with violating 18 USCS § 1001 by making a false material statement to the United States Customs Service; and (3) sought forfeiture of the $357,144 pursuant to 18 USCS § 982(a)(1), which required a court, in imposing sentence upon a person convicted of an offense

259

under 31 USCS § 5316, to order the person to forfeit to the United States any property involved in the offense or traceable to such property. The individual pleaded guilty to the first count, while the government agreed to dismiss the § 1001 count and the individual elected a bench trial on the forfeiture count. After the trial, the United States District Court for the Central District of California (1) expressed the view that forfeiture of the full $357,144, as directed by § 982(a)(1), would violate the Eighth Amendment's excessive fines clause by being grossly disproportionate to the offense in question; and (2) instead ordered the forfeiture of $15,000, in addition to a sentence of 3 years' probation and a $5,000 fine, the maximum fine under the United States Sentencing Guidelines (18 USCS Appx). On appeal by the government, the United States Court of Appeals for the Ninth Circuit, in affirming with respect to the forfeiture, expressed the view that (1) § 982(a)(1) could never satisfy the excessive fines clause in cases involving forfeitures of currency, for such currency was not an "instrumentality" of the crime of failure to report; and (2) while this conclusion might otherwise mean that the individual could not be ordered to forfeit any of the currency at issue, the Court of Appeals lacked jurisdiction to set aside the District Court's forfeiture order of $15,000, because the individual had failed to cross-appeal (84 F3d 334, 1996 US App LEXIS 11464).

On certiorari, the United States Supreme Court affirmed. In an opinion by THOMAS, J., joined by STEVENS, SOUTER, GINSBURG, and BREYER, JJ., it was held that (1) the forfeiture, pursuant to § 982(a)(1), of the full $357,144 involved in the case at hand would constitute punishment and thus would be a "fine" within the meaning of the excessive fines clause; (2) a punitive forfeiture violates the excessive fines clause if the amount of the forfeiture is grossly disproportional to the gravity of a defendant's offense; and (3) in the case at hand, the forfeiture of the full $357,144 would violate the excessive fines clause, because such full forfeiture would be grossly disproportional to the gravity of the individual's reporting offense.

KENNEDY, J., joined by REHNQUIST, Ch. J., and O'CONNOR and SCALIA, JJ., dissenting, expressed the view that the excessive fines clause did not forbid the forfeiture of all $357,144, for—while the Supreme Court's test of gross disproportion would be a proper way to apply the excessive fines clause if the court were faithful in applying that test—(1) Congress had fixed a fine in the amount of the currency which the individual had sought to smuggle or to transport without reporting; (2) if a fine calibrated with this accuracy failed the court's test, then the court's decision portended serious disruption of a vast range of statutory fines; and (3) the court, in order to make its rationale work, improperly appeared to remove important classes of fines from any excessiveness inquiry at all.

COUNSEL

Irving L. Gornstein argued the cause for petitioner. James E. Blatt argued the cause for respondent.

PENNSYLVANIA BOARD OF PROBATION AND PA-
ROLE, Petitioner

v

KEITH M. SCOTT

524 US —, 141 L Ed 2d 344, 118 S Ct 2014

[No. 97-581]

Argued March 30, 1998.
Decided June 22, 1998.

Decision: Federal exclusionary rule held not to bar
introduction at parole revocation hearings of evidence obtained in violation of parolees' rights
under Federal Constitution's Fourth Amendment.

SUMMARY

Based on information that a parolee had violated the
conditions of his parole by such acts as possessing
weapons, parole officers entered the parolee's home
and found firearms, a bow, and arrows. The evidence
obtained during the search was admitted—over the
parolee's objection that the search violated the prohibition, under the Federal Constitution's Fourth
Amendment, against unreasonable searches and
seizures—at the parolee's parole violation hearing, at
which the Pennsylvania Board of Probation and Parole
recommitted the parolee to serve backtime. The Commonwealth Court of Pennsylvania, reversing the
Board's decision, held that the search violated the
Fourth Amendment and that the federal exclusionary
rule, which generally prohibits the introduction at
criminal trial of evidence obtained in violation of a
defendant's Fourth Amendment rights, applied to the

case. The Supreme Court of Pennsylvania, affirming
the judgment of the Commonwealth Court, held that
(1) the search in question was unreasonable, and (2)
the exclusionary rule applied to the case because the
officers who conducted the search were aware that the
parolee was a parolee (548 Pa 418, 698 A2d 32).

On certiorari, the United States Supreme Court
reversed the judgment of the Supreme Court of Pennsylvania and remanded the case. In an opinion by
THOMAS, J., joined by REHNQUIST, Ch. J., and
O'CONNOR, SCALIA, and KENNEDY, JJ., it was held that
the exclusionary rule does not bar the introduction at
parole revocation hearings of evidence obtained in
violation of the parolee's Fourth Amendment rights,
because (1) application of the rule would hinder the
functioning of state parole systems, since the rule,
which precludes consideration of reliable, probative
evidence, imposes significant costs by detracting from
the truthfinding process and allowing many who would
otherwise be incarcerated to escape the consequences
of their actions; (2) the rule is incompatible with the
traditionally flexible administrative process of parole
revocation proceedings, since the rule frequently requires extensive litigation to determine whether particular evidence must be excluded; and (3) the deterrence benefits of applying the rule to parole revocation
hearings would not outweigh these costs, since, in view
of the significant deterrence already provided by the
applicability of the exclusionary rule in criminal trials,
application of the rule at parole revocation hearings
would have little deterrent effect concerning a search
by (a) a police officer, regardless of whether the officer
was aware that the subject of a search was a parolee, or
(b) a parole officer.

STEVENS, J., dissenting, expressed the view that the
exclusionary rule is constitutionally required not as a

right explicitly incorporated in the Fourth Amendment's prohibitions, but as a remedy necessary to insure that those prohibitions are observed.

SOUTER, J., joined by GINSBURG and BREYER, JJ., dissenting, expressed the view that (1) a parole revocation proceeding often serves the same function as a trial, (2) a revocation hearing may present the only forum in which a state will seek to use evidence of a parole violation, even when that evidence would support an independent criminal charge, and (3) the deterrent function of the exclusionary rule is therefore implicated as much by a revocation proceeding as by a conventional trial, and the rule should be applied accordingly.

COUNSEL

D. Michael Fisher argued the cause for petitioner.

Malcolm L. Stewart argued the cause for the United States, as amicus curiae, by special leave of court.

Leonard N. Sosnov argued the cause for respondent.

WISCONSIN DEPARTMENT OF CORRECTIONS, et al., Petitioners

v

KEITH D. SCHACHT

524 US —, 141 L Ed 2d 364, 118 S Ct 2047

[No. 97-461]

Argued April 20, 1998.
Decided June 22, 1998.

Decision: Presence in case of claims that were barred from assertion in Federal District Court by Eleventh Amendment held not to destroy District Court's removal jurisdiction over nonbarred claims.

SUMMARY

An individual who had been dismissed from the position of prison guard filed a complaint in a Wisconsin state court against the Wisconsin department of corrections and several of the department's employees. The employees were sued both in their "personal" and in their "official" capacities. The complaint alleged that the department and its employees had deprived the individual of liberty and property without due process of law, in violation of the Federal Constitution's Fourteenth Amendment and 42 USCS § 1983. The department and employees, relying on 28 USCS § 1441(a), removed the case to the United States District Court for the Western District of Wisconsin. Following removal, the department and employees filed an answer which alleged, in part, that the Constitution's Eleventh Amendment and the doctrine of

265

sovereign immunity barred claims under § 1983 against the state and against the employees in their official capacities. The District Court (1) granted the department and employees' motion for summary judgment on the claims against the employees in their personal capacities, and (2) dismissed the claims against the department and its employees in their official capacities. On appeal, the United States Court of Appeals for the Seventh Circuit—vacating the District Court's judgment and remanding the case to the District Court, with instructions that the District Court remand to the state court—expressed the view that the removal of the case to District Court had been improper because, in view of the presence in the individual's state court complaint of a claim which the Eleventh Amendment prohibited from being asserted in federal court, the District Court lacked subject matter jurisdiction over the case (116 F3d 1151, 1997 US App LEXIS 14640).

On certiorari, the United States Supreme Court vacated and remanded. In an opinion by Breyer, J., expressing the unanimous view of the court, it was held that (1) the presence, in a case otherwise removable to federal court under § 1441(a), of claims that were barred from assertion in federal court by the Eleventh Amendment did not destroy the federal court's removal jurisdiction; and (2) the federal court therefore could decide the claims in the case that were not barred by the Eleventh Amendment.

Kennedy, J., concurring, expressed the view that the Supreme Court had neither reached nor considered the argument that the state, in the case at hand, had waived its Eleventh Amendment immunity by giving its express consent to removal of the case from state court.

COUNSEL

Richard B. Moriarty argued the cause for petitioners.
David E. Lasker argued the cause for respondent.

SWIDLER & BERLIN and JAMES HAMILTON, Petitioners

v

UNITED STATES

524 US —, 141 L Ed 2d 379, 118 S Ct 2081

[No. 97-1192]

Argued June 8, 1998.
Decided June 25, 1998.

Decision: Attorney-client privilege held to protect initial interview notes that were (1) written by White House official's attorney shortly before official's death, and (2) subpoenaed by Independent Counsel in criminal investigation after official's death.

SUMMARY

A Deputy White House Counsel met with an attorney to seek legal representation concerning potential investigations of possible criminal actions in connection with the dismissal of certain White House employees, and the attorney took three pages of handwritten notes of that meeting. Nine days later, the Deputy Counsel committed suicide. An Independent Counsel investigating the dismissals subsequently obtained federal grand jury subpoenas directing the attorney and his law firm to produce the attorney's notes, but the United States District Court for the District of Columbia, granting the firm's motion to quash the subpoena, held that the notes were protected by both the attorney-client privilege and the work product privilege. The United States Court of Appeals for the District of Columbia Circuit, reversing the judgment of the District Court and remanding the case, held that (1) the work product privilege did not apply, and (2) the attorney-client privilege should not automatically apply after the death of the client where the communications are sought for use in a criminal investigation, but should be subject to a balancing test (124 F3d 230, 1997 US App LEXIS 22814). A suggestion for rehearing en banc was denied (129 F3d 637, 1997 US App LEXIS 32954).

On certiorari, the United States Supreme Court reversed. In an opinion by REHNQUIST, Ch. J., joined by STEVENS, KENNEDY, SOUTER, GINSBURG, and BREYER, JJ., it was held that the notes were protected by the attorney-client privilege because both the great body of caselaw and weighty reasons support the position that the attorney-client privilege survives the client's death, even in connection with criminal cases.

O'CONNOR, J., joined by SCALIA and THOMAS, JJ., dissented, expressing the view that (1) a compelling law enforcement need for information may override a client's posthumous interest in confidentiality where the information is not available from other sources, and (2) the attorney-client privilege should not inevitably preclude disclosure of a deceased client's communications in criminal proceedings.

COUNSEL

James Hamilton argued the cause for petitioners.

Brett M. Kavanaugh argued the cause for respondent.

WILLIAM J. CLINTON, President of the United
States, et al., Appellants

v

CITY OF NEW YORK et al.

524 US —, 141 L Ed 2d 393, 118 S Ct 2091

[No. 97-1374]

Argued April 27, 1998.
Decided June 25, 1998.

Decision: Certain parties held to have standing to
challenge validity, under Federal Constitution, of
Line Item Veto Act, 2 USCS §§ 691 et seq.; procedures set forth in Act held to violate Constitution's
presentment clause, Art I, § 7, cl 2.

SUMMARY

The Line Item Veto Act, 2 USCS §§ 691 et seq., which
gave the President of the United States authority to
cancel certain spending and tax benefit measures after
the President had signed such measures into law,
contained an expedited-review provision, 2 USCS
§ 692(a)(1), which authorized any "individual" adversely affected by the Line Item Veto Act to bring a
declaratory judgment action alleging that any provision
of the Line Item Veto Act violated the Federal Constitution. After the President exercised his authority under the Line Item Veto Act to cancel certain
measures—including § 4722(c) of the Balanced Budget
Act of 1997, 111 Stat 515, which waived the Federal
Government's statutory right to recoup certain taxes
levied by the state of New York on Medicaid providers,
and § 968 of the Taxpayer Relief Act of 1997, 111 Stat
270

896, which permitted owners of certain food refiners and processors to defer recognition of capital gains from sales of their stock to eligible farmers' cooperatives—actions seeking a declaratory judgment that the Line Item Veto Act was unconstitutional and thus that a particular cancellation was invalid were brought pursuant to § 692(a)(1) against the President and other federal officials by (1) the city of New York, two hospital associations, a hospital, and two unions representing health care employees with respect to § 4722(c), and (2) a potato farmers' cooperative and one of its individual members with respect to § 968. The United States District Court for the District of Columbia consolidated the two cases and determined that (1) at least one plaintiff in each case had standing under the Constitution's Article III to sue, and (2) the Line Item Veto Act violated the Constitution's present-ment clause, Art I, § 7, cl 2, and the doctrine of separation of powers (985 F Supp 168).

On direct appeal and on expedited review, the United States Supreme Court affirmed the judgment of the District Court. In an opinion by STEVENS, J., joined by REHNQUIST, Ch. J., and KENNEDY, SOUTER, THOMAS, and GINSBURG, JJ., it was held that (1) the District Court's jurisdiction encompassed, in addition to the individual member of the cooperative, the other parties who brought the actions, because Congress intended the word "individual" in § 692(a)(1) to be synonymous with "person," which in the law often had a broad meaning that included such entities as corporations and associations; (2) the city, the hospital associations, the hospital, the cooperative, and the member of the cooperative had satisfied the Article III standing re-quirement of a case or controversy, because the parties had alleged a personal stake in having an actual injury redressed; and (3) the cancellation procedures set

forth in the Line Item Veto Act violated the presentment clause, where if the Line Item Veto Act were valid,
it would authorize the President to create a statute
whose text was not voted on by either House of
Congress or presented to the President for signature.

KENNEDY, J., concurring, expressed the view that by
increasing the power of the President beyond what the
framers of the Constitution envisioned, the Line Item
Veto Act compromised the liberty of the nation's
citizens, liberty which the separation of powers sought
to secure.

SCALIA, J., joined by O'CONNOR, J., and joined as to
points 1 and 2(b) below by BREYER, J., concurring in
part and dissenting in part, (1) agreed with the court
that the New York parties had standing to challenge the
cancellation of § 4722(c); but (2) expressed the view
that (a) the farmers' cooperative and its member
lacked standing to challenge the cancellation of § 968,
as the cooperative's allegations did not establish an
injury in fact that was attributable to the challenged
Presidential action and remediable by the Supreme
Court's invalidation of that action, and (b) the cancellation of § 4722(c) did not violate the presentment
clause.

BREYER, J., joined as to point 1 below by O'CONNOR
and SCALIA, JJ., dissenting, agreed with the court that
the parties had standing, but expressed the view that
the Line Item Veto Act did not violate (1) any specific
textual constitutional command, as the President's
cancellations executed a power conferred upon the
President by Congress, which power was contained in
laws that were enacted in compliance with the exclusive
methods set forth in the Constitution, or (2) any basic
principle concerning the separation of powers.

COUNSEL

Seth P. Waxman argued the cause for appellants.

Louis R. Cohen argued the cause for appellee Snake River Potato Growers.

Charles J. Cooper argued the cause for appellee City of New York

———————

EASTERN ENTERPRISES, Petitioner

v

KENNETH S. APFEL, Commissioner of Social Security, et al.

524 US —, 141 L Ed 2d 451, 118 S Ct 2131

[No. 97-42]

Argued March 4, 1998.
Decided June 25, 1998.

Decision: Provision (26 USCS § 9706(a)(3)) for assessing liability under Coal Industry Retiree Health Benefit Act of 1992 held to violate Federal Constitution as applied to company which had once, but no longer, engaged in coal mining operations.

SUMMARY

Beginning in 1947, various labor agreements between coal operators and a union included provisions concerning health care benefits. Although some health care benefits had been provided to coal industry retirees and their dependents prior to 1974, a 1974 labor agreement was the first one to include express provisions for health care benefits for retirees and their dependents. After two implementing plans, known as the 1950 Benefit Plan and the 1974 Benefit Plan, began to experience serious financial difficulties, Congress eventually enacted the Coal Industry Retiree Health Benefit Act of 1992 (Coal Act) (26 USCS §§ 9701-9722). The Coal Act established a mechanism to fund health care benefits for coal industry retirees and their dependents by assessing premiums against signatory operators, that is, coal industry operators that had signed

274

prior labor agreements. One Coal Act provision (26 USCS § 9706(a)(3)), in describing a premium formula by assigning coal industry retirees to particular signatory operators, provided that if a retiree was not assigned under 26 USCS § 9706(a)(1) or § 9706(a)(2)—both of which referred to signatories of 1978 or later labor agreements—then the liability for the retiree or any person related to the retiree would be assigned to the signatory operator which had employed the retiree for a longer period of time than any other signatory operator prior to the effective date of the 1978 agreement. Meanwhile, a particular company had engaged in coal mining operations for many years—and had been a signatory to coal industry labor agreements—until 1965, when the company had completed the transfer of its coal-related operations to a subsidiary as to which the company, in 1987, had sold its interest. After the enactment of the Coal Act, the Commissioner of Social Security assigned to the company a liability under § 9706(a)(3) for premiums respecting more than 1,000 retirees who had worked for the company before 1966. The company then (1) sued defendants including the Commissioner in the United States District Court for the District of Massachusetts; and (2) included claims that § 9706(a)(3), as applied to the company, (a) effected a taking of the company's property in violation of the takings clause of the Federal Constitution's Fifth Amendment, and (b) violated substantive due process under the Constitution. However, the District Court, in denying the company's motion for summary judgment, expressed the view that § 9706(a)(3) did not appear to be unconstitutional as applied to the company (942 F Supp 684, 1996 US Dist LEXIS 14384). The United States Court of Appeals for the First Circuit, in affirming, rejected the company's takings clause and due process claims (110 F3d 350, 1997 US App LEXIS 6456).

On certiorari, the United States Supreme Court reversed and remanded. Although unable to agree on an opinion, five members of the court agreed that § 9706(a)(3) violated the Constitution as applied to the company.

O'CONNOR, J., announced the judgment of the court and, in an opinion joined by REHNQUIST, Ch. J., and SCALIA and THOMAS, JJ., expressed the view that (1) under the circumstances, the company's takings clause claim was properly filed in the District Court, rather than in the United States Court of Federal Claims; (2) § 9706(a)(3), as applied to the company, effected a regulatory taking in violation of the takings clause, for (a) Congress' solution to what it perceived as a grave problem in the funding of retired miners' health care benefits singled out certain employers, such as the company, to bear a substantial financial burden on the basis of conduct that was far in the past and unrelated to any commitment which the employers had made or to any injury which the employers had caused, and (b) the company could not be forced to bear the expense of lifetime health care benefits for retired miners on the basis of the company's activities decades before those benefits were promised; and (3) it was unnecessary to address the question whether the Coal Act violated substantive due process in light of the Coal Act's severely retroactive impact.

THOMAS, J., concurring, expressed the view that in an appropriate future case, the Supreme Court's precedents might be reconsidered to determine whether a retroactive civil law that passed muster under the takings clause was nonetheless invalid under the ex post facto clause in Art I, § 9, cl 3 of the Constitution.

KENNEDY, J., concurring in the judgment and dissenting in part, expressed the view that (1) with respect to the Constitution, the case at hand was controlled not by the takings clause, but by well-settled due process principles respecting retroactive laws; and (2) applying the Coal Act to the company would violate the proper bounds of retroactivity under those due process principles, where (a) the remedy created by the Coal Act bore no legitimate relation to the interest which the government asserted in support of the statute, and (b) the Coal Act, in creating liability for events which occurred 35 years previously, had a retroactive effect of unprecedented scope.

STEVENS, J., joined by SOUTER, GINSBURG, and BREYER, JJ., dissenting, expressed the view that (1) during the 1950's and 1960's, there was a critically important and implicit understanding on both sides of the bargaining table in the coal industry—which understanding was made explicit in 1974—that coal operators would provide the miners with lifetime health benefits; and (2) accordingly, regardless of whether § 9706(a)(3) was analyzed under the takings clause or as a matter of due process, the company had not carried its burden of overcoming the presumption of constitutionality accorded to an act of Congress by demonstrating that § 9706(a)(3) was unsupported by the reasonable expectations of the parties in interest.

BREYER, J., joined by STEVENS, SOUTER, and GINSBURG, JJ., dissenting, expressed the view that (1) the federal constitutional question involved in the case at hand ought to be analyzed as a matter of due process, rather than under the takings clause; and (2) as a matter of due process, it was not fundamentally unfair for Congress, in the Coal Act, to require the company to pay the health care costs of retired miners who had worked for the company before the company had stopped mining coal in 1965, where (a) for many years, the company had benefited from the labor of those miners, (b) even though the company had not made a contractual promise to pay, the company had helped to create conditions that had led the miners to expect continued health benefits for themselves and their families after the miners retired, and (c) until 1987, the company had continued to draw sizable benefits from the coal industry through a wholly owned subsidiary.

COUNSEL

John T. Montgomery argued the cause for petitioner.

Edwin S. Kneedler argued the cause for federal respondents.

Peter Buscemi argued the cause for private respondents.

NATIONAL ENDOWMENT FOR THE ARTS, et al.,
Petitioners

v

KAREN FINLEY et al.

524 US —, 141 L Ed 2d 500, 118 S Ct 2168

[No. 97-371]

Argued March 31, 1998.
Decided June 25, 1998.

Decision: 20 USCS § 954(d)(1)—directing National Endowment for Arts, in judging arts grant applications, to consider standards of decency and respect for diverse beliefs and values of American public—held not facially invalid under First Amendment.

SUMMARY

The National Foundation on the Arts and Humanities Act (20 USCS §§ 951 et seq.) vests the National Endowment for the Arts (NEA) with discretion to award financial grants to support the arts. Applications for NEA grants are initially reviewed by advisory panels of experts in the relevant artistic field. The panels report to the National Council on the Arts (Council), which, in turn, advises the NEA chairperson. A 1989 amendment directs the chairperson to insure that "artistic excellence and artistic merit are the criteria by which applications are judged, taking into consideration general standards of decency and respect for the diverse beliefs and values of the American public" (20 USCS § 954(d)(1)). Before § 954(d)(1) was enacted, an advisory panel recommended approval of the proj-

279

ects of four performance artists who applied for NEA grants, but the Council subsequently recommended disapproval, and funding was denied. The artists, asserting that the NEA had violated the Federal Constitution's First Amendment and various statutory provisions, filed suit in the United States District Court for the Central District of California for restoration of the recommended grants or reconsideration of the applications. After Congress enacted § 954(d)(1), the artists—joined by an artists' association—amended the complaint to challenge § 954(d)(1) as void for vagueness and impermissibly viewpoint based. The District Court (1) denied the NEA's motion for judgment on the pleadings, (2) granted summary judgment in favor of the artists on their facial constitutional challenge to § 954(d)(1), and (3) enjoined enforcement of § 954(d)(1) (795 F Supp 1457, 1992 US Dist LEXIS 8070). The United States Court of Appeals for the Ninth Circuit, in affirming, (1) concluded that § 954(d)(1) gave rise to the danger of arbitrary and discriminatory application and thus was void for vagueness under the Constitution's First and Fifth Amendments, and (2) alternatively concluded that § 954(d)(1) violated the First Amendment's prohibition of viewpoint-based restrictions on protected speech (100 F3d 671, 1996 US App LEXIS 28837).

On certiorari, the United States Supreme Court reversed the Court of Appeals' judgment and remanded the case for further proceedings. In an opinion by O'CONNOR, J., joined by REHNQUIST, Ch. J., and STEVENS, KENNEDY, and BREYER, JJ., and joined in pertinent part by GINSBURG, J., it was held that (1) § 954(d)(1) was not facially invalid under the First Amendment, for (a) the advisory language of the text of § 954(d)(1) imposed no categorical requirement, (b) the political context surrounding the adoption of the "decency and respect" clause was inconsistent with the assertion that the provision compelled the NEA to deny funding on the basis of viewpoint-discriminatory criteria, (c) the decency and respect clause did not introduce considerations that, in practice, would effectively preclude or punish the expression of particular views, and (d) permissible applications of the decency and respect clause were apparent; and (2) § 954(d)(1), although opaque, was not impermissibly vague under the First and Fifth Amendments, for (a) it was unlikely that speakers would be compelled to steer too far clear of any forbidden area in the context of arts grants, (b) the consequences of imprecision are not constitutionally severe when the government is acting as patron rather than as sovereign, and (c) to accept the vagueness argument in the case at hand would be to call into question the constitutionality of many other valuable government subsidy programs.

SCALIA, J., joined by THOMAS, J., concurring in the judgment, expressed the view that (1) § 954(d)(1) was not merely advisory, but established constitutionally valid content- and viewpoint-based criteria upon which grant applications were to be evaluated; and (2) neither the First Amendment nor the constitutional rule against vague legislation had any application to government funding programs.

SOUTER, J., dissenting, expressed the view that § 954(d)(1), although not unconstitutionally vague, was substantially overbroad—with a significant power to chill artistic production and display—and ought to have been struck down on its face.

COUNSEL

Seth P. Waxman argued the cause for petitioners.
David D. Cole argued the cause for respondents.

RANDON BRAGDON, Petitioner

v

SIDNEY ABBOTT et al.

524 US —, 141 L Ed 2d 540, 118 S Ct 2196

[No. 97-156]

Argued March 30, 1998.
Decided June 25, 1998.

Decision: Dental patient's asymptomatic HIV infection held to be disability under Americans with Disabilities Act provision (42 USCS §.12102(2)(A)); remand held necessary for findings as to health risk to dentist who refused patient in-office treatment.

SUMMARY

The human immunodeficiency virus (HIV) has been identified as the cause of acquired immune deficiency syndrome (AIDS). HIV infection progresses in (1) an initial stage of acute or primary infection; (2) a so-called asymptomatic phase, in which the virus tends to concentrate in the lymph nodes; and (3) a symptomatic stage. A woman whose HIV infection was in the asymptomatic phase went to a dentist's office for a dental examination and disclosed her infection. The dentist discovered a cavity and informed the woman of his policy against filling cavities of HIV-infected patients in his office. The dentist offered to perform the work at a hospital at no extra charge, though the woman would have had to pay for use of the hospital's facilities. The woman declined and filed suit against the dentist in the United States District Court for the District of Maine, in which suit it was alleged, among other matters, that (1)

283

the dentist had violated a provision of the Americans with Disabilities Act of 1990 (ADA) (42 USCS § 12182(a)) which prohibits discrimination against any individual on the basis of disability in the enjoyment of the services of any place of public accommodation; and (2) the woman's HIV infection had deterred her from having children and thus (a) substantially limited her "major life activity" of reproduction, and (b) came within the definition of "disability" for purposes of an ADA provision (42 USCS § 12102(2)(A)). The dentist claimed that his refusal of in-office treatment was covered by another ADA provision (42 USCS § 12182(b)(3)) under which an individual need not be permitted to participate in or benefit from public accommodations where such individual poses a direct threat to the health or safety of others. The District Court, in granting the woman summary judgment, concluded that (1) the woman's asymptomatic HIV infection was a disability under the ADA, and (2) treating her in the dentist's office would not have posed a direct threat to the health and safety of others (912 F Supp 580, 1995 US Dist LEXIS 19312). The United States Court of Appeals for the First Circuit affirmed (107 F3d 934, 1997 US App LEXIS 3870).

On certiorari, the United States Supreme Court vacated the Court of Appeals' judgment and remanded the case for further proceedings. In an opinion by KENNEDY, J., joined by STEVENS, SOUTER, GINSBURG, and BREYER, JJ., it was held that (1) the woman's HIV infection, even in the so-called asymptomatic phase, was a disability under § 12102(2)(A), because the infection was an impairment which substantially limited the major life activity of reproduction; but (2) remand was necessary because, although there were reasons to doubt whether the dentist had advanced sufficient evidence on the question of risk to the health and safety

284

of others, (a) the Court of Appeals, in determining as a matter of law that the woman's infection posed no direct threat to the dentist's health and safety, might have placed mistaken reliance on various items of evidence, and (b) the Supreme Court, in accepting the case for review, had declined to grant certiorari on the question whether the dentist had raised a genuine issue of fact for trial, with the result that the briefs and arguments presented to the Supreme Court did not concentrate on the question of sufficiency of evidence.

STEVENS, J., joined by BREYER, J., concurring, expressed the view that (1) the Court of Appeals' judgment ought to have been affirmed, but (2) the legal analysis in the Supreme Court's opinion was correct, and (3) it was thus appropriate to join the Supreme Court's opinion in order to provide a judgment supported by a majority.

GINSBURG, J., concurring, expressed the view that (1) HIV infection met the statutory and regulatory definitions of disability, for purposes of the ADA, as a physical impairment that (a) substantially limited major life activities, or (b) was so perceived; and (2) it was wise to remand the case for a fully informed determination as to the risk to health care workers' health and safety.

REHNQUIST, Ch. J., joined by SCALIA and THOMAS, JJ., and joined in part (as to point 4 below) by O'CONNOR, J., concurring in the judgment in part and dissenting in part, expressed the view that (1) the ADA's definition of "disability" required an individualized inquiry as to whether the major life activity at issue was one of the individual in question; (2) for purposes of § 12102(2)(A), reproduction was not, as a general matter, a major life activity; (3) even if it were assumed that reproduction was a major life activity of the woman in question, an asymptomatic HIV infection did not

285

substantially limit that activity; and (4) it was proper to vacate the Court of Appeals' judgment, as the dentist's evidence was sufficient to create a triable issue on the question of significant risk.

O'CONNOR, J., concurring in the judgment in part and dissenting in part, expressed the view that (1) the woman's claim of disability ought to have been evaluated on an individualized basis, (2) the woman had not proven that her asymptomatic HIV status substantially limited one or more of her major life activities, and (3) remand was necessary because the Court of Appeals had failed to make a proper determination whether the woman's condition posed a direct threat.

COUNSEL

John W. McCarthy argued the cause for petitioner.

Bennett H. Klein argued the cause for respondents.

Lawrence G. Wallace argued the cause for the United States, as amicus curiae, by special leave of court.

───────────

UNITED STATES, Petitioner

v

ALOYZAS BALSYS

524 US —, 141 L Ed 2d 575, 118 S Ct 2218

[No. 97-873]

Argued April 20, 1998.

Decided June 25, 1998.

Decision: With respect to resident alien's refusal to answer questions stemming from his possible participation in Nazi persecution, alien's fear of foreign criminal prosecution held to be beyond scope of Fifth Amendment privilege against self-incrimination.

SUMMARY

The self-incrimination clause of the Federal Constitution's Fifth Amendment provides a privilege against self-incrimination in "any criminal case." In Malloy v Hogan (1964) 378 US 1, 12 L Ed 2d 653, 84 S Ct 1489, the United States Supreme Court held that under the due process clause of the Constitution's Fourteenth Amendment, the Fifth Amendment privilege is binding on the states as well as the Federal Government. Also, in Murphy v Waterfront Com. of New York Harbor (1964) 378 US 52, 12 L Ed 2d 678, 84 S Ct 1594, which involved some state witnesses who had been granted immunity from state prosecution, the Supreme Court held that the self-incrimination clause barred the Federal Government from using the witnesses' state testimony or its fruits to obtain a federal conviction. The case at hand involved a resident alien who obtained admission to the

United States in 1961 with an application in which the alien said that he had (1) served in the Lithuanian army between 1934 and 1940, and (2) lived in hiding in Lithuania between 1940 and 1944. Later, the Office of Special Investigations of the Criminal Division of the United States Department of Justice (OSI) began an investigation, which could subject the alien to eventual deportation, into the alien's possible participation in Nazi persecution during World War II. In response to an OSI subpoena, the alien (1) gave his name and address, (2) refused to answer any other questions, and (3) invoked his Fifth Amendment privilege against self-incrimination on the basis on an asserted fear of criminal prosecution by foreign nations including Lithuania and Israel. The OSI petitioned the United States District Court for the Eastern District of New York to enforce the subpoena. Although the District Court found that the alien faced a real and substantial danger of prosecution by Lithuania or Israel if he were to provide the information requested, the court granted the enforcement petition, as the court expressed the view that the Fifth Amendment was inapplicable to a claim of self-incrimination that was based solely on a fear of foreign criminal prosecution (918 F Supp 588, 1996 US Dist LEXIS 2739). On appeal, the United States Court of Appeals for the Second Circuit vacated and ordered a remand, as the court expressed the view that a witness who had a real and substantial fear of prosecution by a foreign nation could assert the Fifth Amendment privilege to avoid giving testimony in a domestic proceeding, even if the witness had no valid fear of criminal prosecution in the United States (119 F3d 122, 1997 US App LEXIS 17601).

On certiorari, the Supreme Court reversed and remanded. In an opinion by SOUTER, J., joined by REHN-QUIST, Ch. J., and STEVENS, O'CONNOR, and KENNEDY,

JJ., and joined in pertinent part by SCALIA and THOMAS, JJ., it was held—expressly declining to accept some historical reasoning in Murphy v Waterfront Com. of New York Harbor to the extent that it went beyond a response to Malloy v Hogan—the alien's asserted fear of foreign criminal prosecution was beyond the scope of the Fifth Amendment's self-incrimination clause, where in the context of the Fifth Amendment's other provisions, the most probable reading of the self-incrimination clause limited its principle to concern with prosecution by a sovereign that was itself bound by the clause.

STEVENS, J., concurring, expressed the view that (1) the primary office of the self-incrimination clause is to afford protection to persons whose liberty has been placed in jeopardy in an American tribunal; (2) the Supreme Court's holding would not have any adverse impact on the fairness of American criminal trials; and (3) if the court were to accept the alien's interpretation of the clause, then the court would confer power on foreign governments to impair the administration of justice in the United States.

GINSBURG, J., dissenting, expressed the view that the Fifth Amendment privilege against self-incrimination ordinarily ought to command the respect of United States interrogators, regardless of whether the prosecution reasonably feared by an examinee was domestic or foreign.

BREYER, J., joined by GINSBURG, J., dissenting, expressed the view that pursuant to the precedent of Murphy v Waterfront Com. of New York Harbor—as well as the basic principles underlying the Fifth Amendment privilege against self-incrimination—the privilege ought to encompass not only feared domestic prosecutions, but also feared foreign prosecutions where the danger of an actual foreign prosecution was substantial.

COUNSEL

Michael R. Dreeben argued the cause for petitioner. Ivars Berzins argued the cause for respondent.

ANGEL JAIME MONGE, Petitioner

v

CALIFORNIA

524 US —, 141 L Ed 2d 615, 118 S Ct 2246

[No. 97-6146]

Argued April 28, 1998.
Decided June 26, 1998.

Decision: Application of double jeopardy clause of
Federal Constitution's Fifth Amendment held not
to extend to California court's noncapital sentencing proceeding to determine truth of allegations
supporting enhanced sentence.

SUMMARY

Under California law, (1) where a criminal defendant convicted of a felony has a qualifying prior conviction for one serious felony offense, the court doubles
the defendant's term of imprisonment; and (2) an
assault conviction qualifies as a serious felony if the
defendant either inflicted great bodily injury on another person or personally used a dangerous or deadly
weapon during the assault. A defendant who was
charged under California law with various marijuana
offenses was notified that the state would seek to prove
two sentence enhancement allegations, namely, that
the defendant had previously (1) been convicted of
assault, and (2) served a prison term for that offense.
After a trial in the Superior Court of Los Angeles
County, California, and the jury's entry of a guilty
verdict on the substantive offenses, the truth of the
prior conviction allegations was argued before the

291

Superior Court in a sentencing proceeding. The prosecutor, although asserting that the defendant had personally used a stick in committing the assault, introduced into evidence only a prison record demonstrating that the defendant had been convicted of assault with a deadly weapon and had served a prison term for that offense. The Superior Court found both sentencing allegations true and accordingly imposed an 11-year prison term consisting of 5 years for one of the marijuana offenses, doubled to 10 years for the prior conviction, plus a 1-year enhancement for the prior prison term. On appeal, the Court of Appeal of California, on its own motion, requested briefing as to whether sufficient evidence supported the finding that the defendant had a qualifying prior conviction. The state, conceding that the record of the sentencing proceeding did not contain proof beyond a reasonable doubt that the defendant had personally inflicted great bodily injury or used a deadly weapon, requested another opportunity to prove the allegations on remand. The Court of Appeal, although affirming the marijuana conviction, (1) reversed the Superior Court's finding as to the prior serious felony allegation, on the ground that the evidence was insufficient to trigger sentence enhancement, and (2) concluded that a remand for retrial on the allegation would violate double jeopardy principles. The Supreme Court of California reversed the Court of Appeal's judgment as to the double jeopardy issue. Although the California Supreme Court justices were unable to agree on an opinion, (1) a plurality of justices expressed the view that the double jeopardy clause of the Federal Constitution's Fifth Amendment, though applicable in the capital sentencing context, did not extend to noncapital sentencing proceedings; and (2) an additional justice expressed the view that a second attempt at proving the allegation would not violate the double jeopardy clause, as the factfinder would not be required to re-evaluate the evidence underlying the substantive offense (16 Cal 4th 826, 66 Cal Rptr 2d 853, 941 P2d 1121, 1997 Cal LEXIS 4980).

On certiorari, the United States Supreme Court affirmed. In an opinion by O'CONNOR, J., joined by REHNQUIST, Ch. J., and KENNEDY, THOMAS, and BREYER, JJ., it was held that (1) the applicability of the double jeopardy clause does not extend to noncapital sentencing proceedings; and (2) under the circumstances presented, (a) the double jeopardy clause did not preclude a sentencing proceeding, on remand, to determine the truth of allegations as to the defendant's prior conviction, and (b) the enhanced sentencing determination did not place the defendant in jeopardy for an "offense" for double jeopardy purposes.

STEVENS, J., dissenting, expressed the view that the Supreme Court's opinion failed to recognize the distinction, for double jeopardy purposes, between (1) impermissible resentencing where the evidence in the first proceeding was insufficient, and (2) permissible resentencing where legal errors infected the first proceeding.

SCALIA, J., joined by SOUTER and GINSBURG, J., dissenting, (1) agreed that the double jeopardy clause did not apply to noncapital sentencing proceedings; but (2) expressed the view that in the case at hand, (a) the sentence enhancement was in reality an element of the charged crime, (b) the defendant had been functionally acquitted of the crime when the Court of Appeal of California held that the evidence adduced at trial was insufficient to sustain the enhancement findings, and (c) giving the state a second chance to prove

293

the defendant guilty of the crime would violate the double jeopardy prohibition.

COUNSEL

Clifford Gardner argued the cause for petitioner.

David F. Glassman argued the cause for respondent.

Matthew D. Roberts argued the cause for the United States, as amicus curiae, by special leave of court.

BURLINGTON INDUSTRIES, INC., Petitioner

v

KIMBERLY B. ELLERTH

524 US —, 141 L Ed 2d 633, 118 S Ct 2257

[No. 97-569]

Argued April 22, 1998.

Decided June 26, 1998.

Decision: Under Title VII, employer held (1) subject, without showing of negligence, to vicarious liability to sexually harassed employee for supervisor's creation of hostile environment, but (2) able, when no tangible employment action is taken, to raise affirmative defense.

SUMMARY

Allegedly, (1) a female worker, while employed by a company as a salesperson in a two-person Illinois office, was subjected to constant sexual harassment by a male vice president; (2) the vice president's office was in New York; (3) the vice president was a midlevel manager of the worker; (4) the worker's immediate supervisor reported to the vice president; (5) the vice president repeatedly made boorish and offensive remarks and gestures; and (6) in three incidents, the vice president's comments could be construed as threats to deny the worker tangible job benefits, but these threats were not carried out, and the worker, despite knowing that the company had a policy against sexual harassment, did not inform anyone with authority about the vice president's conduct. After the worker received a right-to-sue letter from the Equal Employment Opportunity Com-

mission, she filed suit in the United States District
Court for the Northern District of Illinois and included
allegations that the company had engaged in sexual
harassment, in violation of Title VII of the Civil Rights
Act of 1964 (42 USCS §§ 2000e et seq.). The District
Court, granting summary judgment in favor of the
company, expressed the view that (1) although the
worker's complaint was framed as one involving a
hostile work environment, there was a quid pro quo
"component" to the hostile environment; and (2)
while the vice president's conduct, as described by the
worker, had been severe and pervasive enough to
create a hostile work environment, the company had
not known and should not have known about the
conduct (912 F Supp 1101, 1996 US Dist LEXIS 594).
On appeal, a panel of the United States Court of
Appeals for the Seventh Circuit initially ordered a
reversal and remand (102 F3d 848, 1996 US App LEXIS
31180). On rehearing en banc, the Court of Appeals
instead—in a decision which had a majority result
without a majority rationale for all of the issues
involved—(1) affirmed the District Court's judgment
with respect to what was called the claim of hostile
environment harassment, (2) reversed the District
Court's judgment with respect to what was called the
claim of quid pro quo harassment, and (3) ordered a
remand for further proceedings (123 F3d 490, 1997 US
App LEXIS 22266).

On certiorari, the United States Supreme Court
affirmed. In an opinion by KENNEDY, J., joined by
REHNQUIST, Ch. J., and STEVENS, O'CONNOR, SOUTER,
and BREYER, JJ., it was held that with respect to Title VII
sexual harassment claims, (1) although the two labels
quid pro quo and hostile work environment are relevant when there is a threshold question whether a
plaintiff can prove discrimination, the two labels are
296

not controlling for purposes of establishing employer liability; (2) an employee who refuses the unwelcome and threatening sexual advances of a supervisor, yet suffers no adverse and tangible job consequences, can recover against an employer without showing that the employer is negligent or otherwise at fault for the supervisor's actions; (3) thus, an employer is subject to vicarious liability to a victimized employee for an actionable hostile environment created by a supervisor with immediate, or successively higher, authority over the employee, but may, when no tangible employment action is taken, raise an affirmative defense to liability or damages; (4) this defense comprises the two necessary elements that (a) the employer exercised reasonable care to prevent and correct promptly any sexually harassing behavior, and (b) the plaintiff employee unreasonably failed to take advantage of any preventive or corrective opportunities provided by the employer or to avoid harm otherwise; and (5) in the case at hand, (a) the company is subject to vicarious liability for the vice president's alleged activity, but should have an opportunity to assert and prove the affirmative defense announced above, and (b) on remand, the District Court will have the opportunity to decide whether it would be appropriate to allow the worker to amend her pleading or supplement her discovery.

GINSBURG, J., concurring in the judgment, agreed with the Supreme Court's (1) ruling in holding 1 above that the labels quid pro quo and hostile work environment were not controlling for purposes of establishing employer liability, and (2) statement in holdings 3 and 4 above of the rule governing employer liability.

THOMAS, J., joined by SCALIA, J., dissenting, expressed the view that (1) as a result of the rule which the Supreme Court inappropriately manufactured in the case at hand, employer liability under Title VII for a hostile work environment would be judged by different standards depending on whether a sexually or racially hostile environment was alleged; (2) instead, the standard of employer liability for a hostile work environment should be the same in both instances, that is, an employer should be liable if, and only if, a plaintiff proves that the employer was negligent in permitting a supervisor's conduct to occur; and (3) under this standard as applied to the worker's allegations, the company could not be held liable for the vice president's conduct.

COUNSEL

James J. Casey argued the cause for petitioner.

Ernest T. Rossiello argued the cause for respondent.

Barbara D. Underwood argued the cause for the United States, as amicus curiae, by special leave of court.

BETH ANN FARAGHER, Petitioner

v

CITY OF BOCA RATON

524 US —, 141 L Ed 2d 662, 118 S Ct 2275

[No. 97-282]

Argued March 25, 1998.

Decided June 26, 1998.

Decision: Employer held (1) subject to vicarious liability, under Title VII of Civil Rights Act of 1964, for supervisor's actionable sexual harassment, but (2) able to raise affirmative defense looking to reasonableness of conduct of employer and victim.

SUMMARY

After resigning from her employment by a city as a lifeguard, a woman brought, in the United States District Court for the Southern District of Florida, against two of her immediate male supervisors and the city an action asserting sexual harassment claims under Title VII of the Civil Rights Act of 1964 (42 USCS §§ 2000e et seq.). The lifeguard, asserting that the two supervisors were agents of the city and that their conduct, which allegedly had created a sexually hostile atmosphere, constituted discrimination in the lifeguard's terms, conditions, and privileges of employment, in violation of 42 USCS § 2000e-2(a)(1), sought a judgment against the city for nominal damages. The District Court, concluding that the harassment was pervasive enough to support an inference of knowledge or constructive knowledge by the city and that the city was liable to the lifeguard under traditional agency

299

principles, awarded the lifeguard nominal damages of one dollar on her Title VII claim (864 F Supp 1552). After a panel of the United States Court of Appeals for the Eleventh Circuit reversed the District Court's judgment against the city (76 F3d 1155), the Court of Appeals, en banc, again reversing the judgment against the city, concluded that (1) in harassing the lifeguard, the supervisors had acted outside the scope of their employment and had not been assisted by their agency relationship with the city, and (2) the city lacked constructive knowledge of the harassment (111 F3d 1530).

On certiorari, the United States Supreme Court reversed the judgment of the Court of Appeals and remanded the case for reinstatement of the judgment of the District Court. In an opinion by SOUTER, J., joined by REHNQUIST, Ch. J., and STEVENS, O'CONNOR, KENNEDY, GINSBURG, and BREYER, JJ., it was held that (1) an employer is subject to vicarious liability under Title VII to a victimized employee for an actionable sexually hostile environment created by a supervisor with immediate or successively higher authority over the employee; (2) when no tangible employment action is taken, a defending employer may raise an affirmative defense to liability or damages, subject to proof by a preponderance of the evidence; (3) this defense comprises the two necessary elements that (a) the employer exercised reasonable care to prevent and correct promptly any sexually harassing behavior, and (b) the plaintiff employee unreasonably failed to take advantage of any preventive or corrective opportunities provided by the employer or to avoid harm otherwise; and (4) under the circumstances in the case at hand, (a) as a matter of law, the city could not be found to have exercised reasonable care to prevent the supervisors' harassing conduct, and (b) there was no reason to remand for consideration of the lifeguard's efforts to mitigate her own damages, since her award was nominal.

THOMAS, J., joined by SCALIA, J., dissenting, expressed the view that (1) absent an adverse employment consequence, an employer cannot be held vicariously liable if a supervisor creates a hostile work environment, and (2) thus the city was not vicariously liable for the conduct of the two supervisors, as the lifeguard suffered no adverse employment consequence from such conduct.

COUNSEL

William R. Amlong argued the cause for petitioner.

Irving L. Gornstein argued the cause for the United States, as amicus curiae, by special leave of court.

Harry A. Rissetto argued the cause for respondent.

GLOSSARY OF COMMON LEGAL TERMS

Abatement
The extinguishment of a lawsuit.

Abstention doctrine
The doctrine whereby a federal court may decline to exercise, or may postpone the exercise of, its jurisdiction, where a case involves a controlling question of state law.

Action
A lawsuit.

Administrative determination
A decision by a government board, agency or official, rather than by a court.

Administrator
One appointed by a court to settle the estate of a deceased person. The feminine form is "administratrix."

Admiralty
The body of law governing maritime cases.

Affidavit
A sworn written statement.

Amicus curiae
One who, not being a party to a lawsuit, assists the court in deciding the case.

Antitrust laws
Laws prohibiting restrictions on competition.

Appealable
That which may be taken to a higher court for review.

Appellant
One who appeals to a superior court from the order of an inferior court.

Appellee
A party against whom a case is appealed from an inferior court to a superior court.

Arbitration
The submission of a dispute to a selected person—not a court—for decision.

Arraign
To call a person before a judge or commissioner to answer criminal charges made against him.

Array
The whole body of persons, summoned to attend court, from whom a jury will be selected.

Assignee
One to whom property or a right is transferred.

Assignor
The transferor of property or a right.

Bill of Rights
The first ten amendments to the United States Constitution.

Brief
A written legal argument submitted to the court deciding the case.

Calendar
A list of cases awaiting decision in a court.

Capital crime
An offense punishable by death.

Cause of action
A right to legal redress.

Cease-and-desist order
An order to stop doing specified acts.

Certiorari
A superior court's order to a lower court to send up the record of a case for review by the superior court.

Choice of remedies
An election of which form of legal redress to seek.

Civil
Not criminal, as a civil lawsuit.

Class action
A lawsuit on behalf of persons too numerous to participate actively therein.

Commerce clause
The provision of the United States Constitution giving Congress power to regulate commerce with foreign nations, among the states.

Common law
The body of the law apart from constitutions, treaties, statutes, ordinances, and regulations.

Contempt
An exhibition of scorn or disrespect toward a judicial or legislative body.

Continuance
A postponement of proceedings.

Copyright
The exclusive privilege of publishing literary or artistic productions.

Coram nobis
A means of challenging a court's judgment, especially in criminal cases.

Court of Appeals
See United States Court of Appeals.

Cross Appeal
An appeal filed by the person against whom an appeal is taken.

De novo
Anew or over again, such as a trial de novo.

Devise
A will provision making a gift of land.

Disputes clause
A provision in a government contract for the settlement of disputes between the contractor and the government by decision of a government board or official.

District court
See United States District Court.

Diversity case
A case decided by a federal court because the parties are citizens of different states.

Double jeopardy
Placing a person twice in jeopardy of conviction for the same offense.

Due process clause
The provision of the United States Constitution that no person shall be deprived of life, liberty, or property without due process of law.

En banc
With all the judges of the court sitting.

Equal protection
The guaranty of the United States Constitution that no person or class of persons shall be denied the same protection of the laws that is enjoyed by other persons or classes of persons in like circumstances.

Establishment clause
The provision of the United States Constitution that Congress shall make no law respecting an establishment of religion.

Federal District Court
See District court.

Federal question jurisdiction
The jurisdiction of federal courts over cases presenting questions of federal law.

Felony
A crime punishable by death or by imprisonment in a state prison.

Forma pauperis
Without the payment of legal fees in advance.

Full faith and credit clause
The provision of the United States Constitution that full faith and credit shall be given in each state to the public acts, records, and judicial proceedings of every other state.

Habeas corpus
A judicial inquiry into the legality of the restraint of a person.

Indictment
A grand jury's accusation of crime.

Interlocutory
That which settles an intervening matter but does not decide a case.

Intestate
One who dies without leaving a valid will.

Jurisdiction of subject matter
The power to decide a certain type of case.

Just compensation clause
The provision of the United States Constitution that no private property may be taken for public use without just compensation.

Laches
Delay barring the right to special forms of relief.

Legatee
One to whom personal property is given by will.

Lessee
A tenant.

Lessor
A landlord.

Libel
Written defamation; in maritime cases, a suit in court.

Lien
A charge upon property for the payment of a debt.

Local action
A lawsuit, especially one involving rights to land, which can be brought only in the place where the wrong was committed.

Maintenance and cure
The legal duty of a seaman's employer to care for him during his illness.

Mandamus
A judicial command to perform an official duty.

Misdemeanor
Any crime not punishable by death or by imprisonment in a state prison.
308

Patent
The exclusive right of manufacture, sale, or use secured by statute to one who invents or discovers a new and useful device or process.

Per curiam
By the court as a whole.

Per se
By itself.

Plaintiff
A person who brings a lawsuit.

Plenary
Full or complete.

Police power
The power inherent in the states as sovereigns and not derived under any written constitution.

Prima facie
At first sight; with regard to evidence, that which, if unexplained or uncontradicted, is sufficient to establish a fact.

Privileges and immunities clause
The provision of the United States Constitution that no state shall make or enforce any law which abridges the privileges or immunities of citizens of the United States.

Pro hac vice
For this occasion.

Pro se
For himself; in his own behalf.

Proximate cause
The immediate cause of injury.

Public defender
A lawyer employed by the public to defend persons accused of crime.

Recognizance
A bail bond.

Remand
To order to be sent back.

Res judicata
The doctrine that a final judgment is binding on the parties to the lawsuit and the matter cannot be relitigated.

Respondent
The defendant in an action; with regard to appeals, the party against whom the appeal is taken.

Sanction
The penalty to be incurred by a wrongdoer.

Saving clause
A statutory provision preserving rights which would otherwise be annihilated by the statute.

Seaworthy
The reasonable fitness of a vessel to perform the service which she has undertaken to perform.

Statute of frauds
A statute rendering certain types of contracts unenforceable unless in writing.

Statute of limitations
A statute fixing a period of time within which certain types of lawsuits or criminal prosecutions must be begun.

Subpoena
Legal process to require the attendance of a witness.

Substantial federal question
A question of federal law of sufficient merit to warrant decision of the case by a federal court.

Substantive offense
An offense which is complete in itself and does not depend on the establishment of another offense.

Summary judgment
A judgment without a trial.

Supremacy clause
The provision of the United States Constitution that the Constitution, federal laws enacted pursuant thereto, and federal treaties shall be the supreme law of the land, binding the judges in every state, notwithstanding any state law to the contrary.

Surety
One who binds himself with another, called the principal, for the performance of an obligation with respect to which the principal is already bound and primarily liable.

Surrogate
The judge of a court dealing largely with wills and decedents' estates.

Tort
A wrong independent of contract; a breach of duty which the law, as distinguished from a mere contract, has imposed.

Tortfeasor
One who commits a tort; a wrongdoer.

Transitory action
An action which may be brought wherever the defendant may be served with process.

Trespass
An injury intentionally inflicted on the person or property of another.

Trier of fact
One who decides questions of fact.

United States Code
The official compilation of statutes enacted by Congress.

United States Court of Appeals
The intermediate level of federal courts above the United States District Courts but below the Supreme Court of the United States.

United States District Court
A federal trial court.

Unseaworthy
See Seaworthy.

USC
See United States Code.

USCS
The abbreviation for United States Code Service, Lawyers Edition, which is a publication annotating the federal laws, arranged according to the numbering of the United States Code.

Venue
The place where a case may be tried.

Writ of certiorari
See Certiorari.

Writ of error coram nobis
See Coram nobis.

TABLE OF CASES

313

TABLE OF CASES

TABLE OF CASES

315

TABLE OF CASES

TABLE OF CASES

317

TABLE OF CASES

INDEX

A

ABSTENTION DOCTRINE.
Jurisdiction.
  Federal courts declining jurisdiction, 139 L Ed 2d 525, 118 S Ct 523.
ABUSE OF DISCRETION OR POWER.
Appeals court, recall of mandate denying federal habeas corpus relief, 140 L Ed 2d 728, 118 S Ct 1489.
Expert scientific testimony.
  Standard of review on decision to exclude, 139 L Ed 2d 508, 118 S Ct 512.
ACCIDENT AND HEALTH INSURANCE.
Pensions and retirement.
  Continued coverage, 141 L Ed 2d 64, 118 S Ct 1869.
ACCOUNTS AND ACCOUNTING.
Attorneys at law.
  Lawyers trust accounts.
    Private property of client, 141 L Ed 2d 174, 118 S Ct 1925.
ADMINISTRATIVE LAW.
Adverse effect.
  Who may sue for violation of the Multiemployer Pension Plan Amendments Act, 139 L Ed 2d 553, 118 S Ct 542.
Double jeopardy.
  Indictments where civil sanctions previously administered, 139 L Ed 2d 450, 118 S Ct 488.
Exhaustion of remedies requirement, 140 L Ed 2d 1070, 118 S Ct 1761.
Federal credit union act.
  Challenge to common bond requirement interpretation, 140 L Ed 2d 1, 118 S Ct 927.
Federal Election Commission.
  Standing to challenge decision that an organization is not a political committee, 141 L Ed 2d 10, 118 S Ct 1777.
Review of agency decisions.
  Substantial evidence test, 139 L Ed 2d 797, 118 S Ct 818.
Ripeness for review.
  Logging provisions of forest service's land and resource management plan for national forest, 140 L Ed 2d 921, 118 S Ct 1665.
ADMIRALTY.
Death and death actions.
  Decedent's predeath pain and suffering, 141 L Ed 2d 102, 118 S Ct 1890.

INDEX

ADMIRALTY —Cont'd
In personam and in rem proceedings.
Shipwreck claimed by state, 140 L Ed 2d 626, 118 S Ct 1464.

ADVERSE POSSESSION.
Boundaries between sovereign states, 140 L Ed 2d 993, 118 S Ct 1726.

AFFIRMANCE OR AFFIRMATION.
Sentence and punishment.
Conspiracy with intent to distribute cocaine and crack, 140 L Ed 2d 703, 118 S Ct 1475.

AGE DISCRIMINATION.
Release of future claims against employer, 139 L Ed 2d 849, 118 S Ct 838.

AGENTS AND AGENCY.
Apparent authority, 141 L Ed 2d 633, 118 S Ct 2257.

ALIENS.
Equal protection.
Paternity requirement as gender classification, 140 L Ed 2d 575, 118 S Ct 1428.

AMBASSADORS AND OTHER CONSULAR OFFICERS.
Executive branch, authority under Vienna Convention, 140 L Ed 2d 529, 118 S Ct 1352.

AMERICANS WITH DISABILITIES ACT.
Applicability to inmates in state prisons, 141 L Ed 2d 215, 118 S Ct 1952.
HIV infection in asymptomatic phase, 141 L Ed 2d 540, 118 S Ct 2196.

AMICUS CURIAE.
Extradition.
Fugitive from justice, 141 L Ed 2d 131, 118 S Ct 1860.
Interstate boundaries.
Filled land around Ellis Island, 140 L Ed 2d 993, 118 S Ct 1726.

ANTITRUST.
Price fixing.
Vertical maximum price fixing, 139 L Ed 2d 199, 118 S Ct 275.

APPEAL AND ERROR.
Americans With Disabilities Act.
Applicability to inmates in state prisons, 141 L Ed 2d 215, 118 S Ct 1952.
Cleanup of hazardous waste.
Liability of parent corporation for subsidiary, 141 L Ed 2d 43, 118 S Ct 1876.
Damages reduced without option for new trial, 140 L Ed 2d 336, 118 S Ct 1210.
Due process.
Failure to consider prior due process decision, 139 L Ed 2d 888, 118 S Ct 904.

APPEAL AND ERROR —Cont'd

Federal election commission.

Standing to challenge decision that an organization is not a political committee, 141 L Ed 2d 10, 118 S Ct 1777.

Felony murder, 141 L Ed 2d 76, 118 S Ct 1895.

Filed rate doctrine.

Communications Act of 1934, 141 L Ed 2d 222, 118 S Ct 1956.

Forest service's land and resource management plan for national forest, 140 L Ed 2d 921, 118 S Ct 1665.

Forfeiture violating excessive fines clause.

Scope of review, 141 L Ed 2d 314, 118 S Ct 2028.

Frivolous petitions, 140 L Ed 2d 310, 118 S Ct 1124.

Issue decided on other grounds.

Indian land ceded to United States, 139 L Ed 2d 773, 118 S Ct 789.

Judgments reviewed on grounds not previously raised, 140 L Ed 2d 710, 118 S Ct 1478.

Multidistrict litigation, 140 L Ed 2d 62, 118 S Ct 956.

Non-final state court judgment, 139 L Ed 2d 433, 118 S Ct 481.

Open issues.

Abandoned shipwreck, 140 L Ed 2d 626, 118 S Ct 1464.

Parole revocation proceedings.

Review of state court decision, 141 L Ed 2d 344, 118 S Ct 2014.

Question presented on certiorari, consideration, 139 L Ed 2d 797, 118 S Ct 818.

Recall of mandate denying federal habeas corpus relief, 140 L Ed 2d 728, 118 S Ct 1489.

Remand.

Affirmative defense or amendment of pleadings, 141 L Ed 2d 633, 118 S Ct 2257.

Sentencing.

Mistake of law, 140 L Ed 2d 271, 118 S Ct 1135.

Specificity of lower court findings, 141 L Ed 2d 540, 118 S Ct 2196.

Ripeness for review.

Environmental organizations challenging logging provisions of resource management plan for national forest, 140 L Ed 2d 921, 118 S Ct 1665

Labor and employment, nonunion employees in agency shop, use of agency fees, 140 L Ed 2d 1070, 118 S Ct 1761

Preclearance under Voting Rights Act, 140 L Ed 2d 406, 118 S Ct 1257.

Showing of actual innocence.

Hearing on merits to relieve procedural default in failing to contest guilty plea, 140 L Ed 2d 828, 118 S Ct 1604.

Standard of review.

Expert scientific testimony, decision to exclude, 139 L Ed 2d 508, 118 S Ct 512.

INDEX

INDEX

BRIBERY.
Proof for conviction under RICO, 139 L Ed 2d 352, 118 S Ct 469.

C

CAPITAL OFFENSES AND PUNISHMENT.
Clemency interviews.
Due process issue, 140 L Ed 2d 387, 118 S Ct 1244.
Felony murder.
Culpable mental state, 141 L Ed 2d 76, 118 S Ct 1895.
Mitigation of sentence.
Failure to instruct capital sentencing jury on concept of mitigation, 139 L Ed 2d 702, 118 S Ct 757.

CASE OR CONTROVERSY.
Line item veto act, declaration of constitutionality, 141 L Ed 2d 393, 118 S Ct 2091.

CEDED PROPERTY OR TERRITORY.
Indians.
Jurisdiction, savings clause in cession treaty, 139 L Ed 2d 773, 118 S Ct 789.

CERCLA.
Clean up of hazardous waste.
Liability of parent corporation for subsidiary, 141 L Ed 2d 43, 118 S Ct 1876.

CERTIFICATES AND CERTIFICATION.
Appeal and error.
Certificate of appealability, 141 L Ed 2d 242, 118 S Ct 1969.

CERTIORARI.
Attorney trust accounts.
Private property of client, 141 L Ed 2d 174, 118 S Ct 1925.
Certificate of appealability.
Jurisdiction of supreme court to review denial of, 141 L Ed 2d 242, 118 S Ct 1969.
Civil Rights actions.
Non-final state judgment, 139 L Ed 2d 433, 118 S Ct 481.
Conspiracy conviction under RICO, 139 L Ed 2d 352, 118 S Ct 469.
Cross-petition, failure to, 139 L Ed 2d 215, 118 S Ct 285.
Extradition.
Review of fugitive status, 141 L Ed 2d 131, 118 S Ct 1860.
Filed rate doctrine.
Communications Act of 1934, 141 L Ed 2d 222, 118 S Ct 1956.
Filing fees, failure to pay.
In forma pauperis appeals denied, 139 L Ed 2d 1, 118 S Ct 1.
Frivolous petitions, 139 L Ed 2d 892, 118 S Ct 903.
Indians.
Indian Nonintercourse Act.
Sale and reacquisition of land by tribe, 141 L Ed 2d 90, 118 S Ct 1904.

Ind-5

COAL.
Taxes.
Restitution to Crow tribe of taxes paid, 140 L Ed 2d 898, 118 S
Ct 1650.

COCAINE.
Sentencing.
Conspiracy with intent to distribute cocaine and crack, 140 L Ed
2d 703, 118 S Ct 1475.

COLLATERAL ATTACK.
Guilty plea.
Hearing on merits of collateral claim upon necessary showing to
relieve prior procedural default, 140 L Ed 2d 828, 118 S Ct
1604.
Necessary showing of actual innocence to relieve procedural
default in failing to contest guilty plea, 140 L Ed 2d 828, 118
S Ct 1604.

COLLECTIVE BARGAINING.
Jurisdiction.
Failure to allege employer violated collective bargaining
agreement, 140 L Ed 2d 863, 118 S Ct 1626.

COLLEGES AND UNIVERSITIES.
Guaranteed student loans.
Misapplication of funds by university, 139 L Ed 2d 215, 118 S Ct
285.

COMMERCE.
Filed rate doctrine.
Communications Act of 1934, 141 L Ed 2d 222, 118 S Ct 1956.

COMMON LAW.
Boundaries.
Filled land around Ellis Island, 140 L Ed 2d 993, 118 S Ct 1726.

COMMUNICATION OR CONVERSATION.
Filed rate doctrine.
Communications Act of 1934, 141 L Ed 2d 222, 118 S Ct 1956.

COMPACTS.
Congressional consent to interstate compact, effect, 140 L Ed 2d
993, 118 S Ct 1726.

CONFESSIONS.
Admissibility.
Nontestifying codefendant, redacted confession, 140 L Ed 2d 294,
118 S Ct 1151.

CONGRESS.
Criminal conduct, ability to make, 140 L Ed 2d 828, 118 S Ct 1604.
Elections.
Open primary statutory scheme, 139 L Ed 2d 369, 118 S Ct 464.

CONSPIRACY.
Bribery under RICO, 139 L Ed 2d 352, 118 S Ct 469.

INDEX

CORPORATIONS —Cont'd
Liability of parent corporation for subsidiary, 141 L Ed 2d 43, 118 S Ct 1876.
Piercing the corporate veil.
Liability of parent corporation for subsidiary, 141 L Ed 2d 43, 118 S Ct 1876.

COST OR EXPENSE.
Clean up of hazardous waste.
Liability of parent corporation for subsidiary, 141 L Ed 2d 43, 118 S Ct 1876.

COURT OF INTERNATIONAL TRADE.
Harbor maintenance tax.
Application to exports, 140 L Ed 2d 453, 118 S Ct 1290.

COURTS.
Judicially implied private right of action.
Remedies, statutory construction, 141 L Ed 2d 277, 118 S Ct 1989.

COURTS-MARTIAL.
Polygraph evidence, admissibility.
Right to present defense, 140 L Ed 2d 413, 118 S Ct 1261.

CRIMINAL LAW.
Showing of innocence.
Hearing on merits to relieve procedural default in failing to contest guilty plea, 140 L Ed 2d 828, 118 S Ct 1604.

CRUEL AND UNUSUAL PUNISHMENT.
Deliberately indifferent conduct.
Jailee awaiting trial on due process claim, 140 L Ed 2d 1043, 118 S Ct 1708.
Mitigation of sentence.
Failure to instruct capital sentencing jury on concept of mitigation, 139 L Ed 2d 702, 118 S Ct 757.

CUSTOMS DUTIES AND IMPORT REGULATIONS.
Harbor maintenance tax, 140 L Ed 2d 453, 118 S Ct 1290.

D

DAMAGES.
Appeal and error.
Death on the high seas act, 141 L Ed 2d 102, 118 S Ct 1890.
Pain and suffering.
Death on the high seas act, 141 L Ed 2d 102, 118 S Ct 1890.

DEATH AND DEATH ACTIONS.
Civil rights actions against municipality.
Non-final state judgments, 139 L Ed 2d 433, 118 S Ct 481.

DEATH ON THE HIGH SEAS ACT.
Survival action for decedent's predeath pain and suffering, 141 L Ed 2d 102, 118 S Ct 1890.

INDEX

DEBATES.
Private televised debate was not public forum, 140 L Ed 2d 875, 118 S Ct 1633.

DECLARATORY JUDGMENT.
Case or controversy.
Habeas corpus, expedited review process, 140 L Ed 2d 970, 118 S Ct 1694.
Line item veto act, constitutionality, 141 L Ed 2d 393, 118 S Ct 2091.
Ripeness of issues.
Preclearance under Voting Rights Act, 140 L Ed 2d 406, 118 S Ct 1257.

DEPORTATION OR EXCLUSION OF ALIENS.
Unlawful return after convictions.
Recidivist sentencing provisions, 140 L Ed 2d 350, 118 S Ct 1219.

DISABLED PERSONS.
HIV infection, asymptomatic phase.
Protection under Americans with Dsiabilities Act, 141 L Ed 2d 540, 118 S Ct 2196.

DISCOVERY PROCEEDINGS.
Immunity of public official, 140 L Ed 2d 759, 118 S Ct 1584.

DISMISSAL, DISCONTINUANCE, AND NONSUIT.
Jurisdiction, 140 L Ed 2d 210, 118 S Ct 1003.

DISTRICT AND PROSECUTING ATTORNEYS.
Privileges and immunities.
False statements of fact supporting probable cause determination, 139 L Ed 2d 471, 118 S Ct 502.

DIVERSITY OF CITIZENSHIP.
Federal jurisdiction over Eleventh amendment claim, 141 L Ed 2d 364, 118 S Ct 2047.

DOUBLE JEOPARDY.
Administrative sanctions previously administered, 139 L Ed 2d 450, 118 S Ct 488.
Noncapital sentencing of repeat offenders, 141 L Ed 2d 615, 118 S Ct 2246.

DRUGS AND NARCOTICS.
Questions of law or fact.
Conspiracy.
Possession with intent to distribute cocaine and crack, 140 L Ed 2d 703, 118 S Ct 1475.
Sentence and punishment.
Conspiracy with intent to distribute cocaine and crack, 140 L Ed 2d 703, 118 S Ct 1475.

DUE PROCESS.
Clemency procedures, 140 L Ed 2d 387, 118 S Ct 1244.

INDEX

DUE PROCESS —Cont'd
Employee false statements in misconduct action.
Adverse action against employee, 139 L Ed 2d 695, 118 S Ct 753.
High speed chase with no intent to harm.
Substantive due process claim, 140 L Ed 2d 1043, 118 S Ct 1708.
Mitigation of sentence.
Failure to instruct capital sentencing jury on concept of
mitigation, 139 L Ed 2d 702, 118 S Ct 757.
Tax refund for payment of unconstitutional tax.
Deprivation of remedy by state, 139 L Ed 2d 888, 118 S Ct 904.

E

ELECTIONS.
First amendment.
Private televised debate was private forum, candidates exclusion
from was no first amendment violation, 140 L Ed 2d 875, 118
S Ct 1633.
Open primary statutory scheme, 139 L Ed 2d 369, 118 S Ct 464.
Preclearance of voting changes under Voting Rights Act, 139 L Ed
2d 339, 118 S Ct 400.

ELEVENTH AMENDMENT.
Removal of cases to federal court.
Nonbarred claims, 141 L Ed 2d 364, 118 S Ct 2047.

ELLIS ISLAND.
Boundary dispute over, 140 L Ed 2d 993, 118 S Ct 1726.

EMINENT DOMAIN.
Attorneys at law.
Lawyers trust accounts.
Private property of client, 141 L Ed 2d 174, 118 S Ct 1925.
Coal industry retiree health benefit act.
Liability for retiree health benefits, 141 L Ed 2d 451, 118 S Ct
2131.

ENVIRONMENTAL LAW.
CERCLA.
Clean up of hazardous waste.
Liability of parent corporation for subsidiary, 141 L Ed 2d 43,
118 S Ct 1876.
Cleanup of hazardous waste.
Liability of parent corporation for subsidiary, 141 L Ed 2d 43, 118
S Ct 1876.
Logging provisions of forest service's land and resource
management plan, 140 L Ed 2d 921, 118 S Ct 1665.
Standing of party to sue, 140 L Ed 2d 210, 118 S Ct 1003.

EQUAL PROTECTION.
Citizenship.
Paternity requirement, 140 L Ed 2d 575, 118 S Ct 1428.

Ind-11

INDEX

INDEX

EXTORTION, BLACKMAIL, AND THREATS.
Conspiracy under RICO, 139 L Ed 2d 352, 118 S Ct 469.

EXTRADITION.
Fugitive from justice, 141 L Ed 2d 131, 118 S Ct 1860.
Scope of permissible inquiry, 141 L Ed 2d 131, 118 S Ct 1860.

F

FEDERAL ELECTION COMMISSION.
Standing to challenge decision that an organization is not a political committee, 141 L Ed 2d 10, 118 S Ct 1777.

FEDERAL QUESTION.
Supplemental jurisdiction.
State law administrative claims including federal constitutional claims, 139 L Ed 2d 525, 118 S Ct 523.

FIFTH AMENDMENT.
Attorneys at law.
Lawyers trust accounts.
Private property of client, 141 L Ed 2d 174, 118 S Ct 1925.
False statements, no right to lie under constitution, 139 L Ed 2d 830, 118 S Ct 805.

FILED RATE DOCTRINE.
Federal preemption of state law, 141 L Ed 2d 222, 118 S Ct 1956.

FINALITY OR CONCLUSIVENESS.
Civil Rights actions.
Non-final state judgment, 139 L Ed 2d 433, 118 S Ct 481.
Social security benefits.
Right of claimant to appeal denial, 141 L Ed 2d 269, 118 S Ct 1984.

FINDINGS OF FACT AND CONCLUSIONS OF LAW.
Constitutional violation suit against public official.
Qualified immunity, 140 L Ed 2d 759, 118 S Ct 1584.

FINES, FORFEITURES, AND PENALTIES.
Excessive fines.
Currency reporting offense, failure to report full amount, 141 L Ed 2d 314, 118 S Ct 2028.
Transporting currency, failure to report amount.
Forfeiture violating excessive fines clause, 141 L Ed 2d 314, 118 S Ct 2028.

FORMA PAUPERIS.
Filing fees, failure to pay.
Certiorari denied in noncriminal matters, 139 L Ed 2d 1, 118 S Ct 1.
Frivolous petitions, 139 L Ed 2d 892, 118 S Ct 903.
Noncriminal matters, 140 L Ed 2d 310, 118 S Ct 1124.

INDEX

FRAUD AND DECEIT.
Bankruptcy, discharge of indebtedness.
  Money arising from fraud, 140 L Ed 2d 341, 118 S Ct 1212.
Employee false statements in misconduct action.
  Adverse action against employee, 139 L Ed 2d 695, 118 S Ct 753.
Exculpatory "no" exception to 18 USCS 1001.
  Denial of wrongdoing, 139 L Ed 2d 830, 118 S Ct 805.
Intent to injure and defraud.
  Misapplication of funds, 139 L Ed 2d 215, 118 S Ct 285.

FREEDOM OF SPEECH AND PRESS.
National Endowment for the Arts.
  Standards of decency, 141 L Ed 2d 500, 118 S Ct 2168.
Retaliation by public official for speech, 140 L Ed 2d 759, 118 S Ct 1584.

FRIVOLOUS APPEALS.
Indigents, 139 L Ed 2d 892, 118 S Ct 903.
  Certiorari denied, failure to pay filing fee, 139 L Ed 2d 1, 118 S Ct 1.
  Forma pauperis petitions, 140 L Ed 2d 310, 118 S Ct 1124.

FULL FAITH AND CREDIT.
Injunction from related case against testifying in product-liability suit, 139 L Ed 2d 580, 118 S Ct 657.

G

GRAND JURY.
Discrimination.
  White accused, standing to raise exclusion of blacks, 140 L Ed 2d 551, 118 S Ct 1419.

GUILTY PLEA.
Voluntariness.
  Hearing on merits allowed after necessary showing of actual innocence, 140 L Ed 2d 828, 118 S Ct 1604.

H

HABEAS CORPUS.
Appeal and error.
  Claim may be reconsidered after previous dismissal as premature, 140 L Ed 2d 849, 118 S Ct 1618.
Exhaustion of remedies.
  Claims may be adjudicated after exhaustion of state remedies even when petition initially dismissed for failure to exhaust, 140 L Ed 2d 43, 118 S Ct 978.
  Prisoners attacking validity or duration of confinement, 140 L Ed 2d 970, 118 S Ct 1694.
Expedited review process.
  Case or controversy requirement, 140 L Ed 2d 970, 118 S Ct 1694.

INDEX

J

JOB DISCRIMINATION.
Same-sex sexual harassment, 140 L Ed 2d 201, 118 S Ct 998.
JUDGMENTS AND DECREES.
Federal tax lien, priority as against perfected liens, 140 L Ed 2d 710, 118 S Ct 1478.
JURISDICTION.
Admiralty.
  Shipwreck claimed by state, 140 L Ed 2d 626, 118 S Ct 1464.
Certificates and certification.
  Denial of certificate of appealability, 141 L Ed 2d 242, 118 S Ct 1969.
Full faith and credit.
  Injunction against testimony in related case in foreign state, 139 L Ed 2d 580, 118 S Ct 657.
Indian land ceded to United States.
  Diminished reservation pursuant to treaty, 139 L Ed 2d 773, 118 S Ct 789.
Merits of claim, 140 L Ed 2d 210, 118 S Ct 1003.
Supplemental jurisdiction.
  State law administrative claims including federal constitutional claims, 139 L Ed 2d 525, 118 S Ct 523.
JURY AND JURY TRIAL.
Copyright action.
  Election to recover damages, 140 L Ed 2d 438, 118 S Ct 1279.
Right to trial by jury.
  Damages remitted on appeal without option of new trial, 140 L Ed 2d 336, 118 S Ct 1210.

L

LABOR AND EMPLOYMENT.
Agency shops.
  Use of agency fee, problem of "free riders," 140 L Ed 2d 1070.
Contracts and agreements.
  Jurisdiction.
    Failure of union to allege violation of collective bargaining agreement, 140 L Ed 2d 863, 118 S Ct 1626.
Declaratory judgment.
  Failure by union to strike allege violation of collective bargaining agreement, 140 L Ed 2d 863, 118 S Ct 1626.
Employee false statements in misconduct action.
  Adverse action against employee, 139 L Ed 2d 695, 118 S Ct 753.
Unfair practice.
  Employee poll as to support of labor union, presumption of support, 139 L Ed 2d 797, 118 S Ct 818.

INDEX

INDEX

PARENT AND SUBSIDIARY CORPORATIONS.
Clean up of hazardous waste.
Liability of parent corporation for subsidiary, 141 L Ed 2d 43, 118 S Ct 1876.

PARTIES.
Standing to seek judicial review.
Banks challenging credit union association, 140 L Ed 2d 1, 118 S Ct 927.
No appropriate relief, application of doctrine, 140 L Ed 2d 210, 118 S Ct 1003.
Raising constitutional rights of another, 140 L Ed 2d 575, 118 S Ct 1428.
Standing to sue.
Declaratory judgment on line item veto act, 141 L Ed 2d 393, 118 S Ct 2091.

PENSIONS AND RETIREMENT.
Employee Retirement Income Security Act.
Continued health insurance coverage, 141 L Ed 2d 64, 118 S Ct 1869.
Health insurance.
Continued coverage, 141 L Ed 2d 64, 118 S Ct 1869.
Limitation of actions commencing when employer misses installment payment, 139 L Ed 2d 553, 118 S Ct 542.

PERSONAL INJURIES.
Federal Election Commission.
Standing to challenge decision that an organization is not a political committee, 141 L Ed 2d 10, 118 S Ct 1777.

PHYSICAL APPEARANCE OR CONDITION.
Americans With Disabilities Act.
Applicability to inmates in state prisons, 141 L Ed 2d 215, 118 S Ct 1952.

POLITICS AND POLITICAL MATTERS.
Speeches.
Private television debate is not public forum, 140 L Ed 2d 875, 118 S Ct 1633.

PORTS AND HARBORS.
Harbor maintenance tax.
Application under constitutions export clause, 140 L Ed 2d 453, 118 S Ct 1290.

PRECEDENTS.
Anti-trust cases.
Rule of reason in per se violation issues, 139 L Ed 2d 199, 118 S Ct 275.

PREEMPTION AND PREEMPTIVE RIGHTS.
State law.
Filed rate doctrine.
Communications Act of 1934, 141 L Ed 2d 222, 118 S Ct 1956.

INDEX

PRIVILEGES AND IMMUNITIES —Cont'd
Self-incrimination.
Fear of foreign prosecution, 141 L Ed 2d 575, 118 S Ct 2218.
Tribal immunity, Indians, 140 L Ed 2d 981, 118 S Ct 1700.

PROBABLE CAUSE.
False statements by prosecutor in supporting documents to arrest
warrant, 139 L Ed 2d 471, 118 S Ct 502.

PROPERTY.
Attorneys at law.
Lawyers trust accounts.
Private property of client, 141 L Ed 2d 174, 118 S Ct 1925.

PUBLIC OFFICERS AND EMPLOYEES.
Qualified immunity.
Constitutional violation of prisoner's rights, 140 L Ed 2d 759, 118
S Ct 1584.

PUNITIVE DAMAGES.
Deprivation of federal and civil rights cases against municipality,
139 L Ed 2d 433.

Q

QUALIFIED IMMUNITY.
High speed police chase.
Due process claim, determination of valid claim before addressing
issue of immunity, 140 L Ed 2d 1043, 118 S Ct 1708.

QUIETING TITLE.
Grave miscarriage of justice, 141 L Ed 2d 32, 118 S Ct 1862.
Judgments and decrees.
Grave miscarriage of justice, 141 L Ed 2d 32, 118 S Ct 1862.

R

RACKETEERING.
Conspiracy to bribe federal officials, prisoners, 139 L Ed 2d 352, 118
S Ct 469.

RADIO AND TELEVISION.
Freedom of speech and press.
Private televised debate was private forum, no first amendment
violation, 140 L Ed 2d 875, 118 S Ct 1633.

REHEARING.
Habeas corpus claim allowed for consideration after being
dismissed as being premature, 140 L Ed 2d 849, 118 S Ct 1618.

REMAND.
Affirmative defense or amendment of pleadings, 141 L Ed 2d 633,
118 S Ct 2257.

INDEX

REMAND —Cont'd
Attorneys at law.
Lawyers trust accounts.
Private property of client, 141 L Ed 2d 174, 118 S Ct 1925.
Cleanup of hazardous waste.
Liability of parent corporation for subsidiary, 141 L Ed 2d 43, 118 S Ct 1876.
Extradition.
Review of fugitive status, 141 L Ed 2d 131, 118 S Ct 1860.
Federal Election Commission.
Standing to challenge decision that an organization is not a political committee, 141 L Ed 2d 10, 118 S Ct 1777.
Hearing on merits allowed after necessary showing of actual innocence, 140 L Ed 2d 828, 118 S Ct 1604.
Social security benefits.
Right of claimant to appeal denial, 141 L Ed 2d 269, 118 S Ct 1984.
Specificity of lower court findings.
Refusal of dental treatment to HIV patient, 141 L Ed 2d 540, 118 S Ct 2196.

REMITTITUR.
Damages reduced on appeal.
Violation of right to jury trial, 140 L Ed 2d 336, 118 S Ct 1210.

REMOVAL OR TRANSFER OF CAUSES.
Eleventh amendment claims.
Jurisdiction over claims not barred, 141 L Ed 2d 364, 118 S Ct 2047.
Multidistrict litigation.
Assignment of case by court to itself under 28 USCS §§1404(a), 1407(a), 140 L Ed 2d 62, 118 S Ct 956.
Prior federal judgment.
Defense must raise claim preclusion to remove, 139 L Ed 2d 912, 118 S Ct 921.
Supplemental jurisdiction.
State law administrative claims including federal constitutional claims, 139 L Ed 2d 525, 118 S Ct 523.

REOPENING.
Habeas corpus claims entitled to adjudication even when previously dismissed for being unripe, 140 L Ed 2d 849, 118 S Ct 1618.

RES JUDICATA.
Defensive plea for removal of case.
Prior federal judgment involved, 139 L Ed 2d 912, 118 S Ct 921.
Full faith and credit.
Injunction in related-case to prevent testimony in product-liability suit, 139 L Ed 2d 580, 118 S Ct 657.

RESTRAINTS OF TRADE, MONOPOLIES AND UNFAIR TRADE PRACTICES.
Vertical maximum price fixing, 139 L Ed 2d 199, 118 S Ct 275.

Ind-23

RULE OF REASON.
Antitrust.
Vertical maximum price fixing, 139 L Ed 2d 199, 118 S Ct 275.

S

SCHOOLS AND EDUCATION.
Sexual harassment and discrimination suit against school district.
Title IX case, 141 L Ed 2d 277, 118 S Ct 1989.

SEARCH AND SEIZURE.
Attorneys at law.
Lawyers trust accounts.
Private property of client, 141 L Ed 2d 174, 118 S Ct 1925.
High speed police chase, freedom of movement restricted.
Intent requirement for coverage under Fourth Amendment, 140 L
Ed 2d 1043, 118 S Ct 1708.
No-knock entry, 140 L Ed 2d 191, 118 S Ct 992.

SECURED TRANSACTIONS.
Perfection of interest.
Motor vehicle loans, "enabling loan" exception to avoid
preferential transfers, 139 L Ed 2d 571, 118 S Ct 651.

SELF-INCRIMINATION.
Clemency proceedings.
Due process issues, 140 L Ed 2d 387, 118 S Ct 1244.
Fear of foreign prosecution, 141 L Ed 2d 575, 118 S Ct 2218.

SENTENCE OR PUNISHMENT.
Conviction.
Conspiracy with intent to distribute cocaine and crack, 140 L Ed
2d 703, 118 S Ct 1475.
Repeat offender sentencing.
Double jeopardy clause applicability to noncapital sentencing, 141
L Ed 2d 615, 118 S Ct 2246.

SETOFF, COUNTERCLAIM AND RECOUPMENT.
Limitation of actions, 140 L Ed 2d 566, 118 S Ct 1408.

SEVERANCE TAXES.
Indians, restitution to Crow tribe of taxes paid, 140 L Ed 2d 898,
118 S Ct 1650.

SEX DISCRIMINATION.
Aliens, citizenship, 140 L Ed 2d 575, 118 S Ct 1428.
Title IX case against school district, 141 L Ed 2d 277, 118 S Ct
1989.

SEXUAL HARASSMENT.
Hostile work environment and quid pro quo labels.
Title VII of civil rights act, 141 L Ed 2d 633, 118 S Ct 2257.
Same-sex coworkers, 140 L Ed 2d 201, 118 S Ct 998.

INDEX

INDEX

5186